Judaism in a Digital Age

T0349442

Danny Schiff

Judaism in a Digital Age

An Ancient Tradition Confronts a Transformative Era

palgrave
macmillan

Danny Schiff
Federation Scholar
Jewish Federation of Greater Pittsburgh
Pittsburgh, PA, USA

ISBN 978-3-031-17991-4   ISBN 978-3-031-17992-1   (eBook)
https://doi.org/10.1007/978-3-031-17992-1

This Palgrave Macmillan imprint is published by the registered company Springer Nature
Switzerland AG.
The registered company address is: Gewerbestrasse 11, 6330 Cham, Switzerland

PREFACE

Somewhere around 1990, everything changed. Back then, of course, nobody realized that any sort of transformation was underway, but, with hindsight, the revolutionary shift now seems clear. The revolution started with technology, but it didn't end there. Ultimately, a new era emerged that led to a reevaluation of many fundamental ideas, altering the way we think about much of what is important.

At first, none of this seemed central to the project that I was working on. I had begun writing about the noticeable decline in the strength of Conservative and Reform Judaism. Having grown up as a non-Orthodox Jew, I wanted to understand what was happening to these two movements that had nourished my Judaism, as well as that of countless others. Why were these streams struggling? The more I investigated, the more I understood that it wasn't that the Reform and Conservative movements were doing anything markedly different from what they had done previously. The main problem was not internal, it was external. Almost overnight, the world around them had been reconfigured.

It seemed logical, therefore, to construct a fuller picture of the far-reaching modifications to human life that have accumulated since 1990. In the process of undertaking that task, I realized two things: First, in virtually every area that matters in Judaism, the new era in which we find ourselves poses weighty questions that deserve serious Jewish responses. Second, the extraordinary developments that we have already experienced in this era will ultimately seem small when compared with what is likely to unfold in the decades to come.

This analysis led me to conclude that, if history is any guide, new iterations of Judaism will probably arise sooner than we expect. While such transitions are never easy, they are vital if Judaism is to achieve one of its major purposes: to elevate the human condition by helping to enhance civilization.

This book discusses what has happened to the once dominant movements of modernity. But it goes further. It explores the reshaped contours of our age, and it attempts to describe the challenges that future iterations of Judaism will need to address. It considers the refashioned reality of our time through a Jewish lens, examining what Jewish teachings and traditions might have to offer in this period of great flux. It proposes that a countercultural Judaism might have renewed relevance and could generate potential solutions to some of the pressing issues that confront humanity in the twenty-first century.

I am deeply grateful to all those who have provided me with their insights, their thoughtfulness, and their support during the production of this work:

To my esteemed colleagues: A significant number of outstanding rabbis, leaders, and friends (most from the Conservative and Reform movements) read the manuscript and offered valuable observations, astute comments, and welcome corrections. Each one enriched the text and did so with care and intellectual rigor. I am truly fortunate to have benefitted from their wisdom and experience. Naturally, any errors, omissions, or deficiencies in the final work are mine alone.

To those who provided outstanding editorial assistance: Phil Getz, Senior Editor at Palgrave Macmillan who immediately took an interest in the book, spent countless hours discussing it from every angle, provided me with wise insights, and expertly guided me through the entire process. Eliana Rangel, Susan Westendorf, Arun Prasath, and Divya Anish at Palgrave Macmillan who supplied skilled editorial support and ably handled the intricacies of production. Ed Levy, who professionally edited the work with an eye to refining the writing and the reasoning. My mother, Judi Schiff, who proofread an early version of the manuscript and rectified multiple imperfections.

To my son, David Schiff, and my daughter, Adina Schiff, who for years have amiably tolerated endless conversations about twenty-first-century Judaism around the Shabbat table and in many other locations—for all their understanding and patience and for their encouragement and caring. They are the future.

To my wife, Anne Schiff, for her boundless devotion and love, for the countless hours she gave as the first one to read and improve each section, for her careful editing and re-editing of each chapter, for her unending belief in me and for her companionship every step of the way. She knew this subject matter would become a book even before I did. "She speaks with wisdom, and kindness is on her lips" (Proverbs 31:26).

Words are inadequate to express the fullness of my appreciation to each of these extraordinary individuals.

Finally, I give thanks to God for the gift of life itself, for the manifold blessings bestowed upon me, and for having been granted the ability to embark upon and to complete this project.

Jerusalem, Israel   Danny Schiff

Contents

CHAPTER 1

Beyond the Mist

By the end of the twenty-first century, it is plausible that humans of our kind will be rare. In just a few decades, our descendants could well be genetically modified, with brains that are hooked into gigantic reservoirs of knowledge, enhanced physical bodies, life expectancies way beyond our own, and an understanding of the world that will make our current perspectives seem decidedly limited. Significantly augmented, they may live alongside a range of beings possessing artificial intelligence with powerful capacity. They will certainly inhabit a vastly altered cultural, technological, and communications landscape that will inevitably refashion their ideas and reactions in every sphere of human functioning. Put simply, if the current trajectory holds, what it means to be human will be radically transformed.

The world around us is changing at breakneck speed. We are hurtling toward the future at a velocity sufficient to ensure that the challenges of tomorrow arrive before we have adequately addressed yesterday's issues. Already, our lives bear little resemblance to what human existence was like as recently as 1990. Profound changes have reshaped not just our technology but the way we interact, form relationships, join communities, configure our economies, distribute power, curate our life experiences, and so much more. Little has been left untouched.

All of this raises a vital question for Judaism: Are the views, structures, and approaches of contemporary Jewish life adequately prepared for what lies ahead? Imagine for a moment being transported back in time for a

© The Author(s), under exclusive license to Springer Nature
Switzerland AG 2023
D. Schiff, *Judaism in a Digital Age*,
https://doi.org/10.1007/978-3-031-17992-1_1

conversation with a Jew in the year 1800. The French Revolution has just ended. Decades of Enlightenment thought have resulted in extensive societal adjustments. Eleven years after the great turning point of 1789, the Jew you encounter may well have a sense that an unprecedented historical era is underway. The early steps toward Jewish emancipation are fresh news. Assuming that your Jewish interlocutor was lucky enough to be among the emancipated, the tangible gains would have been few. But the year is 1800, and a new century of hopeful promise lies ahead.

So, at this pivotal moment in history, you pose a forward-looking inquiry to the Jew you have come to meet: "What do you think the Judaism of the nineteenth century will look like?" Even if the Jew with whom you are conversing is educated and knows of the thinkers of the early *Haskalah* (Jewish Enlightenment), how prescient is the answer likely to be? Will you hear confident predictions that emancipation will ultimately spread all over Europe? Will you be told that self-governing *kehillot* (communities) will become a thing of the past? Maybe. What about the notion that the first liberalizing congregation will be established just ten years hence in Seesen, Germany? Or that ultimately a substantial modern movement that will be known as "Reform" will crystallize? Or that another modern movement known as "Conservative" will follow? Or that many traditional Jews will come to describe themselves as "Orthodox" in reaction to the Reform and Conservative expressions of Judaism? Or that political and cultural Zionism will coalesce as major schools of thought, ultimately culminating in a Zionist movement before the end of the century? You are not likely to hear any of that. The chances that the Jew you are visiting in 1800 can foresee these remarkable forthcoming changes are virtually nil. All these extraordinary developments, each a direct outgrowth of burgeoning modernity, each a powerful institution destined to become central to nineteenth- and twentieth-century Judaism, would very soon remake Jewish life. Yet despite the fact that this thoughtful Jew is aware of the tumultuous events that are going on in the surrounding environment, these new forms of Judaism are scarcely conceivable…even though they are right around the corner.

A little over 200 years later, twenty-first-century Jews are again at an "1800 moment." Like then, Jews today live in a dramatically altered reality from that which characterized the recent past, and there is evidence that a transformative era is underway. Just as then, a significant shift has taken place in the level of acceptance of Jews in free societies. At the same time, familiar Jewish institutions that have withstood the test of time are crumbling, seemingly no longer responsive to current realities. The Jewish ideas and approaches that were devised to cope with modernity, and that were preeminent for more than a hundred years, are in decline. The broader civilization has moved on, and it is, therefore, appropriate to consider "what's next" for Judaism. Many suppose that the future will simply be an updated extension of what went before. But this ignores the message of 1800: Fundamental reconfigurations of human circumstances will, more likely than not, elicit discontinuous ways of thinking about Judaism.

Though the impact of such societal dislocations inevitably has repercussions for all forms of Judaism, nowhere is the effect more pronounced than in that part of the Jewish spectrum broadly titled "non-Orthodox." The brunt of epochal change is disproportionately felt among non-Orthodox Jews because those who attempt to take the teachings of non-Orthodox Judaism seriously often live with a greater identity tension than do either those Jews who have decided to blend into society more extensively or those who are Orthodox. For secular Jews, the ambient culture dominates; it shapes their worldview, their ethical responses, their beliefs, the way they structure time, and the nature of their commitments. There may be elements of "Jewish flavoring" sprinkled into their life mix, but the culture of the surrounding society governs many of their responses. For practicing Orthodox Jews, the opposite is true; the worldview they embrace, their ethics, beliefs, time, and allegiances are predominantly structured by Judaism.

In contrast to these two groups, those committed to living by the philosophies of the non-Orthodox streams of Judaism have historically endeavored to heed both the voice of the ambient culture and that of Judaism. Non-Orthodox Judaism encompasses several contemporary movements, but the two oldest and largest streams, Reform and Conservative, most fully reflect the arc of change that has occurred during modernity.[1] The Conservative and Reform movements came into being with the goal of helping Jews and Judaism adapt to the thought and mores of modern culture and society while at the same time maintaining a commitment to a range of Jewish traditions and practices. For much of late modernity, this mixture was so successful that in twentieth-century America, the two movements became the overwhelmingly preferred option for Jewish affiliation. For decades, the Reform and Conservative streams established hundreds of congregations, educated millions in religious schools, welcomed overflowing crowds to holiday services, constituted popular venues for social interaction and coupling, and imparted

Jewish home practices. But there came a moment when the magic began to fade.

In 2020, the Pew Research Center conducted a comprehensive study of American Jewry. The results made grim reading for those committed to non-Orthodox Judaism. When asked about their Jewish identity, only 54 percent of Jews said they identified with Reform or Conservative Judaism.[2] On the face of it, this statistic might not seem overly disconcerting. However, when compared with the 1990 National Jewish Population data that showed fully 73 percent of Jewish households declaring affinity for the two largest movements, the results represented a steep fall.[3]

The portents for the future are even more worrying for the major non-Orthodox movements. Since 2010, enrolment at non-Orthodox rabbinic schools has declined by 15 percent, with even more precipitous drops at the seminaries sponsored by the Reform and Conservative movements.[4] At the same time, the Orthodox share of American Jewry continues to increase meaningfully: The Pew report showed that 3 percent of Jews over the age of 65 identify as Orthodox, while that proportion is more than fivefold higher—17 percent—for Jews aged 18–29.[5] Perhaps the most significant warning sign is the rise in the number of Jews who no longer identify with any denomination. In 1990, only 10 percent of Jews described themselves as "just Jewish";[6] by 2020, those reporting no particular movement identity had more than tripled to 32 percent, with rates as high as 41 percent for those under the age of twenty-nine.[7]

The contraction of the non-Orthodox denominations could suggest that religious life is unappealing, that the current streams on offer are no longer compelling, or that Jews are rejecting the whole idea of identifying with Jewish movements, preferring instead to create their own personalized approaches to Judaism. Whatever the reason, the trends appear certain to bring further substantial shrinkage to Reform and Conservative Judaism. It is noteworthy, moreover, that birth rates for non-Orthodox Jews have been appreciably below replacement levels for more than a generation. Hence, unlike Orthodoxy, the Reform and Conservative streams have little foreseeable chance of being replenished by natural population increase.

What led to this weakening of Reform and Conservative Judaism? The key to understanding what happened is the "1800 moment" in which we now find ourselves. Not only is it hard to foresee new forms of Judaism that might soon materialize, but, as was the case in 1800, a major transition in history is underway. The period of modernity which began around 1789—and produced so many innovations—lasted for two centuries. Around 1990, a digital revolution arrived, accompanied by a comprehensive rethinking of ideas concerning the nature of human functioning that is proving to be every bit as significant, if not more so, than the disruptions that began in the late eighteenth century. Modernity had come to an end. It follows that Conservative and Reform Judaism—movements that represent responses to modernity—would wane in relevance as a new era, with radically different concerns and demands, began to take hold. Viewed this way, the Reform and Conservative movements lost altitude not because they were unsuccessful responses to modernity but because modernity itself yielded the stage of history.

It is true, of course, that some sections of Orthodoxy are also responses to modernity. But the fealty of Orthodoxy to a codified *halakhah*[8] made it less exposed to the buffeting upheavals taking place in the surrounding society. Unlike the Conservative and Reform movements, Orthodoxy attempted to keep modernity at arm's length and, as a result, was less impacted by its eclipse. Given that the inflection point of the 1990s was not as decisive for Orthodoxy, the chapters ahead will primarily focus on what the arrival of the digital era means for non-Orthodox Judaism; there can, however, be little doubt that many of the challenges and opportunities faced within the non-Orthodox world exist in Orthodoxy as well.

What are the characteristics of this new digital age? Here is a brief sampling: In the space of one generation, a planet without personal computers, where virtually nobody had heard the word "Internet," has been filled with sophisticated computing gadgets, all interconnected. A virtual environment that never existed before has become indispensable to government, businesses, organizations, and individuals. Mobile communications devices that can track positioning and connect universally—previously the stuff of science fiction—have become ubiquitous. The Internet has extensively erased the tyrannies of time and distance, leading to remote work and long-distance collaborations that were once fantasies. A worldwide ethos of sharing, collaborating, and crowdsourcing has produced remarkable leaps forward. Phones and social media have reshaped human interactions, politics, relationships, families, and sexuality. Algorithms have been deployed that invisibly mold human choices. Privacy has largely evaporated. Authority structures have been challenged. And much more. In short, human existence has been remade with breathtaking speed.

In the Jewish context, it is plain that adapting to these profoundly altered circumstances has been problematic for the movements of modernity. This difficulty became even tougher in 2020, when the arrival of the coronavirus pandemic caused much of Jewish life to move online for an extended period, bringing lasting organizational and attitudinal shifts. Developments that might have unfolded over a decade or more were compressed into a period of months, making the struggles of the non-Orthodox movements more manifest. With the Reform and Conservative movements already contracting, the destabilizing effects of the pandemic resulted in a conspicuous public discussion about the survival of Jewish denominations in the Internet era.[9] Understandably, these conversations concentrated on the immediate challenges of preserving the functional elements of existing Jewish life. Hence, the perceived importance of addressing declining affiliation, organizational configurations, and online opportunities led to proposals ranging from movement mergers to the creation of post-denominational virtual communities.[10] The assumption underlying these initiatives appeared to be that the problems ailing non-Orthodox Judaism could be tackled by streamlining institutions, upgrading to more compelling technologies, or rebranding messaging to connect better with the interests and styles of younger generations.

It seems unlikely, however, that these strategies will fix the malaise because the reason the movements of modernity are struggling is not primarily due to their institutions, programs, or procedures. Fundamentally, their challenge is one of ideas. The vitality of any enterprise is inseparable from the relevance, importance, and vibrancy of its core vision. The foundational ideas of the Conservative and Reform movements were crafted as cutting-edge concepts for a societal and intellectual milieu that existed when horses were the dominant mode of transportation. They were designed to enable Judaism to contribute its wisdom for uplifting humanity as effectively as possible within the realities of that period. Since then, the insights of that earlier age have been patched and tweaked to adapt to the conditions of the passing decades. It is, however, unrealistic to expect that ideas that are derivatives of a nineteenth-century response to modernity will be well calibrated to a vastly transformed epoch in which self-driving cars controlled by artificial intelligence ply the streets.

This book, then, explores two transitions, both triggered by the historic turning point that occurred when modernity gave way to the digital age. The first transition is already apparent, while the second is yet to take shape. The first is the journey of Conservative and Reform Judaism from a century of growth to a period of decline. A close examination of this transition reveals some of the factors that affected the non-Orthodox movements in the twentieth century: The modern movements flourished in part because they surfaced at a time when Jews were admitted to society but not fully embraced—before the onset of the "hyper-emancipation" of the digital period. When peak Jewish acceptance in the broader society arrived, the non-Orthodox movements began to steadily lose ground. Another reason for the transition is that the movements had largely achieved their goals of helping Jews adapt to being citizens of nation states and of harmonizing the pivotal intellectual developments of modernity with Jewish life. There was, consequently, less call for their assistance in integrating modernity and Judaism. Perhaps even more importantly, the core attributes that made the movements of modernity successful were not translatable to the challenges of an epoch characterized by "hyper-connectivity," "hyper-individualism," and "hyper-ethics." The Conservative and Reform movements remained inexorably linked to modernity, to its thought and its structures, so that the paradigm shift to a new age, made the leap to the next mountaintop nigh impossible.

The second transition has scarcely begun: the crystallization of a significant Jewish response to the digital age. The discussion of this second transition begins with a detailed exploration of the astounding transformations that have occurred since 1990 and asks how Judaism should tackle these tectonic shifts. Consideration of this question is followed by examples of a number of concerns that have arisen in the digital age which Judaism might be well placed to address.

The book proceeds to investigate the future trajectory of technology as viewed through the lenses of several key thinkers. These futurists concur that the decades ahead will lead to additional seismic change. For example, the computer scientist and futurist Ray Kurzweil observes that given the "explosive power of exponential growth," the rate of progress in every field during the twenty-first century will be thousands of times greater in magnitude than that experienced in the late twentieth century.[11] This has sizable implications. If technological growth is increasing exponentially, then the number of novel ethical dilemmas and uncertainties that will arise from these advances will similarly rocket higher.

The ramifications for Judaism are vast. Given that Judaism is a system that calls upon Jews to live in a way that is exemplary, Judaism will soon confront a host of issues that have not previously been central to the Jewish agenda. As artificial intelligence (AI) becomes ever more sophisticated, as gene editing makes the unexpected possible, and as medical discoveries extend longevity, Judaism will need to grapple with the parameters of what it means to be human—and even whether there should be humans at all. And this is just the tip of the iceberg. Soon enough, the terms "non-Orthodox" and "Orthodox" will become passé. The core debates of twenty-first-century Judaism will revolve around how to respond to an avalanche of new existential challenges and whether to bless whatever the broader society finds acceptable or to offer countercultural perspectives.

This book discusses how Judaism might respond to these conundrums and how it might prepare for what lies ahead. It proposes that the answers to the urgent human questions of our day should not only be in the hands of scientists, politicians, think tanks, and philosophy departments but ought to be a core project of the Jewish collective. Working proactively with age-old sources, Judaism might thus resume its role as an ideas generator that has appreciable relevance and importance. Specifically, the book considers the enhancement of three areas of Jewish functioning—Jewish practice, Jewish community, and Jewish ideas—to ready Jewish life for the era of exponential change that has already begun.

Not far down the road are iterations of Judaism that we cannot yet anticipate. It is possible, nevertheless, to determine some of their parameters and the themes they will have to address. First, though, it is important to ascertain what brought us to this point, what exactly has shifted so dramatically, and how the contours of the road ahead are being shaped; only then will we have some inkling of the new vehicles we will need for the extraordinary journey on which we are now embarked.

NOTES

1. Reform and Conservative Judaism are distinct from one another in important ways. Most notably, the Conservative movement defines itself as *halakhic*, while the Reform movement does not.
2. Pew Research Center, "Jewish Americans in 2020," May 11, 2021, accessed August 1, 2022, https://www.pewforum.org/2021/05/11/jewish-identity-and-belief/
3. Sidney Goldstein, "Profile of American Jewry: Insights from the 1990 National Jewish Population Survey," Table 19, May 1993, accessed August 1, 2022, https://www.jstor.org/stable/23605965?read-now=1&seq=94#metadata_info_tab_contents

4. Arno Rosenfeld, "As movements recede in Jewish life, Reform and Conservative seminaries shrink." *The Forward*, March 25, 2022, accessed August 1, 2022, https://forward.com/news/484575/as-movements-recede-in-jewish-life-reform-and-conservative-seminaries/

5. Pew Research Center, "Jewish Americans in 2020," https://www.pewforum.org/2021/05/11/jewish-identity-and-belief/

6. Goldstein, "Profile of American Jewry: Insights from the 1990 National Jewish Population Survey," Table 19.

7. Pew Research Center, "Jewish Americans in 2020," https://www.pewforum.org/2021/05/11/jewish-identity-and-belief/

8. Usually understood as "Jewish law" or "the Jewish way of going." See Chap. 8 for a fuller discussion.

9. Forward Staff, "Will Jewish denominations survive the pandemic? 30 Rabbis weigh in," *The Forward*, May 19, 2020, accessed August 1, 2022, https://forward.com/opinion/446714/will-jewish-denominations-survive-the-pandemic-30-rabbis-weigh-in/?fbclid=IwAR3_DCnHzzSY06-h660xLtLuxBvvwgPM3S2ZBjrLfl0rVe1G_DO5kOOhLP8

10. Ibid.

11. Ray Kurzweil, as quoted in Thomas Friedman, *Thank You for Being Late: An Optimist's Guide to Thriving in the Age of Accelerations* (New York: Farrar, Straus and Giroux, 2016), 187.

References

Forward Staff, "Will Jewish denominations survive the pandemic? 30 Rabbis weigh in," *The Forward*, May 19, 2020, accessed August 1, 2022, https://forward.com/opinion/446714/will-jewish-denominations-survive-the-pandemic-30-rabbis-weigh-in/?fbclid=IwAR3_DCnHzzSY06-h660xLtLuxBvvwgPM3S2ZBjrLfl0rVe1G_DO5kOOhLP8.

Goldstein, Sidney. "Profile of American Jewry: Insights from the 1990 National Jewish Population Survey," Table 19, May 1993, accessed August 1, 2022, https://www.jstor.org/stable/23605965?read-now=1&seq=94#metadata_info_tab_contents.

Friedman, Thomas. *Thank You for Being Late: An Optimist's Guide to Thriving in the Age of Accelerations* (New York: Farrar, Straus and Giroux, 2016).

Pew Research Center, "Jewish Americans in 2020," May 11, 2021, accessed August 1, 2022, https://www.pewforum.org/2021/05/11/jewish-identity-and-belief/.

Rosenfeld, Arno. "As movements recede in Jewish life, Reform and Conservative seminaries shrink." *The Forward*, March 25, 2022, accessed August 1, 2022, https://forward.com/news/484575/as-movements-recede-in-jewish-life-reform-and-conservative-seminaries/.

CHAPTER 2

Hyper-Emancipation

Emerging into the World

Reform and Conservative Judaism began as responses to the tremendous challenges that modernity posed to Judaism and the Jewish people. These challenges presented themselves in two ways: First, there was the upheaval brought about by the political emancipation that liberated Jews from the rigid confines of the separated, autonomous communities that had typified Jewish life for centuries. Emancipation would open the door to Jewish citizenship in the nascent nation states that were emerging across Europe and beyond. Second, there were the remarkable developments in thought spawned by the ongoing scientific revolution, together with new understandings of philosophy and history that called into question long-held tenets of Judaism. Neither of these historic ruptures could be ignored.

Emancipation prompted a "drastic and far-reaching"[1] reconceptualization of Jewish life. It led to the "destruction of the old corporate status of Jewry" and "the end of the quasi-political functions of the kehillot."[2] Perhaps more crucially, it "was to make Jewish identity a private commitment rather than a legal status, leaving it a complex mix of destiny and choice."[3] Given the newfound freedoms that emancipation brought, one might have expected that the elimination of the ghetto walls would have led to a rush of assimilation. It did not. The overwhelming majority of Jews "rejected this path to assimilation and remained loyal to Judaism and the Jewish people."[4]

© The Author(s), under exclusive license to Springer Nature Switzerland AG 2023
D. Schiff, *Judaism in a Digital Age*,
https://doi.org/10.1007/978-3-031-17992-1_2

It is important to inquire why this was so. Were the Jews of the nineteenth century markedly more devoted to the Jewish cause than their future descendants would be? Given their cultural context, it is possible that they may have been more attentive to their heritage, but this hardly explains their predominant choice to remain within the fold. Rather, the more plausible answer can be summarized in one word: conversion.

When twenty-first-century Jews think about assimilation, the image that usually comes to mind is one of a painless path toward voluntarily jettisoning Judaism. This assimilation process most often results in becoming a "secular Jew" or one who has replaced the descriptor of "Jewish" with "nothing." These options were unavailable in the nineteenth century. The secular persona was still undeveloped, and to become "nothing" effectively meant cutting oneself off from communal life and any realistic aspiration for economic security. Even in France, where Jews had begun to adopt lifestyles similar to those of the surrounding society, "the religious chasm separating Jews and gentiles remained unbridged."[5] As one scholar put it succinctly, "The fact that the Jews were invited to join a society that was not religiously neutral, but Christian, exerted a powerful influence on Jewish identity."[6] The effective choice for the Jew was either to remain Jewish or to become a Christian—formally, by means of the baptismal font. Given the long and deeply painful history of Jewish suffering at the hands of Christians, the prospect of becoming one held little appeal. Consequently, emancipation did not open the floodgates of assimilation—far from it.

Yet another consideration was apt to encourage Jews to remain within the Jewish fold: antisemitism. Whether in its overt form of hatred, abuse, or murder or in its softer form of social exclusion, antisemitism was an ever-present feature of European, Russian, and American Jewish life at least through the nineteenth and the first half of the twentieth centuries. Its impact in Europe was sufficiently frightening that it gave rise to waves of *aliyah* (emigration to the land of Israel) and to Theodore Herzl's vision of a Jewish state as logical paths toward solving the problem of the violent rejection of Jews. In Germany, one country where Jews did have some success in assimilating, quotas attested to the limits placed upon tolerance, and Nazism ultimately gave rise to the most horrifying eruption of genocidal antisemitism ever known.

In the US, which, in the early twentieth century, would become the destination for so many seeking to leave Europe behind, antisemitism was well entrenched. In the 1930s, as Jewish numbers headed toward their highest ever percentage of the US population,[7] "antisemitism peaked" and was practiced even by "highly respected individuals and institutions. Private schools, camps, colleges, resorts, and places of employment all imposed restrictions and quotas on Jews, often quite blatantly."[8] [9] Indeed, one way to chart antisemitism and Jewish exclusion in the US is by examining the rise and fall of Jewish hospitals, country clubs, places of higher learning, and social organizations that were established by Jews to deal with their ostracism from general society. These institutions were started as a direct response to persistent antisemitism that resulted in exclusion.[10]

The antisemitism of the period may well have been the most significant factor that worked to keep Jews Jewish. A large number of American Jews had little interest in their Judaism and may have abandoned the Jewish community altogether had such a move been truly feasible. One survey showed that in 1935, only 8 percent of Jews regularly attended synagogue, and "three-quarters of young Jews…had not attended any religious services at all during the previous year—not even, apparently, on the High Holidays."[11] Instead, Jews turned their attention in multiple external directions: to the Ethical Culture Movement, to Marxism, to Communism, and to "automobiles, golf clubs, radios, bridge parties, extension lectures, and the proceedings of various learned and pseudo-learned societies."[12] Rabbis bemoaned that American Judaism was being "invaded by secularism."[13] Much like their counterparts in the twenty-first century, Jewish leaders held that a deepening interest in "universalism" and the "cosmopolitan spirit" would soon sap Judaism of all vitality.

Jews, then, were not short of external causes to pursue, and their varying interests readily turned their attention away from Jewish concerns. Yet the fact that intermarriage[14] rates remained well under 10 percent throughout this period is ample evidence that most did not stray far from the Jewish community; at a minimum, they maintained their social connections. The sense of being an outsider was always just below the surface. As the American Jewish historian Jonathan Sarna expressed it, their Judaism was "temporarily secured by the antisemitism of non-Jewish neighbors."[15]

In the US, this type of antisemitism would last for decades and would not begin to wane until the horrors of the Holocaust became known: "Between 1946 and 1950, the percentage of Americans who claimed even to have heard 'any criticism or talk against the Jews in the last six months' dropped from 64 percent to 24 percent."[16] By the early 1960s, while antisemitism had not disappeared, "almost all resorts and housing developments had dropped their restrictive clauses; antisemitic college quotas had mostly ended; and professional fields like law, medicine, and banking proved more receptive to Jews."[17] As antisemitism weakened, its impact on Jews evaporated rapidly. It would not take long for Jews to wonder why they needed separate Jewish institutions. "By the 1980s and 1990s, many people in the Jewish community were questioning 'whether, with the passing of time, the Jewish hospital remains a necessary concept.'"[18] Similarly, when one of Miami's Jewish country clubs closed in 2011, it was reported that it had served "Jewish families who were once barred from joining, as recently as the early 1980s, similarly upscale clubs." As the club president explained, when "barriers in the community came down… Jewish people were accepted at other clubs and there were many competing social engagements."[19]

The evidence, then, suggests a turning point in the emancipation process: by the early 1960s, American antisemitism had begun to weaken, and by the early 1980s, antisemitism—though its presence was still felt—was largely insignificant to the functioning of Jews in American society. Reflecting on this change, Alan Dershowitz, professor of law at Harvard, wrote that "the good news is that American Jews—as individuals—have never been more secure, more accepted, more affluent, and less victimized by discrimination or anti-Semitism."[20] A number of societal transitions led to this long-awaited shift from entrenched antisemitism to near full acceptance of Jewish participation. Beyond the Holocaust, the civil rights movement of the 1960s ameliorated discrimination, as the negative implications of exclusionist policies became more apparent. Feminism arose as a serious force, challenging long-held assumptions about "appropriate" societal roles. The interest in "roots" that surfaced in the 1970s expanded pride in group identity and laid the foundations for social structures that would later embrace diversity.[21]

Whatever the cause, the impact on Jews, particularly in America, was noticeable. In the mid-1990s, Dershowitz described it this way:

> Bill Clinton's presidency marked the end of discrimination against Jews in the upper echelons of government. For the first time in American history, the fact that an aspirant for high appointive office was a Jew became irrelevant in his or her selection. President Clinton…selected several Jewish cabinet members, two Jewish Supreme Court justices, numerous Jewish ambassadors and other high-level executive and judicial officials… It is fair to say that in today's America, a Jew can aspire to any office, any job, and any social status.[22]

Soon, Clinton's Vice President, Al Gore, would select Senator Joe Lieberman as the first Jew to run on a presidential ticket, and President Clinton's daughter, President Trump's daughter (who converted to Judaism), and each of President Biden's three children would marry Jews, as would Vice President Kamala Harris. The very fact that these marriages came to be regarded as unremarkable was a sure sign of the astonishing progress in Jewish acceptance by non-Jewish society since the 1980s.

Indeed, the intermarriage rate through the decades presents a barometer of this shift in attitudes. In the years prior to 1960, intermarriage did not rise above 7 percent. In the 1960s, the rate nudged up to 13 percent. Between 1970 and 1979, the rate more than doubled to 28 percent, but in-marriage remained normative. Between 1980 and 1984, intermarriage climbed quickly to 38 percent. From 1985 to 1995, the rate escalated to 43 percent. From 1996 to 2001, the rate went up further to 47 percent.[23] By 2008, the rate was estimated to have reached 55 percent.[24] In 2020, the Pew report found an intermarriage rate of 61 percent, with a 72 percent rate for non-Orthodox Jews.[25] Intermarriage had become the norm. No matter what the reaction of Jews might be to intermarriage, the numbers demonstrate conclusively that from around 1980 on, there was no shortage of non-Jews who were ready to marry Jews. There could hardly be a better demonstration of the broad social acceptance that Jews had come to enjoy.

This cursory sketch of the parameters of Jewish social exclusion illustrates something crucial about the nature of emancipation up until the elimination of the antisemitic barriers that occurred between 1960 and 1980: it was only partial. To be sure, a revolution had taken place in the nineteenth century: Jews had achieved citizenship, were full economic participants, had non-Jewish friends, attended prestigious institutions, and some attained positions of communal prominence. Any societal obstacles that remained for Jews were rarely highlighted, so Jews lived with the sense that they had been accepted; and, compared with the long centuries of seclusion, modernity unquestionably provided expanded freedoms, commercial opportunities, and possibilities for social interaction.

Yet it is now apparent that this first stage of emancipation was anything but complete. Insofar as European emancipation required a Jew to become a Christian to be fully accepted, a largely insurmountable hurdle to full emancipation remained in place. Even when that obstruction disappeared, the exclusion from colleges, professions, institutions, and clubs that remained—both in Europe and the US—restricted emancipation. Jews continued to lack the type of complete social penetration that might have been expected had emancipation been allowed to reach its ultimate logical conclusion.

During this period of "partial emancipation," Jews not only worked hard to build institutions to serve Jewish needs, they also created social structures that would allow young Jews to meet and marry. Since, during the first half of the twentieth century, Jews and gentiles had little interest in marrying each other, a Jew who wanted to marry needed to meet other Jews. Encountering other Jews occured primarily at synagogues, youth organizations, and other communal bodies that promoted such interactions. The desire to marry essentially compelled Jews to look inward, to depend on their own communal institutions, and to socialize within a Jewish context. The ghetto walls might have fallen, but invisible barriers remained. Given that Jews were still required to form their principal social contacts within the Jewish community, Jewish emancipation was still a "work in progress." Jews were free, yet not wholly accepted; liberated, but not totally admitted. So long as exclusion remained a practical problem with which Jews had to grapple, Jews were not truly able to move in society with the same range of options as those that existed for non-Jews. Hence, insofar as the goal of emancipation was to make Jewish identity into a wholly "private commitment"—a choice of the individual, without external pressures or social dictates—it was unfinished.

It follows that the effective ending of most all social exclusion that took place between 1960 and 1980 represented a notable opening. From that point on, no longer were affiliations with Jewishness or with the Jewish community predicated upon a reality of limited alternatives. Jews became fully free, without external constraints on their choices to remain within the Jewish fold or to leave. The outcome that emancipation had originally portended, but had never wholly delivered, had arrived.

The response of a vast number of Jews to this new reality was unambiguous: Given that the intermarriage rate was no more than 7 percent prior to 1960 but was in the vicinity of 40 percent—and rising quickly—in the 1980s, it is clear that emancipation and assimilation were linked. Many Jews who intermarried did not intend to abandon Judaism; some hoped to raise Jewish children and stay connected. Given the nature of intermarriage, however, this resolve often remained an aspiration.[26] Despite the fact that it became increasingly plain that intermarriage was a likely pathway to assimilation, Jews continued to marry non-Jews in ever greater numbers.

It would be a mistake, however, to limit consideration of assimilation to the phenomenon of intermarriage. Intermarriage is, after all, an indicator of a broader phenomenon. The 2020 Pew study found that around one quarter of US Jews are Jews of "no religion," meaning that they have a Jewish parent or were raised Jewish, but do not identify Judaism as their religion, regarding themselves instead as cultural or ethnic Jews. Tellingly, the report observes that "Jews by religion are far more likely than Jews of no religion to say that being Jewish is very important to them (55% vs. 7%); 55% of Jews of no religion say being Jewish is of little importance to them."[27] These numbers demonstrate that in an environment where the barriers to leaving Jewish life are virtually non-existent, a large number of American Jews are prone to assimilate.

There seems to be little prospect that trends in the surrounding society will turn in a direction that will make assimilation less likely. Indeed, in the twenty-first century, it is possible to assert that Jews have gone beyond full acceptance. Various cultural signs suggest that Jews and Jewish folkways are "trendy" in American culture. Thus, Jon Stewart, one of America's most watched early twenty-first-century comedians, liberally inserted Jewish references into his daily delivery of mock news with the reasonable expectation that they would be widely appreciated. Some non-Jews, not content with merely attending *Bar* and *Bat Mitzvah* observances for their Jewish friends, adopted such celebrations for themselves.[28] And President Obama, enthusiastic to practice a quintessential Jewish tradition, introduced an annual seder ritual to the White House.[29] Indeed, a 2014 study showed that, of all the religious groups in the US, Americans felt most warmly toward Jews.[30] When the study was repeated in 2017 and again in 2019, it came up with the same result: Jews continued to receive the "warmest ratings."[31] In a brief three decades, Jews went from being unwelcome at the country club to drinking four cups of wine in the home of the leader of the free world. Perhaps not since Joseph in Egypt rose from being a foreign prisoner to a national leader had Jews leaped in standing so far, so fast.

The embrace of the trappings of Jewish culture by the wider society has caused Jews to feel more accepted in America, not more attached to Judaism or the Jewish community. It is, consequently, reasonable to assert that the twenty-first century has become a period of what might be termed "hyper-emancipation." In the US, home to more than 70 percent of the

Jewish diaspora, not only have the barriers to full Jewish participation been removed, but the wider society now exerts a magnetic attraction upon Jews to move beyond the Jewish orbit. This age of hyper-emancipation that began post-1980 represents a break with the Jewish past almost as significant as the initial move toward partial emancipation two centuries ago.

The Rise and Decline of Reform and Conservative Judaism

In the nineteenth century, even though full acceptance remained a distant prospect, the changes brought about by emancipation were significant. Jews were offered citizenship in the emerging nation states of modernity, provided that they dissolved their autonomous communal existence in which Jewish law held sway. For the most part, it was an offer they could not refuse. But accepting the bargain meant that Judaism needed to adapt to a new environment and, in the process, had to be remade. It could no longer be the lived expression of a separate nation with its own laws, customs, and practices. Becoming a nation within a nation was not an option. The solution for Judaism was, in short order, to become a religion. Judaism effectively became "Christianized," with its parameters and its relationship with the state modeled on those of the church.[32]

Hence, virtually simultaneously, Judaism was recast as a religion, and Jews became citizens of nation states with broader societal access than they had experienced in centuries. The vast majority who remained Jews sought to maximize the gains of citizenship by demonstrating that they could be loyal, productive citizens and that their reformulated Judaism was ready for smooth incorporation into mass society, no longer encumbered by its "shtetl" past. Not only did Judaism have to become a religion, it had to become the type of religion that was conducive to the zeitgeist of the modern state.

Reform, Conservative, and Orthodox Judaism represent the three major nineteenth-century solutions to making Judaism function on religious terms within the non-Jewish states of modernity. There would, of course, be other responses. Some groups attempted to enshrine Judaism within the framework of cultural or benevolent organizations. Some attempted to resist the advances of the state, preferring to continue a cloistered existence on the margins of society, to the extent that it was possible. Zionists proposed an altogether different solution: to recreate an autonomous Jewish polity within a Jewish state.

From a sociological perspective, Reform and Conservative Judaism began as attempts to forestall assimilation while embracing the ethos of modernity. To be sure, the two movements approached these goals with considerably different solutions: The Reform movement made the individual the arbiter of Jewish practice. The Conservative movement, by contrast, committed itself to *halakhah* and effected its changes through the mechanism of rabbinic decisions. Both movements emphasized that "visionary change" was necessary to adapt Judaism to modern times. Orthodoxy took a different path. Having come into being in reaction to the modernizing movements, Orthodoxy distinguished itself by its determination to offer an "orthodox" form of traditional Judaism, that was to some extent impervious to the currents of modernity, but still operated within the new "religionized" structures necessitated by the nation state.

Reform and Conservative Judaism were both products of Western Europe, where they established solid foundations. But their real success came in post-war America. Reform Judaism had been a rising force in nineteenth-century American Jewish life. However, between 1880 and 1924, some two million Jews from Russia and Eastern Europe, most of them Orthodox, fled persecution and made their way to America.[33] As a result, in the first decades of the twentieth century, despite the growth of Reform and Conservative Judaism, Orthodoxy was the largest movement in American Jewish life.[34] That reality changed swiftly. By the middle of the twentieth century, a new generation, largely born in America, turned away from Orthodoxy, associating it with an old world that lay in ruins. Orthodoxy seemed less well suited to the freedoms of America and the spirit of rebirth and renewal that animated post-Holocaust American Jewry: "They had, after all, immigrated not only to escape poverty and anti-Semitism but in pursuit of 'modernity.'"[35]

Not surprisingly, the most popular destination for those leaving Orthodoxy was the Conservative movement, where the philosophy and aesthetics were more familiar than those of the Reform movement. Between 1945 and 1965, the Conservative movement added 450 new congregations, "more than the number of new Reform and Orthodox synagogues combined."[36] While the Reform movement was not in first place, it too made strides. From the mid-1940s to the mid-1960s, the number of Reform congregations doubled, and the number of affiliated families tripled.[37] By the late 1950s, the synagogue affiliation rate reached 60 percent, "a figure never exceeded."[38] America was moving to the suburbs, and Jewish life was going through a renaissance: "Between 1945 and 1965, well over one thousand synagogues and temples were built or rebuilt."[39] Secularism was not in vogue, belonging to a congregation was fashionable, a "baby boom" of young Jews needed to be educated in new synagogue education buildings, and post-Holocaust theological inquiry was popular.[40] By 1970, a national survey reported that 42 percent of Jews identified as Conservative, 33 percent as Reform, and 11 percent as Orthodox.[41] As noted earlier, this level of non-Orthodox vigor lasted till somewhere around 1990, by which time the Reform movement at 38 percent had overtaken the Conservative movement at 35 percent, with Orthodoxy at a low of 7 percent.[42] It is clear that by the third quarter of the twentieth century, the Reform and Conservative movements had become the foremost hubs of Jewish life in the US, the world's largest Jewish community.

In truth, though, it is unlikely that the strength of non-Orthodox Judaism between 1950 and 1990 was due to widespread enthusiasm for the ideological core of what the movements offered. Ironically, even as Reform and Conservative Judaism were ascending, there was "every indication" that their adherents were "actually becoming more lax in their religious practice."[43] It was not "belief, synagogue attendance, [or] the regular practice of Jewish rituals" that best described the reasons why Jews built, buttressed, and belonged to non-Orthodox institutions.[44] Rather, it was because the reality of exclusion, or perceived exclusion, left little choice.

It was in the synagogues—the Conservative and Reform synagogues—that Jews found the education that would lead to *Bar Mitzvah* and where youth groups would open the door to marriage partners. The more people that joined synagogues, the more magnetic the synagogues became as places where social and business connections were forged. This was particularly true in the mushrooming suburbs and in the newer urban communities, where the non-Orthodox synagogue was often the only outpost of Judaism and regularly served as a substitute for far-distant family ties. Jewish cultural organizations were not nearly as adept at filling these roles. By the time Jewish exclusion began to evaporate, the synagogue building boom was in full swing, and non-Orthodox synagogues were simply "the place to be." Momentum, and long-embedded habits, ensured that robust non-Orthodox identification continued for some time even after the social ostracizing of Jews had diminished. Yet it cannot be an accident that the noticeable decline of Conservative and Reform Judaism began little more than a decade after Jewish exclusion had effectively come to an end.

A generation later, with the non-Orthodox proportion of the American Jewish pie shrinking, it is worth reflecting on what happened. Looking back, it seems clear that the manifold twentieth-century successes of the Conservative and Reform movements ought to be considered within the reality of the partial emancipation that prevailed when the two movements became ascendant. The rise of the non-Orthodox movements essentially took place behind a firewall of social separation and was fueled by the need to build families and communities in multiple locations. Hundreds of thousands of Jews belonged to these movements more by default than by devotion, such that their ongoing exposure to the movements did not reliably result in durable commitments to the practices or the institutions of Conservative or Reform Judaism—or even to the importance of transmitting Judaism itself.

In 1990, with 73 percent of American Jews identifying as Reform or Conservative, only 10 percent of American Jews attended synagogue weekly, only 12 percent reported that they kept kosher, and only 19 percent "usually" lit candles on Friday night.[45] Given that some of the Jews who engaged in these practices must have been Orthodox, these were plain indicators that the religious eagerness of Conservative and Reform Jews was low. It is hard to imagine that intermarriage rates would have risen as steeply or that the pace of movement contraction would have been as pronounced had there been a robust dedication to the positions of the movements.[46] After all, both movements continued to express plain opposition to intermarriage throughout the last quarter of the twentieth century.[47] Yet hundreds of thousands of Reform and Conservative Jews paid no heed. The same held true for fidelity to ideology: Many Jews who described themselves as Conservative did not have a systematic approach to Judaism that might be described as *halakhic*, and few Reform Jews were "committed to the ongoing study of the whole array of *mitzvot*" or "to the fulfillment of those *mitzvot* that spoke to them."[48] In short, while describing themselves as Reform or Conservative, a considerable proportion was rarely interested in more than a glancing involvement with movement practices or philosophies. Small wonder, then, that when hyper-emancipation arrived, many would detach themselves from these affiliations. While non-Orthodox Judaism had thrived behind a barrier of exclusion that impeded assimilation, there was insufficient loyalty to stop the outflow once the levee was breached. As one scholar put it, a large number of American Jews had "lost all religious basis for sustaining a distinctive identity, and the protective encapsulation once provided by their Jewishness collapsed."[49]

It is easy to level blame at the Conservative and Reform movements themselves for their contraction. Voices from within Orthodoxy sometimes opine that American Jewry would not have experienced such sustained assimilation were it not for the positions taken by the "compromising" non-Orthodox movements. This claim has little credibility. It assumes that the main reason why Orthodoxy fell from its peak in the first half of the twentieth century was because of the alluring siren song of non-Orthodox Judaism, and that if Orthodoxy had been the sole option the situation would have been healthier. In reality, had Orthodoxy been the sole option available, a more moderate alternative would have been invented; many Jews living in free societies would not have constrained themselves within traditional boundaries. It is certainly possible that, for some, identifying with a non-Orthodox approach made abandoning Judaism an easier step. It is equally possible that, for others, being non-Orthodox kept them involved in Jewish life in a way that otherwise would not have been a consideration.

There is yet another criticism that is sometimes advanced. According to this viewpoint, the Conservative and Reform movements are in decline principally because they did not do enough to be accommodating to the needs of those who sought intermarriage; if only they had been more responsive, the argument maintains, many more might have remained connected to their Jewishness. It is, of course, impossible to know what might have happened, but what did happen in response to every act of amelioration and accommodation is clear: the intermarriage rate never plateaued but continued to rise no matter what was attempted. The Reform movement introduced patrilineal descent and an outreach program in the 1980s, and an ever greater number of Reform rabbis moved to officiate at intermarriages. The Conservative movement introduced a *keruv* (drawing close) program and made sure that every social barrier to acceptance of the intermarried melted away. In the final analysis, none of it mattered. The intermarriage rate climbed ever higher, no matter what the movements did. Hyper-emancipation offered extensive possibilities for connecting beyond the Jewish milieu and that reality proved far more powerful than the decisions of non-Orthodox rabbis.

Though the twenty-first century has been marked by a discernible uptick in antisemitism, the hyper-emancipation thesis remains intact.

Societal doors continue to be almost fully open to Jews in a way that was not the case a century earlier. Just as the Reform and Conservative movements flourished within the conditions of partial emancipation, they are plainly now struggling in a world of hyper-emancipation where Jews have virtually unrestricted public opportunities. It was not, however, just the place of Jews in the broader society that was evolving in the last decades of the twentieth century. The world of ideas and the needs of Jews were also shifting. In many ways, those transitions would prove to be even more formidable for the movements of modernity.

NOTES

1. Robert Seltzer, *Jewish People, Jewish Thought* (New York: Macmillan Publishing Company, 1980), 544.
2. Ibid.
3. Ibid.
4. Ibid.
5. Jay R. Berkovitz, *The Shaping of Jewish Identity in Nineteenth-Century France* (Detroit: Wayne State University Press, 1995), 114.
6. Ibid., 117.
7. Ira Sheskin and Arnold Deshefsky, "Jewish Population in the United States, 2010" (North American Jewish Databank, 2011) accessed October 11, 2020, https://www.brandeis.edu/cmjs/conferences/demography-conf/pdfs/Dashefsky_JewishPopulationUS2010.pdf, 3.
8. Jonathan D. Sarna and Jonathan Golden, "The American Jewish Experience in the Twentieth Century: Antisemitism and Assimilation," National Humanities Center, 2000, accessed August 1, 2022, http://nationalhumanitiescenter.org/tserve/twenty/tkeyinfo/jewishexp.htm
9. "By 1922, they [Jews] made up more than a fifth of Harvard's freshman class. The administration and alumni were up in arms. Jews were thought to be sickly and grasping, grade-grubbing and insular. They displaced the sons of wealthy Wasp alumni, which did not bode well for fund-raising. A. Lawrence Lowell, Harvard's president in the nineteen-twenties, stated flatly that too many Jews would destroy the school: 'The summer hotel that is ruined by admitting Jews meets its fate…because they drive away the Gentiles, and then after the Gentiles have left, they leave also.'" See: Malcolm Gladwell, "Getting In," *The New Yorker*, October 10, 2005, accessed August 1, 2022, http://www.newyorker.com/archive/2005/10/10/051010crat_atlarge?currentPage=all
10. Robert A. Katz, "PAGING DR. SHYLOCK!: Jewish Hospitals and the Prudent Re-Investment of Jewish Philanthropy," in *Religious Giving for*

Love of God, ed. David H. Smith (Bloomington: Indiana University Press, 2010), 162.

11. Jonathan D. Sarna, *American Judaism: A History* (New Haven: Yale University Press, 2004), 224–225.

12. Ibid., 226.

13. Ibid.

14. "Intermarriage" refers to a marriage between a Jew and a non-Jew. "In-marriage" refers to a marriage between a Jew and a Jew. "In-marriage" includes marriages between a Jew and an individual who has converted to Judaism.

15. Sarna, *American Judaism*, 227.

16. Ibid., 276.

17. Ibid.

18. Katz, "PAGING DR. SHYLOCK!" 176.

19. Howard Cohen, "Changing Times Cited as Jewish Country Club Closes," *The Miami Herald*, May 1, 2011, accessed October 11, 2020, http://articles.sun-sentinel.com/2011-05-01/entertainment/mh-westview-country-club-20110501_1_social-club-family-oriented-club-jewish-members

20. Alan Dershowitz, *The Vanishing American Jew—In Search of Jewish Identity for the Next Century* (New York: Touchstone, 1997), 1.

21. Sarna, *American Judaism*, 317.

22. Dershowitz, *The Vanishing American Jew*, 9–10.

23. The National Jewish Population Survey, 2000–01, A United Jewish Communities Report, accessed August 1, 2022, https://cdn.fedweb.org/fed-34/136/National-Jewish-Population-Study.pdf, Table 14.

24. Kobi Nahshoni, "Intermarriage rates among Diaspora Jews at all-time high," Ynet News.com, November 17, 2010, accessed August 1, 2022, http://www.ynetnews.com/articles/0,7340,L-3984935,00.html.   The findings, reported by the Knesset Information and Research Center, showed that "while in the United States 55% of all Jews married non-Jewish partners, intermarriage rates in Australia, Canada and Turkey fluctuate between 25%–30%. An intermarriage rate of 35%–45% was recorded among the Jewish Diaspora in France, Britain and most of Latin America. The study revealed much higher figures in Eastern Europe and the former Soviet Union, where 65% of Jews exchanged nuptials with non Jews, while Russia came out on top of the list with a 75% rate of intermarriage."

25. Pew Research Center, "Jewish Americans in 2020," https://www.pewresearch.org/religion/2021/05/11/marriage-families-and-children/

26. The 2020 Pew research shows that 28 percent of Jews with non-Jewish spouses were raising their children as "Jews by religion," whereas 93 percent of Jews with Jewish spouses were doing so. See Pew Research Center,

"Jewish Americans in 2020," https://www.pewresearch.org/religion/2021/05/11/marriage-families-and-children/

27. Pew Research Center, "Jewish Americans in 2020," https://www.pewresearch.org/religion/2021/05/11/jewish-identity-and-belief/
28. Elizabeth Bernstein, "You Don't Have to Be Jewish to Want a Bar Mitzvah Party," *The Wall Street Journal*, January 14, 2004, accessed August 1, 2022, https://www.wsj.com/articles/SB107404276295131300
29. Jodi Kantor, "Next Year in the White House: A Seder Tradition," *The New York Times*, March 27, 2010, accessed August 1, 2022, http://www.nytimes.com/2010/03/28/us/politics/28seder.html?_r=0
30. "How Americans Feel About Religious Groups," Pew Research Center, July 16, 2014, accessed August 1, 2022, http://www.pewforum.org/2014/07/16/how-americans-feel-about-religious-groups/
31. "Americans Express Increasingly Warm Feelings Towards Religious Groups," Pew Research Center, February 15, 2017, accessed August 1, 2022, http://www.pewforum.org/2017/02/15/americans-express-increasingly-warm-feelings-toward-religious-groups/
    "What Americans Know About Religion," Pew Research Center, July 23, 2019, accessed August 1, 2022, https://www.pewresearch.org/religion/2019/07/23/feelings-toward-religious-groups/
32. Seltzer, *Jewish People, Jewish Thought*, 523–527.
33. Joellyn Zollman, "Jewish Immigration to America: Three Waves," *My Jewish Learning*, accessed August 1, 2022, https://www.myjewishlearning.com/article/jewish-immigration-to-america-three-waves/
34. Sarna, *American Judaism*, 278.
35. Rodney Stark, *One True God* (Princeton: Princeton University Press, 2001), 211.
36. Sarna, *American Judaism*, 284.
37. Ibid.
38. Ibid., 277.
39. Ibid., 279.
40. Ibid.
41. Samuel C. Heilman, *Portrait of American Jews* (University of Washington Press, 1995), 71.
42. Sidney Goldstein, "Profile of American Jewry: Insights from the 1990 National Jewish Population Survey," May 1993, accessed August 1, 2022, https://www.jstor.org/stable/23605965?read-now=1&seq=94#metadata_info_tab_contents Table 19.
43. Sarna, *American Judaism*, 278.
44. Ibid., 279.
45. "The National Jewish Population Survey, 1990" as cited in Stark, *One True God*, 213.

46. The Pew report of 2013 showed that the Conservative movement had around half the percentage of American Jewish identification that it had in 1990: from 35 percent, it had fallen to 18 percent. The Reform movement, by contrast could claim that its contraction had been slight and that it remained the largest movement by a considerable margin, having experienced a decline from 38 percent to 35 percent ("A Portrait of American Jews: Overview," Pew Research Center, October 1, 2013, accessed August 1, 2022, https://www.pewforum.org/2013/10/01/jewish-american-beliefs-attitudes-culture-survey/, 10).

When examined a little closer, however, these figures do not tell the full story. The Pew research goes on to show that fully 30 percent of those raised Conservative a generation earlier had become Reform as adults. The Reform movement, meanwhile, had lost 28 percent who had become "Jews of no religion" or non-Jewish; the corresponding figure for the Conservative movement was appreciably lower at 17 percent. It is reasonable, therefore, to surmise that, because of the Conservative movement's ban on rabbinic officiation at intermarriages, many Conservative Jews who sought intermarriage began to identify as Reform. At the same time, the Reform movement was losing a larger percentage to assimilation than was true for the Conservative movement.

47. The Conservative movement could hardly have a plainer position: "Rabbis may not officiate at, participate in, or attend an intermarriage." "A Code of Professional Conduct," Rabbinical Assembly, October 21, 2004, accessed August 1, 2022, http://www.rabbinicalassembly.org/sites/default/files/public/ethical_guidelines/Code%20of%20conduct-2011-public.pdf, 2

The position of the Reform movement is more complex. The official position of the Reform rabbinate, not revisited since 1973, is that rabbis should not officiate at intermarriages. Over the years, a rising percentage of Reform rabbis have turned their backs on that ruling. Nevertheless, for most of the twentieth century, even those who wanted to accept the intermarried sought to prevent intermarriage (see Mark Washofsky, *Jewish Living: A Guide to Contemporary Reform Practice*, New York: URJ Books and Music, 2001, 155–156). Thus, when Rabbi Alexander Schindler launched his effort of "outreach" to the mixed marriage, he declared "Let no one misinterpret and infer that I am here endorsing intermarriage. I deplore intermarriage, and I discourage it. I struggle against it, as a rabbi and as the father of five children" ("Schindler's 1978 Speech Establishing Outreach," December 2, 1978, accessed April 20, 2015, http://urj.org/about/union/history/schindler/?syspage=article&item_id=61140). Explicit discouragement of intermarriage would remain a part of Reform discourse for at least the next two decades.

48. "A Statement of Principles for Reform Judaism," Central Conference of American Rabbis, May 1999, accessed August 1, 2022, https://www.ccarnet.org/rabbinic-voice/platforms/article-statement-principles-reform-judaism/
49. Stark, *One True God*, 214.

References

Americans Express Increasingly Warm Feelings Towards Religious Groups, Pew Research Center, February 15, 2017, accessed August 1, 2022, http://www.pewforum.org/2017/02/15/americans-express-increasingly-warm-feelings-toward-religious-groups/.

A Code of Professional Conduct, Rabbinical Assembly, October 21, 2004, accessed August 1, 2022, http://www.rabbinicalassembly.org/sites/default/files/public/ethical_guidelines/Code%20of%20conduct-2011-public.pdf.

A Portrait of American Jews: Overview, Pew Research Center, October 1, 2013, accessed August 1, 2022, https://www.pewforum.org/2013/10/01/jewish-american-beliefs-attitudes-culture-survey/.

A Statement of Principles for Reform Judaism, Central Conference of American Rabbis, May 1999, accessed August 1, 2022, https://www.ccarnet.org/rabbinic-voice/platforms/article-statement-principles-reform-judaism/.

Bernstein, Elizabeth. "You Don't Have to Be Jewish to Want a Bar Mitzvah Party," *The Wall Street Journal*, January 14, 2004, accessed August 1, 2022, https://www.wsj.com/articles/SB107404276295131300.

Berkovitz, Jay. *The Shaping of Jewish Identity in Nineteenth-Century France* (Detroit: Wayne State University Press, 1995).

Cohen, Howard. "Changing Times Cited as Jewish Country Club Closes," *The Miami Herald*, May 1, 2011, accessed October 11, 2020, http://articles.sun-sentinel.com/2011-05-01/entertainment/mh-westview-country-club-20110501_1_social-club-family-oriented-club-jewish-members.

Dershowitz, Alan. *The Vanishing American Jew—In Search of Jewish Identity for the Next Century* (New York: Touchstone, 1997), 1.

Gladwell, Malcolm. "Getting In," *The New Yorker*, October 10, 2005, accessed August 1, 2022, http://www.newyorker.com/archive/2005/10/10/051010crat_atlarge?currentPage=all.

Goldstein, Sidney. "Profile of American Jewry: Insights from the 1990 National Jewish Population Survey," May 1993, accessed August 1, 2022, https://www.jstor.org/stable/23605965?read-now=1&seq=94#metadata_info_tab_contents.

Heilman, Samuel. *Portrait of American Jews* (University of Washington Press, 1995).

How Americans Feel About Religious Groups, Pew Research Center, July 16, 2014, accessed August 1, 2022, http://www.pewforum.org/2014/07/16/how-americans-feel-about-religious-groups/.

Kantor, Jodi. "Next Year in the White House: A Seder Tradition," *The New York Times*, March 27, 2010, accessed August 1, 2022, http://www.nytimes.com/2010/03/28/us/politics/28seder.html?_r=0.

Katz, Robert. "PAGING DR. SHYLOCK!: Jewish Hospitals and the Prudent Re-Investment of Jewish Philanthropy," in *Religious Giving for Love of God*, ed. David H. Smith (Bloomington: Indiana University Press, 2010).

Nahshoni, Kobi. "Intermarriage rates among Diaspora Jews at all-time high," Ynet News.com, November 17, 2010, accessed August 1, 2022, http://www.ynetnews.com/articles/0,7340,L-3984935,00.html.

Pew Research Center, "Jewish Americans in 2020," https://www.pewresearch.org/religion/2021/05/11/marriage-families-and-children/.

Sarna, Jonathan. *American Judaism: A History* (New Haven: Yale University Press, 2004).

Sarna, Jonathan and Golden, Jonathan. "The American Jewish Experience in the Twentieth Century: Antisemitism and Assimilation," National Humanities Center, 2000, accessed August 1, 2022, http://nationalhumanitiescenter.org/tserve/twenty/tkeyinfo/jewishexp.htm.

Schindler's 1978 Speech Establishing Outreach, December 2, 1978, accessed April 20, 2015, http://urj.org/about/union/history/schindler/?syspage=article&item_id=61140.

Seltzer, Robert. *Jewish People, Jewish Thought* (New York: Macmillan Publishing Company, 1980).

Sheskin Ira and Deshefsky, Arnold. "Jewish Population in the United States, 2010" (North American Jewish Databank, 2011) accessed October 11, 2020, https://www.brandeis.edu/cmjs/conferences/demographyconf/pdfs/Dashefsky_JewishPopulationUS2010.pdf.

Stark, Rodney. *One True God* (Princeton: Princeton University Press, 2001).

The National Jewish Population Survey, 2000–01, A United Jewish Communities Report, accessed August 1, 2022, https://cdn.fedweb.org/fed-34/136/National-Jewish-Population-Study.pdf.

Washofsky, Mark. *Jewish Living: A Guide to Contemporary Reform Practice* (New York: URJ Books and Music, 2001).

What Americans Know About Religion, Pew Research Center, July 23, 2019, accessed August 1, 2022, https://www.pewresearch.org/religion/2019/07/23/feelings-toward-religious-groups/.

Zollman, Joellyn. "Jewish Immigration to America: Three Waves," *My Jewish Learning*, accessed August 1, 2022, https://www.myjewishlearning.com/article/jewish-immigration-to-america-three-waves/.

CHAPTER 3

Embracing Modernity

HARMONIZING TWO WORLDS

The initial Jewish challenge of the nineteenth century was emancipation. But the second and more complex struggle was focused on how to respond to the revolution in thought that was emblematic of modernity. As they emerged from their previously isolated communities, Jews encountered a burgeoning world of Enlightenment:

> [They] found themselves faced with new intellectual challenges that could not be ignored. What were the implications of the ongoing scientific revolution to the Jewish conception of God, the world, the nature of man? Modern philosophical thought had to be considered if Judaism was to remain intellectually respectable. A new historical awareness that appeared in the late eighteenth century, and especially in the nineteenth, raised the question of how the concept of progress and the understanding of the origins of Judaism were to affect Jewish theology.[1]

These were hardly esoteric matters that could be left to scholars alone. They had deep implications for anybody who wanted to live in the modern world and remain Jewish at the same time. Seemingly every nineteenth-century intellectual discipline offered an array of unprecedented conundrums for Jews:

> [Science] contradicted classic Judaism on matters of fact, like the age of the earth, or in the likely understanding of nature...and made the demonstra-

D. Schiff, *Judaism in a Digital Age*, https://doi.org/10.1007/978-3-031-17992-1_3

tion of God's power by miracle seem mythological. It provided a simpler, more integrated view of the world than Judaism knew, one where mathematically describable patterns, not God's immediate rule, were to be found.[2]

Modern history instituted new tools that were "chronological" and "contextual." It postulated that Jewish law and Jewish practice had developed through the centuries in response to the economic and social circumstances in which Jews found themselves. It taught that Jewish tradition was not, as most Jews had hitherto believed, largely unchanged since Sinai. Even more shattering, the Torah and the Bible, when subject to historical scrutiny, appeared to be "a compilation and harmonization of a number of different traditions about Israelite religions and origins"[3] inconsistent with a singular act of Divine revelation. And, in an age of reason, there were very real questions surrounding Divine revelation itself: If Divine revelation could not be assumed as an "accepted truth," what need was there to practice the commandments that flowed from it? There was, furthermore, a real sense that hope relied more on humanity and less on Divinity and that human beings alone could "radically improve things."[4] The impediments to a better future for all people were either "ignorance or thoughtless tradition," and both could be "swept away by education and knowledge."[5]

Another feature of modernity also represented a pivotal change: the rise of individualism. An enhanced emphasis on the individual was an inevitable byproduct of modernity's key social innovations:

> Capitalism, through the operation of the free market, breaks down traditional communities and bonds of social solidarity, thereby both freeing individuals and forcing them to become self-reliant for their own well-being, either to succeed or fail in competition with others in the open market. The state seconds this individualizing propensity of the market by treating people as citizens who are individually responsible in meeting its obligations and by stipulating that contracts—freely entered into—should constitute the basis of relationships between citizens in a civil society... Finally, science is also conducive to individualism by promoting critical thought and breaking the controlling hold over the minds exercised by traditional beliefs and collective ideas previously utilized by both spiritual and political authorities to keep individuals in check.[6]

In the premodern era, the life of the individual was subordinate to the group and was heavily constrained by conventions and social standing.

Conformity in deed and thought was expected, especially within Jewish life. As the excommunication of Spinoza demonstrated, approaches that strayed from the circumscribed path were unwelcome.[7] The arrival of modernity challenged the premise of this structure. Slowly at first, but with widening impact, modernity decoupled individuals from their social station and from conformity requirements that were not demanded by law. Individualism and a focus on individual desires were on the rise.

If all this was not challenging enough, any attempt to think about religious concepts within the framework of modernity also had to contend seriously with the revolutionary positions of Immanuel Kant. Kant maintained that true religion, the religion of the future, required "steadfast diligence in leading a morally good life [and] in fulfilling one's duties to fellow human beings."[8] The implication of this was clear: morality was what really counted. In the twenty-first century, this might seem obvious, but prior to modernity, there was no general sense that the primary value of religion lay in its moral essence or that religion might be critiqued for its moral worth. This is, however, precisely the direction in which Kant's thinking pointed. In Kant's view, the "statutory laws" of religious observance were of little merit if they "made no claims upon conscience"; they amounted to little more than "ceremonial and symbolic expressions" that were "ultimately superfluous."[9] Kant essentially rejected the significance of any law that did not have moral intent grounded in reason and held that ceremonies conducted with no better motive than "to please God" were "representative of paganism."[10] He went one step further: Kant argued that an externally imposed law could not be moral because it was forced upon the recipient without consent or voluntary acceptance. Hence, "to be pure, a moral law must be autonomous, or self-imposed."[11]

Kant's position is essentially synonymous with the central tenet of what it means to be liberal. At the core of classic liberalism is a commitment to equal liberty for all: "to be human means being a rational and moral agent, a free chooser with responsibility for one's own actions. It puts a premium on conscience rather than the 'blind' following of rules."[12] Insofar as this came to be a central feature of what it meant to be a member of a liberal society, it raised the obvious question for Jews: Why shouldn't the theory of liberalism apply to Judaism as well? After all, Jews "did not want to be freely human in one part of themselves and constrainedly Jewish in another realm of their existence. They wanted no dividing line between what constituted the modern and the Jewish in the answer they were seeking."[13]

This background provides critical context for understanding what the Reform and Conservative movements were really trying to achieve. It is simplistic to perceive these two streams as just sociological structures designed to create a post-emancipation religious home for modern Jews who had lost the shtetl but still wanted a community. The non-Orthodox movements addressed the challenges of modernity fully: they sought to engage with its intellectual currents and to deal directly with the philosophical hurdles that nineteenth-century Jews could not ignore. Their primary mission was not just to help Jews live as Jews in an unprecedented era but to rethink Judaism in order to incorporate the new insights of modernity.

Each movement took a different path to achieve this goal. In Reform thought, a succession of platforms articulating foundational principles could not have been clearer about the primacy of modern thought. The Pittsburgh Platform of 1885 stated it directly:

> We hold that the modern discoveries of scientific researches in the domain of nature and history are not antagonistic to the doctrines of Judaism, the Bible reflecting the primitive ideas of its own age, and at times clothing its conception of divine Providence and Justice dealing with men in miraculous narratives.[14]

It is not by accident that the Bible is the "primitive" reflection of a bygone era when compared to the "modern discoveries" of scientific research in "nature and history." And with more than a passing nod to Kant, the Platform writers had no difficulty in establishing which parts of the Jewish legal structure had outlived their usefulness: "Today we accept as binding only its moral laws, and maintain only such ceremonies as elevate and sanctify our lives, but reject all such as are not adapted to the views and habits of modern civilization." The Pittsburgh Platform conceived of Judaism not as a nation attempting to cleave to a divinely revealed Torah but as "a progressive religion, ever striving to be in accord with the postulates of reason." And modernity was not just a new epoch but heralded an opening that was little short of messianic: "We recognize, in the modern era of universal culture of heart and intellect, the approaching of the realization of Israel's great Messianic hope for the establishment of the kingdom of truth, justice, and peace among all men."[15]

The 1937 Columbus Platform also held that Judaism was thoroughly compatible with modernity: "The new discoveries of science, while replacing the older scientific views underlying our sacred literature, do not conflict with the essential spirit of religion as manifested in the consecration of man's will, heart and mind to the service of God and of humanity."[16] By 1976, however, when the Reform movement produced its first post-Holocaust platform, signs of doubt began to appear. Accepting modernity's centrality was still a given: "It now seems self-evident to most Jews: that our tradition should interact with modern culture; that its forms ought to reflect a contemporary esthetic; that its scholarship needs to be conducted by modern, critical methods; and that change has been and must continue to be a fundamental reality in Jewish life." But modernity was no longer an unmitigated good:

> The widespread threats to freedom, the problems inherent in the explosion of new knowledge and of ever more powerful technologies, and the spiritual emptiness of much of Western culture have taught us to be less dependent on the values of our society and to reassert what remains perennially valid in Judaism's teaching.[17]

There is, though, little evidence that the Reform movement became less enchanted with the zeitgeist. While preparing the Pittsburgh Principles of 1999, the chief author, Rabbi Richard Levy, proposed a new approach: "Looking back at a century which has witnessed some of the greatest gifts and the most awful consequences of modernity, we proclaim that the *mitzvot* of the Torah are our center, and Judaism is the scale by which we shall judge the modern world."[18] In what amounts to an about-face from classic nineteenth-century attitudes, Levy advocated reversing the approach of the 1885 Pittsburgh Platform: No longer would Torah be judged by its suitability to modernity—modernity would instead be judged by its suitability to Torah. Not a word, however, of Levy's reversal found its way into the final version of the Principles. To be sure, unease about modernity is articulated in the document: "We continue to have faith that, in spite of the unspeakable evils committed against our people and the sufferings endured by others, the partnership of God and humanity will ultimately prevail."[19] Beyond this expression of pain, however, the drafters rejected Levy's relegation of modernity to a subordinate position. While they expressed ambivalence about modernity, they refused to subject the values of modern society to the type of Jewish accountability that Levy had encouraged. The message was clear: For the Reform movement, the voice of modernity would continue to outweigh the expectations of Judaism.

In the Conservative movement, adapting Judaism to modernity was a more measured project. After all, as befits its name, the Conservative movement sought to "conserve" Jewish tradition within the context of modernity. The original goal of the founders was not to start a new denomination but to represent the continuity of that "true" Judaism which, in their view, had always been both traditional and developing. They regarded Reform as a "revolutionary deviation from Jewish tradition" and Orthodoxy as "stultifying the inner dynamism of Judaism"; they hoped to provide Jews with a Judaism that suffered from neither excess.[20]

But no matter how traditional the founders intended to be, modern elements were at the heart of Conservative thought. Unlike the Reform movement's multiple platforms, the Conservative movement issued few position statements.[21] Nevertheless, Conservative attitudes are readily discernible from the decisions, debates, and scholarship of the movement. From the start it was clear that, basing itself on the thought of the rabbi and historian, Zacharias Frankel, Conservative Judaism would embrace what it called a "positive-historical" approach, devoted to both tradition and change.[22] The "positive" part of the term was a reference to the "authentic, unchanging skeletal kernel of Jewish continuity." The "historical" part acknowledged "the reality of change, newness, and adaptability."[23] As one of the Conservative movement's eminent thinkers, Mordechai Waxman, described it, the concept of historical Judaism represented "a recognition of the fact that Judaism has changed through the ages and…an understanding of why and how it has changed."[24] This openness to change was balanced by a positive loyalty to Jewish law. As we have seen, though, the study of history and the acknowledgment that Judaism could "develop" were quintessentially modern notions. Hence, giving history the weight that the Conservatives afforded it inevitably meant evaluating Judaism with the tools of modernity. The nineteenth-century Hungarian Orthodox rabbi, Moses Sofer (the "Chatam Sofer"), spoke for the traditional view when he articulated "chadash assur min haTorah" (whatever is new is forbidden by the Torah)—effectively foreclosing any recognition of change.[25] The Conservative movement, by contrast, did not only accept modern historical analysis, it acknowledged its indebtedness to the discipline. Rabbi Solomon Schechter, one of the leaders of Conservative Judaism, wrote of the "historical school": "The main strength of this school lies in its scientific work, for which Judaism will always be under a deep sense of gratitude."[26]

It was, though, more than just the utilization of historical perspectives that conveyed the modernist impulse within Conservative Judaism. The movement also incorporated biblical criticism into its worldview. Indeed, the primary reason why the early twentieth-century Union of Orthodox Rabbis issued a *herem* (religious ban) against the employment of rabbis emerging from the Conservative-run seminary was "the acceptance of modern critical methods for Bible study by Professor Louis Ginzberg of the Seminary faculty."[27] Nor was the methodology of biblical criticism intended to be limited to the academy. When the Conservative movement published its own Torah commentary for synagogues, biblical criticism was described as the salient feature that distinguished Conservative Judaism from Rabbinic Judaism: "Conservative Judaism is based on Rabbinic Judaism. It differs, however, in the recognition that all texts were composed in given historical contexts. The Conservative movement, in short, applies historical, critical methods to the study of the biblical text."[28]

Perhaps the clearest sign of the embrace of modernity by the Conservative movement is evident in the struggle over how to approach *halakhah*. From early on, there was a divergence between those who wanted to make relatively minor adjustments through responding narrowly to specific questions as they arose and those who thought that proactive "legislation" was required to effect real change. This led to tensions, as Rabbi Morris Adler described in 1948:

> We stand with one foot in the very heart of the "actions and passions" of our time, aware of the imperious demands, pressures and dissolutions with which it confronts us, and with the other foot we stand reverently and loyally in the sanctuary of an old tradition. It is because we are alive to the rights of both that our movement seems to be marked by self-contradiction, indecisiveness, and ambiguity, and draws the strictures of both the traditional and untraditional elements.[29]

A couple of years later, when the movement's Committee on Jewish Law and Standards (CJLS) tackled the seemingly intractable problem of the *agunah*,[30] the chair of the committee described the motivation for acting in this way:

> …[O]ur own profession of the adequacy of historic Judaism for modern life importunately waits to be squared with the facts. If we fail to make Judaism as expressed at least in its procedure for divorce accord with our deepest sense of justice and equity, we shall permanently become spiritual schizophrenics who talk one way and feel quite another.[31]

According to this view, Judaism had to be made acceptable to modern life, even if it required revolutionary *halakhic* steps.

At a conference devoted to the subject of Jewish law, Rabbi Ira Eisenstein, a former president of the Conservative Rabbinical Assembly, elucidated the position of those in favor of legislation:

> The fact that we have come together to discuss the adjustment of Jewish law to life indicates that we do not share the same mentality as our ancestors. We are consciously attempting to make the law serve our needs. We cannot, therefore, any longer pretend that what we are doing is merely to reaffirm our allegiance to the law. Any changes we suggest will be deliberate and conscious... The fact that we take our needs into consideration constitutes a psychological revolution.[32]

Jewish law, Eisenstein continued, must allow for "the consent of the governed," and Conservative Judaism should explicitly move from "pure interpretation of an unalterable law to free and revocable legislation."[33] Clearly, "making the law serve needs" through legislation represents a bold move designed to ensure that the *halakhah* would conform to contemporary sensibilities.

It is important to recall that there was a competing approach that saw *halakhah* within Conservative Judaism quite differently. This alternative school held that "the thrust of the Jewish tradition and the Conservative community is to maintain the law and the practices of the past as much as possible, and the burden of proof is on the one who wants to alter them."[34] However, an examination of the movement's *halakhic* actions since 1950 indicates that the Eisenstein wing had the upper hand. Whatever one's view of the rulings, the movement's decisions permitting some driving and electricity use on Shabbat, mixed seating, women rabbis, homosexual relationships, and online prayer *minyanim*, inter alia, appear to represent actions "to serve needs" far more than attempts to "maintain the law and the practices of the past."[35] It seems, therefore, reasonable to assert that the movement's philosophy extensively incorporated modern predilections.

A word is in order about the place of the individual within the Reform and Conservative worldview. Traditionally, the individual was regarded as being subservient to the law. The Reform movement, however, embarked upon a different path. While affirming the need to study the law, Reform Judaism became almost synonymous with the vision of a community of autonomous Jews, each imbued with the power of knowledgeable decision-making: "Reform Jews respond to change in various ways according to the Reform principle of the autonomy of the individual."[36] Embracing Kantian thought, Reform Judaism taught that individuals were free to adopt or reject elements of the law according to their own subjective evaluations.

The Conservative movement did not seek to emulate Reform's commitment to autonomy. Conservative Judaism's *halakhic* structure called upon the local rabbi to act as the legal decision-maker for the community. The rabbi had the option to rule on the basis of traditional *halakhic* stances or on those positions authorized by the CJLS. At face value, it appears to have been a structure with little room for individual decision-making. The reality was not so simple. Rabbi Louis Epstein offered a glimpse of the complexity in a 1941 speech:

> A man in my congregation suffered amputation of his legs as a result of illness. He took his verdict manfully and read his Sabbath prayers at home. But on one Sabbath he had Yahrzeit and his desire to say the Kaddish in public...created pressure upon him too powerful to resist. The discipline of the law was yielding to personal conscience. He asked me whether it would be terribly sinful for him to ride to the synagogue, and I, frankly, shirked the responsibility of giving a direct answer. My answer was: If you ask me the law, you know what my answer will be... Is it up to me or to yourself to decide a matter of your own conscience? He took the responsibility upon himself and he was in the synagogue on Sabbath morning.
>
> Did he make the proper decision or not? I suppose some of us will say "yes," some will say "no." But who of us would condemn him for giving his own conscience a voice in a matter pertaining to his own soul?[37]

It was appropriate, according to Epstein, for the man's conscience to replace the voice of his rabbi in what was plainly a *halakhic* decision. There were, therefore, instances in which individual conscience could supersede the law itself. Judging by the conduct of Conservative Jews through the decades, there has been little disagreement with Epstein's perspective.[38] When conscience occupies a credible place in evaluating *halakhic* matters, the individual gains an augmented role in the process. There can be little doubt, therefore, that Conservative Judaism, like Reform, enhanced the standing of the individual.

All of this leads to the following conclusion: Both the Reform and the Conservative movements were, from their inception, intended to be intertwined with the intellectual currents of modernity—where modernity means not just a specific epoch in history but a characteristic set of ideas. Orthodoxy, for the most part, sought to exclude those ideas. The Conservative and Reform movements, seeing these ideas as requisite features of what it meant to be "enlightened" and part of modern society, embraced them. Hence, while the two movements started off as initiatives to accommodate the aesthetics, music, language, and religious structure of modernity, they became more than that. They became places where the weltanschauung of modernity held sway, where the intellectual agenda of modernity—science, history, biblical criticism, the primacy of morality, and an expanded focus on the individual—was the assumed intellectual scaffolding to which Judaism had to be molded (and not the other way around). As one philosopher described the outcome of the balancing act between Judaism and modernity for the non-Orthodox movements: "…modern ideas proved so attractive that most of the concessions were made on the Jewish side."[39] Modernity and non-Orthodox Judaism were indivisibly linked.

DIMINISHING IMPACT

An analogy: An old town has existed for centuries. Its inhabitants are steeped in the long-practiced customs and ways of their town. Their world, however, changes dramatically when a new town is established nearby. "New Town" is spacious and is open to newcomers. They do things completely differently in New Town; it is a place that knows little about the ways and customs of "Old Town." Sadly, for its residents, Old Town is slated for demolition. Soon, Old Town will be no more. Fortunately, the residents of Old Town are willing to move to New Town. But there are challenges: How will the move of the Old Town residents to New Town be facilitated? How will Old Town residents learn and adapt to the unfamiliar practices of their new location? In response to these needs, "movements" arise that see it as their purpose to help move Old Town residents to their new homes. Not only do the movements offer assistance to relocate physically, but they also provide a process of adaptation to the ways of New Town. Thus, the movements promise to help acclimatize the Old Towners to the approaches of their new environment. Helpfully, the movements have developed various creative strategies so that the Old Towners can preserve cherished elements of Old Town culture in a manner that is compatible with New Town mores and acceptable to the New Towners. In large measure, the movements are successful in moving Old Town residents to their new neighborhoods, as well as in adapting their thinking and behavior to "New Town style." The Old Towners are deeply grateful to the movements for their invaluable help.

Decades pass. The task of moving Old Town residents from Old Town to New Town was completed long ago. After the last residents moved, Old Town was razed and is all but forgotten. In New Town, the former Old Towners have added generations to their families. The grandchildren and great-grandchildren of the former Old Towners have no knowledge of Old Town or its ways. They are New Towners through and through. They are thoroughly savvy in the ways of New Town. They are not seen as Old Town immigrants; they are just New Towners like everybody else. While they appreciate some of the foods, distinctive celebrations, and literature that their great-grandparents brought with them from Old Town, they are in every way New Towners. They need no assistance in adapting their thinking to New Town style; they know no other.

Hence, while these younger generations still hold some nostalgic loyalty and gratitude to the movements that were once so helpful to their families, they wonder who or what the movements are now trying to move. If anything, they are somewhat bemused by the movements. For while the movements usually seem to find a way to approve of the dominant new trends in New Town, utilizing concepts from Old Town literature and culture, they sometimes seem late to the party. For example, when members of the younger generations first started to marry into original New Town families, the movements said that this would threaten the continuation of Old Town traditions. But as members of the younger generations married into original New Town families in ever greater numbers, the movements changed their tune. They explored ways to show approval and to encourage the "intermarrieds" to continue Old Town practices within their new families. To the younger generations, it often seemed like the movements were reacting after the fact in response to societal developments.

The movements recalled the time when they had really been the "movers"—those days when they had moved people from the old to the new town and had opened the immigrants' eyes to how a new culture could be embraced and harmonized with old traditions. Now, it had to be admitted that they no longer played such an indispensable role. For better or worse, the younger generations were adopting the latest intellectual currents of New Town without much regard to whether those trends could be adapted to Old Town values.

So the movement leaders pondered: How could the movements regain relevance? If they simply advocated following Old Town practices in a New Town setting, they would appear out of touch. Instead, they tweaked their approach: The movements would speedily engage the latest intellectual currents of New Town and would, as best they could, base their positions in language drawn from Old Town sources. They noted, for example, that there was ongoing interest in cleaning up and beautifying New Town. So, drawing on Old Town sources that spoke of the importance of cleaning and beautifying, they aligned themselves with the campaign. The younger generations seemed happy that the movements had become more responsive, though many acknowledged that they did not really look to the movements to help them in matters that the public was already advancing. They could, after all, help beautify New Town in the company of other more broad-based groups. Although they had no objection to the movements, why did they really need them? True, they were a valued bridge between the fast-paced realities of New Town and the enriching culture of Old Town—but was that enough to make them important?

No analogy should be pushed too far. This "tale of two towns" elucidates something of the challenge for the Conservative and Reform movements once the move to modernity was accomplished. At their inception, Reform and Conservative Judaism were truly movements: they pursued social change by assisting Jews to integrate the intellectual and societal realities of modernity into their lives.[40] Both movements enabled Jews to move to New Town and retool their Judaism so as to be simultaneously Jewish, wholly modern, and fully integrated. The Reform movement helped Jews conceptualize Judaism as a religious community committed to a progressive religious outlook, in accord with "the postulates of reason" that emphasized autonomy, morality, and the voice of the prophets. The Conservative movement helped Jews commit to both tradition and change by remaining loyal to *halakhah*, adapting Jewish thought and Jewish law to contemporary circumstances, and strengthening the Jewish people. For both movements, the main objective was to assist Jews in navigating a transition that individuals would have been hard pressed to traverse alone.

A century and a half later, what remains of this endeavor? Jews long ago adapted to modernity. Few look to either the Conservative or Reform movements for insights on how to become part of post-Enlightenment society. As for the process of adapting Judaism to modern thought, it is, if anything, difficult for the great majority of Jews to conceive of Judaism without modernity's prism. The majority of non-Orthodox Jews believe that the Bible was written by multiple hands over an extended period, that science is fact while miracles are fiction, that one can be a practicing Jew and yet be autonomous, that morality and conscience are paramount concerns of religion, and that the needs of the individual occupy an elevated place. The Conservative and Reform movements are no longer moving anybody to uncharted territory. In the twenty-first century, they are addressing native New Towners for whom the viewpoint of modernity is a given.

This post-revolutionary challenge is not unusual. It is also seen in political revolutions. But the difference between successful political revolutions and the transformations overseen by the Conservative and Reform movements is that political revolutions usually end up with the revolutionaries in control of the political, social, and cultural environment in which they seek to implement their philosophy. The same cannot be said for the non-Orthodox movements. As Jews became citizens of mass nation states and Jewish identity became a voluntary phenomenon, the movements entered a world in which they were not in control of the broader environment. From the self-governing reality of Old Town, they had helped move Jews to a place where the real governing work was in the hands of others, the real action was to be found in engaging New Town issues directly, and the power of Old Town traditions was waning.

Even more significantly, since the movements were so closely tied to the outlook of modernity, their adherents have tended to adopt the positions of contemporary culture with little consideration of the fact that inherited Jewish viewpoints might differ markedly. To be sure, Reform and Conservative rabbis have at times spoken against modern trends or passed dissenting resolutions. But the movements have largely desisted from mounting campaigns against disquieting aspects of modernity, even when such campaigns would have been in line with non-Orthodox thought. Initiatives with the potential to create real distance or dissonance between non-Orthodox Jews and their surrounding culture have rarely been on the agenda.

Consider the subject of family size: Judaism regards childbearing as a commandment. Rabbinic texts encouraged large families, and, in the centuries prior to birth control, having multiple children was the norm.[41] Modern society had other ideas. The advent of contraception allowed for the effective limiting of family size, and the Zero Population Growth (ZPG) movement of the 1970s counseled that, given the Earth's limited resources, no family should have more than two children. For a tiny people like the Jews, this was problematic. Cut in size by one-third during the Holocaust, with growing assimilation rates depleting Jewish numbers, it was in the interests of the Jewish community to keep the "supply side" high. Conservative and Reform leaders recognized this but never seriously campaigned for larger families. In 1963, the American Jewish Committee's Milton Himmelfarb complained about the stance of non-Orthodox rabbis:

> The rabbis, more than anyone else, are worried about our survival, but they seem to prefer not to know that we are failing to reproduce ourselves. When they do turn their attention to Jewish fertility, it is to invoke the support of Jewish tradition or law for birth control. There are famous Reform and Conservative responsa of that kind, and recently a well-known rabbi felt it necessary to say the same things again—as if we needed the encouragement... If the rabbis wanted us to have more children, would they make a point of telling us that Jewish law favors birth control?[42]

As ZPG became a communal issue, Himmelfarb told a 1975 seminar of the Women's League for Conservative Judaism that "disinterest in having children" represented a "greater threat to the future of the Jewish people than intermarriage."[43]

Yet, even though a drive for increasing family size was in keeping with Jewish tradition and would have strengthened the non-Orthodox community, no such project materialized. Why not? Why did the movements expend great energies in outreach to non-Jews and other areas that required appreciable changes in behavior but did little to promote larger families? The answer is that such a move would have run counter to fundamental currents in modernity. Not only did ZPG, women joining the workforce, and simple economics argue strongly for having fewer children, but family size had come to be viewed as an individual, almost private, decision where autonomy (even for Conservative Jews) was expected. Jewish tradition and Jewish interests might have been unambiguous on the subject but promoting a perspective that did not blend well with the ideas of modernity was unpalatable. Hence, the movements tended to highlight those policies that were in keeping with modern thought, like permitting certain contraceptives, but downplayed that which modernity regarded as problematic.

There are additional examples: As the divorce rate rose quickly during the twentieth century, neither movement worked strenuously to stem the tide. Judaism, of course, has always permitted divorce, albeit within a societal context in which divorce was rare. But with divorce rates at all-time highs, the movements invested little rhetorical or practical energy in trying to keep marriages together. Socially acceptable divorce worked well for individuals, and the culture simply adjusted to seeing divorce as a sad but unremarkable feature of modernity. In the area of *tzedakah* (charitable giving), many Christian groups were likely to be more assiduous about tithing than were non-Orthodox Jews in giving 10 percent of their income to *tzedakah*. Despite the fact that Judaism sees the giving of *tzedakah* at a particular level as a commandment, the values of modern culture regard charity as a personal, private, and voluntary decision. The movements did little to counter this attitude. Neither did the movements stand firm against the ongoing encroachment of commercialism on sacred time. There was a general reluctance to cross swords with features of modernity that non-Orthodox Jews had already embraced.

These points are not presented to criticize the Reform and Conservative movements. All organizations prioritize. Rather, these observations are offered in order to clarify why the movements' priorities developed as they did. Mindful of their constituents' desires to fit in and to reap the benefits of full participation in society, non-Orthodox opposition to significant trends in modernity was minimal. It is true that the Conservative and Reform movements were part of a broad range of initiatives that challenged societal inequalities in areas like civil rights, women's equality, and gay marriage. However, these changes were countercultural only in the sense that they challenged certain realities that had been long entrenched in general and Jewish culture. They were not countercultural in the sense of requiring non-Orthodox Jews to differentiate themselves from the liberal setting of which they were already a part. To the contrary, those who fought for such causes as civil rights, women's liberation, or marriage equality joined their Jewish voices to sizable societal initiatives that were underway independent of Jewish efforts. Insofar as these transformations led to unprecedented changes within Conservative and Reform Judaism, such as women rabbis and LGBTQ acceptance, these path-breaking developments represented Jewish versions of phenomena that were already being modeled elsewhere.[44]

There is, consequently, a noticeable pattern to the issues championed by the Reform and Conservative movements. Those issues that are adopted as pivotal societal causes within the societies in which Jews live—particularly if they tend toward liberalizing restrictions on individuals—will likely be given Jewish form and receive support from the Conservative and Reform movements. Those causes that run counter to such societal trends usually will not. In this context it is fully understandable why the non-Orthodox movements provided strong backing for gay marriage, despite the difficulties of justifying such unions on the basis of classic texts, while offering scant encouragement for having additional children, despite the textual injunctions to do so.

Given this pattern, it is plain that the non-Orthodox movements do not wholly control their own agenda. Dwelling in New Town, they respond to New Town's priorities. There is, of course, nothing wrong with following the crowd when the crowd is headed in a worthy direction. Indeed, failing to make judicious adjustments in keeping with contemporary mores has the potential to leave Judaism in a deficient position. A prominent historic example was Rabbeinu Gershom's eleventh-century decision to ban polygamy for the Ashkenazi part of the Jewish people. One of the main causes for this move was the "influence of the reality of the Christian environs, in which it was forbidden by law to marry more than one woman."[45] Hence, a motivating factor for Rabbeinu Gershom was that Judaism needed to do what was seen to be right and should not be perceived as lagging behind the broader culture. There are several contemporary areas in which the Reform and Conservative movements have led the way toward significant Jewish changes, walking in the footsteps of surrounding societal trends.[46] There is, then, a benefit to imitation: Judaism can sometimes be strengthened and refined by suitable adjustments stimulated by external wisdom.

However, in an open society where Jews are entirely free when it comes to their participation in Jewish life, there are also risks. If, for example, an individual is devoted to the environmental cause, the utility of expressing that commitment through a Jewish organization is not obvious. True, the movements can campaign for environmentalism with a Jewish voice. They can muster texts to support the case. But if having an impact on the environment is the goal, there are many specialized organizations that are likely to offer more direct ways to address the cause. If addressing homelessness, the minimum wage, or tackling hunger are priorities, why is it best to "seek justice" through the Reform or Conservative movements? Changing New Town might well be more effectively achieved through organizations that do not have a particularist approach.[47] Skepticism about working within a Jewish context is all the more likely if a particular cause cannot be said to emerge organically from within the Jewish tradition but appears to have been retrofitted to the tradition because of its contemporary appeal.[48]

This leads to a vital question: What do the Reform and Conservative movements stand for that would cause an individual to opt to stay with or connect to them? What is their specific, differentiated vision that makes joining their cause compelling? Frequently, questions of this type are answered with a list of activities. But it is goals, rather than activities, that are pivotal when evaluating the direction, character, and aspirations of a movement. By way of analogy, healthy individuals eat and sleep every day, but this tells us little about their priorities, aspirations, or ambitions. So too, "being more Jewishly engaged," "coming to more Jewish events," or even "living by the *halakhah*" may be Jewish identity markers but reveal little about why certain activities are of greater importance than others.

Conservative and Reform Judaism do not seek members just for the sake of having more members. They seek to transform lives. But in what way? Some will deem the answer to this question obvious: These are synagogue-based movements. They are known for the services they offer, for spirituality, for the celebration of life cycle events and holydays, for urging members to better themselves, for supporting individuals through the travails of life, and for connecting their adherents to the study of texts. The goal is straightforward: to build communities of inspiration around what houses of worship do best. Both the Conservative and Reform movements offer fine rabbis, appealing synagogues, powerful life cycle experiences, enriching holiday observances, substantive support structures, and opportunities for learning.

There are, however, problems with responding in this way. First, it limits the scope of the movements' interests and functioning to the spiritual or ritual realm. While important, this domain is narrow. Second, Jews rarely attend synagogue. More than four-fifths of Reform Jews and more than three-fifths of Conservative Jews appear "a few times a year or less."[49] So if the primary goal of the Conservative and Reform movements is to offer synagogue excellence, most congregants will seldom be exposed to it. Third, while modernity had the effect of narrowing

Judaism to the religious domain, Judaism seeks to have an impact on society beyond the walls of the synagogue. Fourth, in their own descriptions of what they represent, the movements paint a considerably broader picture. While viewing strong synagogues as critical, they do not regard houses of worship as ends in themselves. The articulated goals of the Conservative and Reform movements are manifestly broader than their synagogue networks.

What are these stated goals? The Reform movement offers a succinct listing of priorities in a summary on the movement's flagship website. While not an official movement position, it is a widely accessible statement of what Reform Judaism stands for.[50] First, it declares that the Reform movement "affirms the central tenets of Judaism—God, Torah, and Israel—while acknowledging the diversity of Reform Jewish beliefs and practices." Judaism must "change and adapt to the needs of the day," and consequently Reform Judaism "asks us to renew our living Covenant with God, the people Israel, humankind, and the earth." Second, it affirms a "commitment to the ongoing work of pursuing justice." Highlighting the notion that all humans are "created in the image of God" and are "God's partners in improving the world," the statement affirms that "*Tikkun olam*, the repair of our world, is a hallmark of Reform Judaism as we strive to bring about a world of justice, wholeness, and compassion." Third, acknowledging that there is "more than one authentic way to be Jewish," Reform Judaism is described as unswervingly "committed to inclusion, not exclusion." Inclusion means a complete commitment to gender equality as well as the embracing of "audacious hospitality," a term that conveys the movement's desire to "reach out to those currently not engaged in Jewish life." This goal "includes but is not limited to: Jews-by-choice and those exploring Judaism; Jews of color; LGBTQ+ Jews; Jews with physical, mental, or intellectual disabilities; interfaith and intermarried couples and families; multiracial families; families with young children; as well as those at the intersection of many identities."[51]

The Conservative movement also offers a prominent listing of priorities. Authored by Professor Arnold Eisen, chancellor emeritus of the Jewish Theological Seminary, the work is not an official movement statement but an essay on contemporary "understandings of Conservative Judaism itself."[52] In his analysis, Eisen deals with many features of Conservative Jewish life—covenant, community, "peoplehood & Israel," learning, *mitzvah*, *tefillah* (prayer), and denominations. In the *mitzvah* section, Eisen offers a selection of those *mitzvot* that "seem especially crucial to Conservative Jewish life right now." First, there is study, "because we cannot walk confidently into the future unless we know…the Torah that Jews have lived and taught." Second, there is *tefillah*, "because we need to recover the rich and nuanced conversation with and about God." Third, Eisen posits that Conservative Jews need to observe "Sabbaths, festivals and other holy times" in order to maintain "times and spaces dedicated to our norms, our view of the world, our rituals and texts, the needs of our communities, and our encounter with what is best inside ourselves." Fourth is Israel, because the "State of Israel is essential to Jewish survival." And fifth is "protection of the planet," "because we are the stewards of God's Creation."[53]

Analyzing these lists can help ascertain some of the twenty-first-century aspirations of the movements. The Reform statement begins with a commitment to diversity of belief and practice. The extent to which the Reform movement is committed to such diversity is clarified in an accompanying online article entitled "Authentic Reform Judaism."[54] The article provides examples of what "authentic" Reform Judaism looks like in practice:

> Some Jewish families light Shabbat candles every Friday night. That is authentic Reform Judaism. Some families rarely or never light Shabbat candles. That, too, is authentic Reform Judaism…
>
> …[S]ome in our congregations keep strictly kosher houses, never eating non-kosher food outside the home. That's authentic Reform Judaism. Others cook and enjoy bacon cheeseburgers and other non-kosher fare. That's authentic Reform Judaism too…
>
> Do you come to Friday evening or Saturday morning services to observe a yahrzeit? Do you put on tefillin? Do you attend Torah study? If so, you are an authentic Reform Jew. If you don't know what tefillin are, you are still an authentic Reform Jew…
>
> Such diversity is our strength.[55]

It is clear that the "diversity" intended here goes considerably beyond differences over styles of observance; rather, it includes both those who observe and those who, while aware of the possibilities, do not. According to this view, for the Reform Jew it is just as "authentic" to perform Shabbat rituals as to not perform them, to know about tefillin as to not know, and to observe dietary laws as to bypass them. And, given that some have begun to consider altering the liturgy to make atheists feel included,[56] this type of "diversity" may well extend to Reform's central tenets of "God, Torah, and Israel." Whatever one might think of the merits of this approach, it seems reasonable to posit that this understanding of diversity is both open-minded and lacking in direction. If both "X" and "the inverse of X" are authentic Reform Judaism, then authentic Reform Judaism cannot be said to offer decisive prescriptions of its own. Reform Judaism provides bridges among the differing practices and beliefs of the individuals who comprise the movement, but the movement itself offers no non-negotiable positions beyond diversity itself. Diversity, according to this viewpoint, not only affords each individual free choice, but it also holds that every individual's choice to observe or not to observe should be honored equally.

The second priority the Reform movement stresses is *tikkun olam*. Emerging from the historic Reform commitment to "prophetic Judaism," *tikkun olam* has become sufficiently prominent that it is described as "a hallmark of Reform Judaism." Naturally, those who seek to "repair the world" are worthy of admiration. But questions abound: What exactly are the limits and the primary concerns of *tikkun olam*? Can a non-Jew engage in *tikkun olam*, or is it a Jewish activity? Is any project that is subjectively defined as *tikkun olam* to be considered *tikkun olam*, or are there objective criteria? For example, if individuals decide that saving fetuses from termination constitutes *tikkun olam*, and they work against abortions sought for economic reasons, is that *tikkun olam* because they deem it so? Can a person who works counter to their efforts in support of such abortions similarly claim to be pursuing *tikkun olam*? Is it *tikkun olam* if a Jew performs good works entirely disconnected from the Jewish community or Jewish mandates? By way of illustration, if a Jew goes to Fiji to help improve the fitness of native Fijians, is it *tikkun olam*? Can one claim to be engaged in *tikkun olam* if the project being pursued runs counter to the teachings of Judaism? For instance, could one claim to be doing *tikkun olam* by volunteering to shoot rabbits in order to lessen the effects of an overabundance of rabbits on other species?[57] Can one earn money for acts of *tikkun olam*, or must true *tikkun olam* be uncompensated? Perhaps most significantly: Is there a hierarchy of desirable *tikkun olam* endeavors, or is every act equally worthy? Is a morning spent caring for abused women at a local shelter just as valuable as a morning spent removing pollutants from a local stream, or is one more important than the other?

Individuals may well have responses to these inquiries, but the Reform movement offers no definitive guidance. Some will wonder why answering these questions really matters when promoting *tikkun olam* leads to applaudable results. But the issue at stake is the extent to which these are characteristic Reform Jewish outcomes, expressing a defined goal that epitomizes the distinctive voice of the movement. If, after all, anybody can perform acts of *tikkun olam*, or one can subjectively define what constitutes *tikkun olam*, or one can choose a *tikkun olam* plan without reference to Jewish sources, or one can subjectively choose which acts of *tikkun olam* take precedence over others, then *tikkun olam* is essentially the performance of self-defined acts of individual goodness. And if individuals can perform acts of *tikkun olam* with outcomes that are directly contrary to each other, and where there is no clarity about which activities are more and which are less central, then *tikkun olam* might well be a virtue, but it is hard to see what makes it a coherently Jewish one.

The third priority on the Reform list stresses Reform's commitment to inclusivity. Few in the non-Orthodox world will disagree with this commitment. But should there be any boundaries? Some Reform rabbis are already pointing to the way ahead: "While we should never lose sight of the brilliant integrity of a unified Jewish existence, we must make Judaism available to those who are not seeking such a solitary religious identity."[58] If "inclusion" means making Judaism available to those who might seek to add it to a preexisting religious identity, do any inviolable boundary markers remain? Are non-Jews who belong to Reform congregations to be regarded as members of the "Jewish people?" Does "inclusion" suggest that they are functionally equivalent to Jews? Unless the limits of inclusivity are defined, there is the potential for a blurring of identity categories with weighty implications for our understandings of Jewishness.

Before drawing some overall conclusions about the Reform approach, it is worth comparing the Reform goals to those of the Conservative movement. At first glance, the list of Conservative priorities looks more concrete. This may be because it appears in a section designed to tackle *mitzvot*, but it is worth noting that Eisen's final two selections—supporting Israel and protecting the planet—are not *mitzvot* in the strict sense. Understood as a description of the movement's goals, the Conservative movement seems more directive than the Reform movement. Eisen prescribes that Conservative Jews should study, should engage in a "rich and nuanced conversation with God," and should observe Shabbat and holy times so that it is possible to carve out opportunities "dedicated to our norms, our view of the world." In addition, commitment to Israel is critical to be able "to apply the Torah's teachings in new ways to every aspect of the public sphere." These statements are specific and concrete. They envision an individual who is committed to core Jewish concerns. The one novel item on the list is "protection of the planet." It is the only goal that is universal and contemporary, and Eisen explains his choice by positing that "God's creation" is "threatened with destruction as never before." Hence, it is, according to Eisen, a Conservative movement priority to preserve the physical environment of which we are "stewards."[59]

All of this seems straightforward enough. However, immediately following this list, Eisen adds a final paragraph:

> When all is said and done, I stand with the young rabbinic colleague who told her congregation one day that God does not care "whether or not we spend money on Shabbat or eat a McDonald's cheeseburger," but that God does care "whether or not we live our lives with a sense of purpose, whether or not we have gratitude and seek forgiveness, whether or not we are…compassionate and concerned about social justice." We can't accomplish that as individuals. We need communities animated by shared norms, aspiration, and commitment, and guided by shared practice. *Mitzvah* and *Halakhah* are needed to help Jews bring more meaning to their lives, and more justice and compassion to the world.[60]

What is a member of the Conservative movement to make of these lines? Having just endorsed Shabbat and other *mitzvot*, Eisen now explains that God does not care much about the particulars of *mitzvot* performance but really views Jewish life through a wider lens. True, the wording still endorses *mitzvah* and *halakhah* as "needed" but only insofar as they serve the cause of "bringing meaning to lives" and "justice and compassion to the world." If God is not really concerned about the minutiae of observance, then it is logical for Conservative Jews to attend to the development of their "sense of purpose, compassion, and social justice." In many ways, this sounds more akin to the Reform movement's pursuit of *tikkun olam* than to the endorsement of specific *mitzvot*.

Which approach represents the real Conservative movement? The answer is probably both. Both the specified, traditionalist approach based on delineated injunctions and the more general pursuit of "meaning, justice, and compassion" appear to represent contemporary Conservative Judaism. Even though Eisen does not care for the "tradition and change" slogan,[61] he affirms that the traditional voice and the language of modernity should resonate together:

> We dance around the Torah to new melodies as well as old, and power enduring commitments with new ideas. We hold that the beliefs and prac-

tices of Judaism developed by Jews over many centuries are fully compatible with the best of modern convictions and sensibilities—pluralism and reason, democracy and human rights, global citizenship and social justice—and that our love of Torah, Israel, and God is strengthened, rather than weakened, by full participation in the societies and cultures of which Jews are a part.[62]

While this integration of two strands is attractive, the strands pull in different directions—one toward the more classic agenda of study, prayer, holy times, and Israel and the other toward the more contemporary agenda of social justice, compassion, and care for the world. It is, of course, possible to devote oneself to both simultaneously. But Eisen portrays Judaism as "compatible with the best of modern convictions and sensibilities" and describes "full participation" in society and culture as virtuous because they strengthen Judaism.

What, then, can be gleaned from the stated goals of the two movements? They are, understandably, heavily influenced by the priorities of the surrounding culture. The Reform movement is sufficiently flexible that little is mandated in the realm of thought or deed. It places a heavy emphasis on *tikkun olam* without precisely defining the concept. It emphasizes "adapting to the needs of the day," making it responsive to the agenda of others. It elevates inclusion and equality for all to the extent that it is hard to discern where the boundaries of Jewish identity lie. The Reform movement is open and welcoming, but as it becomes more diverse in its commitments, more modern in its outlook, and more "inclusive," it appears less able to specify a defined Jewish direction. The Conservative movement is not altogether different. It does call for Jews to obligate themselves in specific areas like Torah learning, prayer, sacred times, Israel, and environmental protection. But like the Reform movement, the Conservative movement is centered on the priorities of modernity; it too speaks about "compassion, concern, and social justice," while giving the impression that the distinctively Jewish parts of its agenda are less pressing.

In many ways, both movements are authentic products of their era. In 1989, the political scientist Francis Fukuyama wrote his landmark essay on the end of history. The Cold War was ending, and Fukuyama declared that the great ideological battles between East and West were over and that Western liberal democracy had won:

What we may be witnessing is not just the end of the Cold War, or the passing of a particular period of post-war history, but the end of history as such:

that is, the end point of mankind's ideological evolution and the universal-
ization of Western liberal democracy as the final form of human government.[63]

Time has not been kind to Fukuyama's prediction. With the passing of
the 1990s, sometimes referred to as the "holiday from history,"[64] the
twenty-first century has seen history return undiminished. Though he was
incorrect about the end of history, Fukuyama insightfully observed that
the dominance of the liberal democracies meant that a marketplace ethos
had come to exert a more central influence on culture, while ideologies
were playing a considerably smaller role:

> The end of history will be a very sad time. The struggle for recognition, the
> willingness to risk one's life for a purely abstract goal, the worldwide ideo-
> logical struggle that called forth daring, courage, imagination, and idealism,
> will be replaced by economic calculation, the endless solving of technical
> problems, environmental concerns, and the satisfaction of sophisticated
> consumer demands.[65]

In other words, with the battle over big ideas seemingly won, nations
would be driven extensively by consumer preferences without a discernible overarching philosophy of why one alternative might be better than
another. Deep questions about the direction of human society would
come to be seen as academically interesting but less than vital. Rabbi
Jonathan Sacks, a public intellectual and former chief rabbi of the British
Commonwealth, astutely observed that never before have humans "been
faced with more choices, but never before have the great society-shaping
institutions offered less guidance on why we should choose this way rather
than that."[66]

Broadly speaking, the non-Orthodox movements became part of this
milieu. They had assisted Jews to be "at home" in Western society by
championing a free-choice approach to Judaism that was well-aligned with
the ascendant ethic of maximizing personal fulfillment. In so doing, they
rarely attempted to promote views that might run counter to cultural
trends. The movements remained fundamentally oriented toward providing strategies for harmonizing Judaism with modernity.

However, the case can be made that the process of deliberating about
and initiating ideas that could reshape civilization was historically central
to Judaism. The Jewish aspiration was not that Jews should be comfortable insiders, selecting from the menu and imitating their surroundings;
rather, the classic model was that Jews should be outsiders, standing on

the opposite riverbank, ready to critique the zeitgeist and propose alternatives:

> Jewish tradition has always claimed that Jews need to be different in order that they might play a quasi-subversive role in society… Jews' role is not to second every motion of society, but to second guess society's priorities. It is not only that Jews have an alternative position to espouse; the tradition occasionally insists that Jews have to be prophets, outcasts, harsh critics of prevailing social mores.[67]

From the time when Abraham was told to leave his birthplace and to begin anew somewhere else, turning his back on the dominant culture and establishing a different vision, Judaism held that transforming society requires separating from it. The Hebrew word *kadosh* conveys exactly this perspective: separated for a special purpose. When the Torah specifies (Exodus 19:3–6) that the Jews should be a people who are *kadosh*, it is essentially communicating that Jews should aspire to a distinctive role in society, ready to critique the culture and to help refashion it. When the prophets of the Bible called for justice for the poor, the widow, and the orphan they did not do so as consummate insiders; they did so as outcasts.[68] As much as prophetic Judaism was about a particular message of justice, it was about the iconoclastic position of the messenger as an outsider who could discern society's missteps: "Somehow, feeling too much at home undermines our ability to see what is wrong with the world in which we live."[69]

Ironically, then, as much as Jews thirsted for an end to the isolation forced upon Jewish communities throughout the centuries, the functioning of Judaism is somewhat dependent on being able to analyze surrounding society from a distance. Modernity opened the door to Jewish emancipation and erased the barriers to full participation, but it simultaneously challenged Judaism to demarcate a path that was differentiated from its surroundings. Indeed, the more that Reform and Conservative Judaism embraced modernity, the more difficult it became to articulate the case for a distinctively Jewish approach. It seems reasonable to assert that the current weakness of the Conservative and Reform movements owes as much to an uncertain raison d'être as it does to the circumstances of hyper-emancipation.

Reinvigorating non-Orthodox Judaism will, therefore, require moving away from the founding impulse of "fitting in" towards embracing the complicated work of critically appraising societal directions. If new iterations of non-Orthodox Judaism are to have relevance going forward, they will need to emphasize the historic Jewish task of evaluating contemporary civilization critically and offering a Jewish vision for how elements of society could be constructively reshaped. Developing that message will require a degree of distance from the accepted modes of conventional thinking. This does not imply physical separation. Jews cannot learn from their culture if they are not part of it, nor can they have any impact upon it if they do not engage with it. The complex challenge is to live in society while not yet wholly being "of society," to comprehend society's values while yet questioning them: simultaneously, to be a part and apart.

This transition would be sufficiently difficult to accomplish if the familiar circumstances of modernity had remained constant. It is, however, made far more complex, and considerably more consequential, by the fact that since 1990 much of human civilization has changed beyond recognition. Many of the bedrock assumptions of modernity, upon which the contemporary movements of Judaism were founded, have been superseded, leading to a fundamentally altered landscape. It is this remarkable new reality which non-Orthodox Judaism must now confront.

NOTES

1. Seltzer, *Jewish People, Jewish Thought*, 546.
2. Eugene B. Borowitz, *Choices in Modern Jewish Thought: A Partisan Guide* (New York: Behrman House, 1983), 20.
3. Ibid., 21.
4. Ibid., 22.
5. Ibid.
6. Harry Redner, *Beyond Civilization: Society, Culture, and the Individual in the Age of Globalization* (London: Routledge, 2013), 94.
7. Steven Nadler, "Why Spinoza was Excommunicated," *Humanities*, September/October 2013, Volume 34, Number 5, accessed August 1, 2022, https://www.neh.gov/article/why-spinoza-was-excommunicated
8. Michael A. Meyer, *Response to Modernity* (New York: Oxford University Press, 1988), 65.
9. Ibid.
10. Ibid.
11. Emil L. Fackenheim, "Kant and Judaism," *Commentary Magazine*, December 1, 1963, accessed August 1, 2022, https://www.commentary-magazine.com/article/kant-and-judaism/
12. Larry Siedentop, *Inventing the Individual–The Origins of Western Liberalism* (London: Penguin Books, 2014), 361.

13. Borowitz, *Choices in Modern Jewish Thought*, 23.
14. "The Pittsburgh Platform" 1885, Central Conference of American Rabbis, accessed August 1, 2022, https://www.ccarnet.org/rabbinic-voice/platforms/article-declaration-principles/
15. Ibid.
16. "The Columbus Platform" 1937, Central Conference of American Rabbis, accessed August 1, 2022, https://www.ccarnet.org/rabbinic-voice/platforms/article-guiding-principles-reform-judaism/
17. "Reform Judaism: A Centenary Perspective," Adopted in San Francisco—1976, Central Conference of American Rabbis, accessed August 1, 2022, https://www.ccarnet.org/rabbinic-voice/platforms/article-reform-judaism-centenary-perspective/
18. Richard Levy, "Ten Principles for Reform Judaism," in *Reform Judaism Magazine*, August 1998, accessed May 18, 2015, http://reformjudaismmag.net/rjmag-90s/1198tp.html
19. "A Statement of Principles for Reform Judaism," Central Conference of American Rabbis, accessed August 1, 2022, https://www.ccarnet.org/rabbinic-voice/platforms/article-statement-principles-reform-judaism/
20. Mordechai Waxman, *Tradition and Change–The Development of Conservative Judaism* (New York: The Burning Bush Press, 1958), 12–13.
21. While there have been a number of books describing the movement's stances, the only official "Statement of Principles of Conservative Judaism" published by the movement was "*Emet Ve-Emunah*," released in 1988.
22. "Tradition and change" became something of a motto for the movement, which is why Rabbi Waxman used it as the title for his book that told the story of Conservative Judaism.
23. Herbert Rosenblum, *Conservative Judaism—A Contemporary History* (New York: United Synagogue of America, 1983), 2.
24. Waxman, *Tradition and Change*, 16.
25. Chatam Sofer as quoted in Donniel Hartman, *The Boundaries of Judaism* (New York: Continuum, 2007), 111.
26. Solomon Schechter, "Historical Judaism," as quoted in Waxman, *Tradition and Change*, 97.
27. Rosenblum, *Conservative Judaism—A Contemporary History*, 17.
28. David L. Lieber (Ed.), *Etz Hayim–Torah and Commentary* (Philadelphia: The Jewish Publication Society, 2001), xxi.
29. Morris Adler as cited in Rosenblum, *Conservative Judaism—A Contemporary History*, 119.
30. A wife whose husband refuses to provide a Jewish divorce to conclude their marital relationship.
31. Theodore Friedman as cited in Rosenblum, *Conservative Judaism—A Contemporary History*, 120.

32. Ira Eisenstein, "The Need for Legislation in Jewish Law," as quoted in Waxman, *Tradition and Change*, 448. Later in life, Eisenstein would be among the founders of the Reconstructionist movement. These words, however, come from the time when he was very much an integral part of the Conservative movement. Their content still speaks eloquently for a substantial part of the movement.

33. Ibid., 450.

34. *Emet Ve-Emunah–Statement of Principles of Conservative Judaism* (New York: The Jewish Theological Seminary of America, 1988), 23.

35. As one sympathetic analyst wrote, "While it might be possible to read Jewish law to permit driving on Shabbat or ordaining a woman rabbi, both of those choices seem motivated by a reluctant acquiescence to the demands of the time rather than by a deep and reverent reading of the texts." Samantha Shapiro, "One Mad Rabbi," *Slate Magazine*, August 28, 2006, accessed August 1, 2022, http://www.slate.com/articles/life/faithbased/2006/08/one_mad_rabbi.html

36. "Reform Judaism: A Centenary Perspective," Adopted in San Francisco—1976, Central Conference of American Rabbis, accessed August 1, 2022, https://www.ccarnet.org/rabbinic-voice/platforms/article-reform-judaism-zionism-centenary-platform/

37. Louis M. Epstein, "Freedom versus Discipline in Jewish Law," Report of the CJL—1941, in David Golinkin (Ed.) *Proceedings of the Committee on Jewish Law and Standards of the Conservative Movement 1927–1970*, Volume 1 (Jerusalem: The Rabbinical Assembly, 1997) 131b-c. The incident described clearly took place prior to the Law Committee's decision to authorize driving to synagogue on Shabbat.

38. Allowing "conscience" to play a role can, if not checked, lead to a subjective response to *halakhah* that resembles autonomy. It is telling that, in the twenty-first century, Rabbi Jerome Epstein, in a piece entitled "The 'Ideal' Conservative Jew," would feel the need to remind Conservative Jews that "[m]any people mistakenly believe that Conservative Judaism is 'pick and choose' Judaism—that there are no rules or expectations. In truth, however, Conservative Judaism is committed to Jewish tradition and to the observance of *mitzvot*." Clearly, the role of the individual in decision-making had expanded beyond what had been originally contemplated. Jerome Epstein, "The 'Ideal' Conservative Jew," United Synagogue of Conservative Judaism, accessed May 19, 2015, http://www.uscj.org/JewishLivingandLearning/JewishObservance/TheIdealConservativeJew.aspx

39. Borowitz, *Choices in Modern Jewish Thought*, 24.

40. It is worth noting that it is unusual to hear Orthodoxy described as the "Orthodox movement." Orthodoxy is perceived to be more about preser-

vation of a received tradition than social change in pursuit of a goal. Hence, the "movement" designation is less applicable.

41. For a good summary article, see Ronald H. Isaacs, "Does Judaism Allow Birth Control?" *My Jewish Learning*, accessed August 1, 2022, http://www.myjewishlearning.com/article/procreation-and-contraception/

42. Michael E. Staub, *Torn at the Roots: The Crisis of Jewish Liberalism in Postwar America* (New York: Columbia University Press, 2002), 261.

43. Ibid., 262.

44. In a 2015 graduation speech to students at the Hebrew Union College, the Reform movement's seminary, Richard Siegel reviewed the "revolutionary" experiences of his "Baby Boomer" generation: "We saw how all around us the larger American society was undergoing radical change, almost overnight…civil rights, feminism, the anti-Vietnam movement, the sexual revolution, identity politics, ethnic pride… And we asked, why not the Jewish community, as well?" Richard Siegel, "Bridging the Gap: A New Paradigm for Change," EJewishPhilanthropy, June 2, 2015, accessed August 1, 2022, http://ejewishphilanthropy.com/bridging-the-gap-a-new-paradigm-for-change/?utm_source=June+2+Tues&utm_campaign=Tue+June+2&utm_medium=email. The order here is significant. They "saw" what was going on in surrounding society and then asked, "Why not the Jewish community?" Profound as they were, the changes they sought were echoes of what was already happening on a broader stage.

45. Avraham Grossman, *Pious and Rebellious: Jewish Women in Medieval Europe* (Lebanon NH: Brandeis University Press, 2004), 74. Grossman attributes this explanation to Ze'ev Falk.

46. The changed role of women in Jewish life is clearly the most prominent example.

47. The President of the Union for Reform Judaism expressed this concern unambiguously: "Today, Jacobs said, young people don't necessarily connect their activism with their Judaism." "New Religious Action Center leader aims to sharpen Reform Judaism's stamp on policy," washingtonpost.com, January 7, 2015, accessed August 1, 2022, http://www.washingtonpost.com/local/new-religious-action-center-leader-aims-to-intensify-reform-judaisms-effect-on-policy/2015/01/07/01560fde-9693-11e4-927a-4fa2638cd1b0_story.html.

48. The Washington, DC, Religious Action Center of the Reform movement lists "more than 70 different issues" for which it advocates. Some of these issues emerge powerfully from within the Torah tradition. Others are related to Jewish tradition in a more tangential way. See https://www.rac.org/about-rac accessed October 11, 2020.

49. Pew Research Center, "Jewish Americans in 2020," https://www.pewresearch.org/religion/2021/05/11/jewish-practices-and-customs/ It is

worth noting that there is a marked difference between Conservative and Reform Jews in the attendance rate of those who come "monthly or more": 33 percent of Conservative Jews attend at least monthly, more than double the rate of 14 percent for Reform Jews.

50. "What is Reform Judaism?," ReformJudaism.org, accessed August 1, 2022, http://www.reformjudaism.org/what-reform-judaism

51. Ibid.

52. Arnold M. Eisen, *Conservative Judaism Today and Tomorrow* (New York: The Jewish Theological Seminary of America, 2014), Kindle Location 1. It is important to note that Chancellor Eisen's essay is centrally referenced on the movement's most well-known webpage about Conservative Judaism: http://www.jtsa.edu/conservative-judaism, accessed October 11, 2020.

53. Ibid., Kindle Location 535.

54. Alan Zeichick, "What Is Authentic Reform Judaism," ReformJudaism.org, accessed August 1, 2022, https://reformjudaism.org/what-authentic-reform-judaism. This article represents the views of one individual movement leader. Nevertheless, its featured position on the movement website seems to imply that the movement approves of its content.

55. Ibid.

56. Seth M. Limmer, "Reform Judaism for the 21st Century," June 6, 2015, accessed August 1, 2022, https://rabbilimmer.wordpress.com/

57. Judaism would oppose this practice since it involves animal suffering, *tza'ar ba'alei chayim*.

58. Limmer, "Reform Judaism for the 21st Century," June 6, 2015, accessed August 1, 2022, https://rabbilimmer.wordpress.com/

59. Eisen, *Conservative Judaism Today and Tomorrow*, Kindle Location 530.

60. Ibid., Kindle Location 570.

61. Ibid., Kindle Location 866.

62. Ibid., Kindle Location 893.

63. Francis Fukuyama, "The End of History?," *The National Interest*, Summer 1989, accessed August 1, 2022, https://www.jstor.org/stable/24027184?read-now=1&seq=1#page_scan_tab_contents

64. George Will, "The End of America's Holiday from History," *Orlando Sentinel*, February 23, 1999, accessed October 11, 2020, http://articles.orlandosentinel.com/1999-02-23/news/9902230361_1_north-korea-foreign-policy-domestic-policy

65. Fukuyama, "The End of History?," 25–26.

66. Jonathan Sacks, *The Dignity of Difference* (London: Continuum, 2002), 40.

67. Daniel Gordis, *Does the World Need Jews?* (New York: Scribner, 1997), 177.

68. "[T]he Greek Axial breakthrough contrasts fundamentally with the Israelite one, where the prophets stood outside politics, but judged it from on high. They marked out an inviolable ethical sphere from which they

could launch fierce attacks against political power in the name of a god of truth. They meddled in all affairs of state without restraint and denounced the actions of the kings, whether in internal or external political matters. The early Greek law-givers and reformers, and later the philosophers, took the opposite course; they were intent on changing the constitution of the polis, but never stood against it or removed themselves from it." Redner, *Beyond Civilization*, 72.

69. Gordis, *Does the World Need Jews?*, 182.

References

A Statement of Principles for Reform Judaism, Central Conference of American Rabbis, accessed August 1, 2022, https://www.ccarnet.org/rabbinic-voice/platforms/article-statement-principles-reform-judaism/.

Borowitz, Eugene. *Choices In Modern Jewish Thought: A Partisan Guide* (New York: Behrman House, 1983).

Eisen, Arnold. *Conservative Judaism Today and Tomorrow* (New York: The Jewish Theological Seminary of America, 2014).

Emet Ve-Emunah–Statement of Principles of Conservative Judaism, (New York: The Jewish Theological Seminary of America, 1988).

Epstein, Louis. "Freedom versus Discipline in Jewish Law," Report of the CJL—1941, in David Golinkin (Ed.) Proceedings of the Committee on Jewish Law and Standards of the Conservative Movement 1927–1970, Volume 1 (Jerusalem: The Rabbinical Assembly, 1997).

Epstein, Jerome. "The 'Ideal' Conservative Jew," United Synagogue of Conservative Judaism, accessed May 19, 2015, http://www.uscj.org/JewishLivingandLearning/JewishObservance/TheIdealConservativeJew.aspx.

Fackenheim, Emil. "Kant and Judaism," Commentary Magazine, December 1, 1963, accessed August 1, 2022, https://www.commentarymagazine.com/article/kant-and-judaism/.

Fukuyama, Francis. "The End of History?," The National Interest, Summer 1989, accessed August 1, 2022, https://www.jstor.org/stable/24027184?readnow=1&seq=1#page_scan_tab_contents.

Gordis, Daniel. *Does the World Need Jews?* (New York: Scribner, 1997).

Grossman, Avraham. *Pious and Rebellious: Jewish Women in Medieval Europe*, (Lebanon NH: Brandeis University Press, 2004).

Hartman, Donniel. *The Boundaries of Judaism* (New York: Continuum, 2007).

Isaacs, Ronald. "Does Judaism Allow Birth Control?" My Jewish Learning, accessed August 1, 2022, http://www.myjewishlearning.com/article/procreation-and-contraception/.

Leiber, David (Ed.), *Etz Hayim–Torah and Commentary* (Philadelphia: The Jewish Publication Society, 2001).

Limmer, Seth. "Reform Judaism for the 21ˢᵗ Century," June 6, 2015, accessed August 1, 2022, https://rabbilimmer.wordpress.com/.

Meyer, Michael. *Response to Modernity* (New York: Oxford University Press, 1988).

Levy, Richard. "Ten Principles for Reform Judaism," in Reform Judaism Magazine, August 1998, accessed May 18, 2015, http://reformjudaismmag.net/rjmag-90s/1198tp.html.

Nadler, Steven. "Why Spinoza was Excommunicated," Humanities, September/October 2013, Volume 34, Number 5, accessed August 1, 2022, https://www.neh.gov/article/why-spinoza-was-excommunicated.

New Religious Action Center leader aims to sharpen Reform Judaism's stamp on policy, washingtonpost.com, January 7, 2015, accessed August 1, 2022, http://www.washingtonpost.com/local/new-religious-action-center-leader-aims-to-intensify-reform-judaisms-effect-on-policy/2015/01/07/01560fd e-9693-11e4-927a-4fa2638cd1b0_story.html.

Pew Research Center, "Jewish Americans in 2020," https://www.pewresearch.org/religion/2021/05/11/jewish-practices-and-customs/.

Redner, Harry. *Beyond Civilization: Society, Culture, and the Individual in the Age of Globalization* (London: Routledge, 2013).

Reform Judaism: A Centenary Perspective, Adopted in San Francisco—1976, Central Conference of American Rabbis, accessed August 1, 2022, https://www.ccarnet.org/rabbinic-voice/platforms/article-reform-judaism-centenary-perspective/.

Rosenblum, Herbert. *Conservative Judaism—A Contemporary History* (New York: United Synagogue of America, 1983).

Sacks, Jonathan. *The Dignity of Difference* (London: Continuum, 2002).

Seltzer, Robert. *Jewish People, Jewish Thought* (New York: Macmillan Publishing Company, 1980).

Shapiro, Samantha. "One Mad Rabbi," Slate Magazine, August 28, 2006, accessed August 1, 2022, http://www.slate.com/articles/life/faithbased/2006/08/one_mad_rabbi.html.

Siedentop, Larry. *Inventing the Individual–The Origins of Western Liberalism.* London, Penguin Books, 2014.

Siegel, Richard. "Bridging the Gap: A New Paradigm for Change," EJewishPhilanthropy, June 2, 2015, accessed August 1, 2022, http://ejewishphilanthropy.com/bridging-the-gap-a-new-paradigm-for-change/?utm_source=June+2+Tues&utm_campaign=Tue+June+2&utm_medium=email.

Staub, Michael. *Torn at the Roots: The Crisis of Jewish Liberalism in Postwar America* (New York: Columbia University Press, 2002).

The Columbus Platform 1937, Central Conference of American Rabbis, accessed August 1, 2022, https://www.ccarnet.org/rabbinic-voice/platforms/article-guiding-principles-reform-judaism/.

The Pittsburgh Platform 1885, Central Conference of American Rabbis, accessed August 1, 2022, https://www.ccarnet.org/rabbinic-voice/platforms/article-declaration-principles/.

Waxman, Mordechai. *Tradition and Change–The Development of Conservative Judaism* (New York: The Burning Bush Press, 1958).

What is Reform Judaism?, ReformJudaism.org, accessed August 1, 2022, http://www.reformjudaism.org/what-reform-judaism.

Will, George. "The End of America's Holiday from History," Orlando Sentinel, February 23, 1999, accessed October 11, 2020, http://articles.orlandosentinel.com/1999-02-23/news/9902230361_1_north-korea-foreign-policy-domestic-policy.

Zeichick, Alan. "What Is Authentic Reform Judaism," ReformJudaism.org, accessed August 1, 2022, https://reformjudaism.org/what-authentic-reform-judaism.

CHAPTER 4

A New Era

It is now apparent in hindsight that just as Francis Fukuyama was declaring history to be over, a new era was actually dawning. Variously referred to as the "digital age," the "Internet era," the "great acceleration," or the period of "globalization," it is the unremittingly disruptive time in which we now live. It is an age marked by an unprecedented level of worldwide interconnectedness. This is not, of course, the first era in which dramatic advances have bridged the gaps between continents. The journalist and author Thomas Friedman has written of two previous such periods beginning as far back as the sixteenth century.[1] Nor is the Internet the first technology to shrink the globe and to push back the tyranny of distance; telephone, radio, aircraft, and Earth-orbiting satellites each played their part.

However, the transformations that have truly reordered human civilization have all been of one type: each refashioned the way storable information is transmitted. Prior to our own time, there were three such paradigm-shifting moments: The invention of writing 20,000 to 30,000 years ago introduced pictograms and hieroglyphics which led to the foundation of civilization. Later, the creation of alphabets, 4000 years ago, gave rise to literacy and the spread of knowledge. Then, in the middle of the fifteenth century, the printing press challenged ecclesiastical authority, boosted education, and spurred the growth of science. Indeed, the printing press led directly to "the collapse of strictly hierarchical societies in which only a few were literate and had access to texts" and to a revised

D. Schiff, *Judaism in a Digital Age*,
https://doi.org/10.1007/978-3-031-17992-1_4

"awareness of time," as news pamphlets with dates became possible.[2] So extensively did the printing press expand access to information that it can rightfully be described as a prime catalyst of modernity. Given this background, it is no small matter to postulate that the transformations that began around 1990 have been even more profound:

> Printing was invented in the fifteenth century, became popular a few centuries later, and had a huge impact in that we were able to move cultural knowledge from the human brain into a printed form. We have the same sort of revolution happening right now, on steroids, and it is affecting every dimension of human life.[3]

Our current period, centered around the Internet, is the fourth major information technology transformation in history. It is, therefore, possible to pinpoint with some accuracy when modernity yielded the stage to our new age of hyper-connectivity. Personal computers reached the mass market for the first time in the 1980s and quickly became widespread. The nascent Internet arrived in the 1990s and, almost overnight, a powerful leap in the human ability to transmit, store, and share information in real time refashioned numerous aspects of life irreversibly.

In the fifteenth century, the pace of innovation wrought by the printing press must have felt rapid. Only fifty years after the arrival of the printing press in 1450, there were 35,000 titles in print, and between 15 and 20 million books were in circulation. Within a century, that number expanded tenfold.[4] But the changes in the dissemination of knowledge and the societal upheavals instigated by the printing press were glacial compared to the digital revolution. When Bill Clinton became US president in January 1993, there were less than 100 sites on the World Wide Web. When he left office, eight years later, there were close to 30 million. By the time the web had been accessible for a quarter century, the number of websites exceeded one and a half billion, and the number of users surpassed 3 billion—approaching half the world's population.[5] Never before in history has the extent of change in technology been more far-reaching, and never before has it taken place with such astonishing speed. And as the technological advances developed and spread exponentially, so the remaking of human culture has unfolded with corresponding swiftness. Previous generations needed historians to trace the long-term reworking of societal structures brought about by information technologies; today, societies are being reconfigured before our very eyes.

Indeed, the technology writer Robert Colville has labeled our age "the great acceleration."[6] He justifies this description by detailing the amounts of time that were required to achieve widespread adoption of successive technologies:

> For the printing press, it was centuries; for television and radio, a few decades; for the web, just six or seven years... In 2005, just 5 per cent of American adults used social networking sites; six years later, the figure was at 65 per cent and climbing fast.[7]

As a consequence, Colville asserts that it is no longer appropriate to speak of recent history proceeding in a smooth continuation. Like a jet that morphs from a terrestrial vehicle into an aircraft once it has reached a certain velocity, we have now embarked upon an age that is marked by great acceleration in countless facets of life. Fast-paced innovation has become the norm. The result, writes Colville, "is a mindset in which permanent revolution is not just a business model, but almost the only one that makes sense."[8] One of the triggers for this acceleration has been the steady doubling in computational power roughly every two years. In the decades since 1990, that reality has progressed to the point

> where the doubling has gotten so big and fast we're starting to see stuff that is fundamentally different in power and capability from anything we have seen before—self-driving cars, computers that can think on their own and beat any human in chess, Jeopardy!, or even Go, a 2,500-year-old board game considered vastly more complicated than chess.[9]

We have entered a period in which we are producing technologies that are fundamentally different in their nature from what went before. In the words of Andrew McAfee of MIT's business school, we are in an epoch "when the rate of change and the acceleration of the rate of change both increase at the same time."[10] Small wonder that Friedman observes that we are traversing "one of the greatest leaps forward in history," a period that represents one of the most tumultuous "transformative moments"[11] ever experienced by humans.

It has become clear, moreover, that the sheer pace and scope of change have outstripped the ability of most human beings to adapt. Craig Mundie, the former chief of strategy and research at Microsoft, observes that "*disruption* is what happens when someone does something clever that makes you or your company look obsolete. *Dislocation* is when the whole environment is being altered so quickly that everyone starts to feel they can't keep up."[12] Maybe more than at any other time in human history, it is a feeling of "dislocation" that epitomizes our new era. We are in a period of "dis-location," both in the sense that geographic location has never been less critical and in the sense of the unsettling instability that comes from the requirement to reset constantly. As Dov Seidman, CEO of a global ethics and compliance firm, notes, the speed of civilizational transformation "is happening faster than we have yet been able to reshape ourselves, our leadership, our institutions, our societies, and our ethical choices."[13] Plainly, in a growing number of places, both developed and underdeveloped, this is contributing to social, political, and cultural instability.

Well before the word *globalization* became a politically charged term, its dissemination represented a barometer of the marked transition that was underway.[14] The sociologist Anthony Giddens offered this observation about the use of the word:

> The global spread of the term is evidence of the very developments to which it refers. Every business guru talks about it. No political speech is complete without reference to it. Yet even in the late 1980s the term was hardly used, either in the academic literature or in everyday language. It has come from nowhere to be almost everywhere.[15]

This constant referencing of a novel international interconnectedness signified that history had arrived at a sufficiently disruptive juncture to indicate that a new age had arrived—one that supplanted the period we call modernity. As the philosopher and historian of civilization Harry Redner wrote, "By the close of the twentieth century, Western Modernity was concluding and a new civilizational formation was taking its place. This process is commonly known as globalization, but that term barely conveys the epochal significance of what is now occurring."[16]

This invites the question: What features of this ascendant digital age support the claim that we are living through a time of "epochal significance?" There are many. Clearly, no area has been more consequential than science and technology. Cities that were once hubs of steel manufacturing or centers of agricultural regions now compete to be seen as advanced tech incubators. Mobile communications devices based on sophisticated algorithms, unheard of a generation ago, are ubiquitous: "Nearly all fundamental human pursuits have been touched, if not revolutionized, by mobile."[17] In an eyeblink—less than fifteen years—mobile has become "the most rapidly adopted consumer technology in history."[18] Perhaps most importantly, today every person with Internet access has a world of information at their fingertips that was in large part inaccessible to anyone who lived prior to 1990. This means that every human with a phone is now inundated with as much data in a single day as people used to absorb during all their days on Earth.[19] In the digital age, moreover, we are regularly "in touch with more people in an hour than early humans met in their entire lives."[20] And, if all this were not enough, then consider that "no matter where you are on the planet, except the most remote locations, you are likely being exposed, directly or indirectly, to more contact with more different ideas...than ever before in human history."[21] We are surrounded by a dizzying volume of stimuli delivered on an array of screens, apps, and devices, with powerful new technologies arriving in the hands of the public in a never-ending stream.

This technological fountain has produced breathtaking marvels. As recently as the 1980s, information took days to arrive, or a distant journey to access, or expensive research to unearth, or was nigh impossible to locate. No longer. It is now available with little more than a voice command and often without cost. Those who in any bygone age would have been unreachable, because contacting them was prohibitively expensive or because there was no way of knowing of their existence, are now just clicks or taps away. Had the coronavirus pandemic occurred a decade or two earlier, the social, emotional, educational, and economic costs would have been immeasurably worse. The fact that a large proportion of social connections, classes, meetings, appointments, and much more could take place in virtual settings made the calamity less severe.

The implications of these developments are far-reaching. National borders have come to mean less in a world in which individuals and organizations can work, socialize, and communicate from anywhere. This has inexorably changed the way that many think about lines on maps. As borders have become permeable, and cooperation in real time across the planet has become natural, an ethos of sharing, collaborating, and crowdsourcing has produced impressive leaps forward. One of the most prominent examples of this phenomenon is Wikipedia, the online encyclopedia, which has made print encyclopedias all but obsolete:

Since its creation on January 15, 2001, Wikipedia has grown into the world's largest reference website, attracting 1.7 billion unique-device visitors monthly as of November 2021. It currently has more than fifty-nine million articles in more than 300 languages...Wikipedia is a live collaboration differing from paper-based reference sources in important ways. It is continually created and updated, with articles on new events appearing within minutes, rather than months or years. Because everybody can help improve it, Wikipedia has become more comprehensive than any other encyclopedia.[22]

Wikipedia typifies the technological platforms of the age: It is open to all those who have an internet connection, it is accessible in hundreds of languages, it is constantly updated, and it builds knowledge through the number of participants and their constant refinement of each other's work.

The technology revolution is, then, to a large extent a knowledge revolution. The Internet has effectively democratized access to information. Consequently, advances in the medical field that were once implausible are now moving ahead. The mapping of the human genome that took place in the 1990s is one example.[23] That project would have been inconceivable without the computing power and the communications of the digital age. The amassing of huge data sets in diverse disciplines means that the age of acceleration is also an era of "big data." Mining this data for patterns and trends is producing efficiencies and predictive abilities that were never available before.

Today, societal functioning is dependent on technology in ways that were unimaginable in the 1990s; even a localized Internet failure has the potential to cause major havoc because many systems have no offline replacement. Not only has the Internet become a thoroughly indispensable utility, it has also "technologized" tasks that used to be performed easily without technology. Even the efficient growing of strawberries now requires "data analysis, intelligent sensors, and greenhouse automation."[24] Literally every domain has been impacted.

It is important to emphasize that this technological revolution was neither intended nor planned. It sprouted like a fast-growing jungle that was thrust upon humanity without consultation or consent. Yet opting out has become essentially impossible; it would be tantamount to opting out of society. Contemporary technologies and networks are now unavoidable features of life if one wants to participate in the full range of commercial and social opportunities:

The imposition of information technology on just about everybody in our advanced societies constitutes a gigantic social experiment. It began less than a generation ago, not through any conscious decision on anybody's part that it should be tried, but rather as a creeping process of technological improvement, as piece by piece one after another component of the system was introduced and enthusiastically accepted, first by the computer aficionados and then by nearly everybody else...Now there is no escaping it.[25]

And we are just at the beginning. Wearable technology, the Internet of things,[26] the promise of biotechnology, AI, and the metaverse,[27] to name just the headline areas, all portend further leaps forward. In short, we have arrived at an extraordinary moment in the history of technology:

> If you look back over human history, only a few energy sources fundamentally changed everything for most everyone—fire, electricity, and computing. And now, given where computing has arrived with the cloud, it is not an exaggeration to suggest that it's becoming more profound than fire and electricity. Fire and electricity were hugely important sources of mass energy. They could warm your home, power your tools, or transport you from place to place. But in and of themselves they couldn't help you think or think for you. They could not connect you to all the world's knowledge or all the world's people. We have simply never had a tool like this that could be accessed by people all over the world at the same time via a smartphone.[28]

Like science and technology, global commerce has also been fundamentally reconceived. Hyper-connectivity has combined with the entrepreneurial spirit to recreate whole industries: online travel sites have supplanted travel agents, just as ridesharing has altered urban transportation, and streaming has reshaped entertainment. There is no longer a bank branch on every corner, and online shopping has shuttered many brick-and-mortar stores. Financial and commercial transactions that all required physical exchanges are now handled virtually, and digital currencies are on the rise. In Giddens' words, "geared as it is to electronic money—money that exists only as digits in computers—the current world economy has no parallels in earlier times."[29]

We have become used to the phenomenon of garage startups swiftly remaking business sectors that had been largely unchanged for generations. As enterprises established in dorm rooms have become mighty global brands, established major corporations have stumbled and fallen.[30] Respect for venerable institutions has shriveled, replaced by a startup mentality that suggests that the cutting edge is the only place to be. This has contributed to a burgeoning attitude that nothing needs to be as it was—"that there is always, somewhere and somehow, a better way. It breeds skepticism and mistrust of any authority, and an unwillingness to take any distribution of power for granted."[31] This questioning of traditional structures is a noteworthy feature of the commercial environment that has produced broader ramifications for society as a whole.

The expanded economic interconnectedness of the digital age has yielded both worthy and problematic outcomes. On the positive side, the "multiplier effect" of the Internet has helped bring an end to the period of human history marked by unavoidable scarcity. There is enough wealth, and food to provide for all—if humanity can overcome the challenges of distribution and the unwillingness to share resources. The number of people living in extreme poverty fell from 1.9 billion in 1990 to 836 million in 2015, owing largely to economic growth and allocation improvements.[32] During that period, impressive strides were made in areas of human well-being ranging from infant mortality rates to drinking water access.[33] Urbanization raised the standards of living for many. Today, "for the first time in history, more people live in cities than in farms,"[34] a noteworthy development that has opened new vistas of prosperity for hundreds of millions:

> In emerging economies, incomes are rising faster, and at a greater scale, than at any point in history. As urbanization began to sweep across the emerging world, the consuming class added 1.2 billion new members in 20 years, from 1990 to 2010. By 2025,…the global consuming class [is expected] to add 1.8 billion people, to reach a total of 4.2 billion. Total consumption is expected to reach $64 trillion, nearly half of it in emerging economies.[35]

On the negative side of the ledger, income inequality and wealth gaps have expanded greatly. The globalized digital economy has created a tiny cadre of financial winners—and many losers whose incomes have stagnated. The US typifies the pattern: In 1979, the top 1 percent of wage earners received 7.3 percent of all earnings. By 2018, they were receiving 13.3 percent. In 1979, the bottom 90 percent of wage earners received 69.8 percent of all wages. By 2018, that number had fallen to 61.0 percent. In 1979, the top 1 percent of earners earned an average of 9.4 times the average income of the bottom 90 percent of earners. By 2018, they were earning 19.6 times as much. From 1979 to 2018, the income of the top 1 percent increased, on average, by 158 percent. For the bottom 90 percent, the increase was just 24 percent.[36] In terms of net household

wealth, the disparities are even more pronounced. In 1989, the top 1 percent of households owned 23.7 percent of the wealth, while the bottom
50 percent owned 3.7 percent of the wealth. The top 1 percent had 6.4
times as much wealth as all the households in the lower half. By the end of
2019, the top 1 percent had 31.2 percent of the wealth, while the share of
the bottom half had fallen to 1.8 percent. This meant that the top 1 percent had come to own 17.3 times as much wealth as half the households
in the country.[37]

Clearly, the age of acceleration has turbocharged inequality. These
inequalities have contributed to distortions in power, in politics, in perceived fairness, and in philanthropic priorities. The fact that the 1920s also
saw high income and wealth disparities means that inequality is not unique
to the digital era. Nevertheless, the Internet age has greatly magnified
concentrations of wealth because global technology companies attract
worldwide customers, providing great economies of scale. In the twenty-
first century, a tech startup, created and run by just a few dozen people,
can take off overnight, make money internationally, and be sold for billions within just a couple of years. This funnels massive wealth into tiny
cohorts: "Tech has changed the rules on income inequality…it concen-
trates wealth more effectively than any despot could dream of. After all, a
despot can oppress only his subjects. Tech has a global reach."[38] In the
digital economy, the gaps between rich and poor have become sufficiently
wide that it is inconceivable that they could be overcome through continuing business as usual.[39]

Beyond technology and the marketplace, culture has become globalized. In previous centuries, human culture was composed of hundreds of
distinctive local cultures that had little interaction or overlap. That is over.
Delivered by the Internet, the media, and the "culture industry," an emergent global culture has become all but ubiquitous:

> This is much more than just an industry manufacturing entertainment, con-
> sumer wares and pleasant dreams, as in Hollywood's dream factories. Now,
> an all-embracing global culture envelops people from the cradle to the
> grave. It is culture that has become second nature to us all. We know it inti-
> mately, yet we find it difficult to grasp its full extent and the influence it
> has on us.[40]

In 2010, Netflix operated only in the US; by 2021 it was in 190 countries. A relatively small number of media transnationals have harnessed

technology to spread entertainment, news, and advertising virtually everywhere. Their business model works best when it promotes entertainment that is as broadly appealing to a mass audience as possible—even if it is to the detriment of more serious content:

> One of the most glaring developments of the last two decades has been the transformation of news broadcasts and educational programmes into shallow entertainment shows—many of them ironically touted as 'reality' shows. Given that news is less than half as profitable as entertainment, media firms are increasingly tempted to pursue higher profits.[41]

In most places, local culture still coexists with global culture, but in some locations, global culture has replaced local culture altogether. The optimistic view is that the juggernaut of global culture will not wholly eliminate local cultures but will instead yield distinctive hybrids. This hybridity, however, is unlikely to impede cultural loss. Language offers an example: given that more than 80 percent of the current content of the Internet is in English, it would be no surprise if there were a further decline in the number of languages in the not-too-distant future.[42] Friedman describes the implications: "…because globalization as a culturally homogenizing and environment-devouring force is coming on so fast, there is a real danger that in just a few decades it could wipe out the ecological and cultural diversity that took millions of years of human and biological evolution to produce."[43]

Not only is cultural diversity contracting, but "being cultured" is no longer understood as it once was:

> …[I]n advanced economies, capitalist corporations are increasingly more involved in what amounts to cultural production, the creation of values, rather than economic production, the manufacture of goods… Hence, it is the advertising industry and the Culture Industry in general, those enterprises that set the standards in such matters and determine what the fashions will be, which drive the economy. What we can call global culture assumes overriding economic importance, especially among the elite of global society. This is, of course, culture in a quite different sense to any that was current in past civilizations.[44]

Success in such a commercially driven cultural environment is little connected to virtue or good character or achievements. Redner points to four measures that have become central in today's globalized culture: money, position, power, and celebrity.[45] In the digital age, pursuing this quartet is now promoted by the global purveyors of culture to such an extent that alternatives receive little attention:

> Cultural refinements have become worthless, or at best they figure as eccentric hobbies that some people can allow themselves, provided they keep it to themselves. Moral qualities are almost equally jejune for almost nobody prides himself or herself on having a good name or upright character... The idea that anybody should wish to be taken for a gentleman or lady is laughable.[46]

Even if this is an overstatement, it seems reasonable to assert that our hyper-connected environment is reordering priorities. By way of illustration, at the same time that there is a shortage of clergy in the US, millions now aspire to impact others by becoming Internet marketing influencers. This juxtaposition may well signify that qualities that used to be more central are now being pushed to the margins.

Why is this happening? David Brooks, a cultural commentator and columnist for *The New York Times*, offers an explanation based on our changing perceptions of self. He differentiates between what he calls the "Little Me" and the "Big Me."[47] The "Little Me" version of human life that prevailed for a long time was indebted to a biblical worldview and emphasized that each of us is beset by character challenges that need to be overcome and that human susceptibility, fallibility, and moral struggle are at the core of existence. Hence, Little Me character traits are typified by humility, selflessness, and self-sacrifice. Brooks chronicles how, after World War II, the Little Me perception of the self gradually gave way to a Big Me view, as building self-esteem became a priority. This expansion of Big Me produced a number of positive outcomes in terms of boosting peoples' sense of self. It also changed perceptions about the importance of self:

> The underlying assumptions about human nature and the shape of human life were altered by this shift to the Big Me. If you were born at any time over the last sixty years, you were probably born into what the philosopher Charles Taylor has called "the culture of authenticity." This mindset is based on the romantic idea that each of us has a Golden Figure in the core of our self. There is an innately good True Self, which can be trusted, consulted, and gotten in touch with. Your personal feelings are the best guide for what is right and wrong. In this ethos, the self is to be trusted, not doubted. Your

desires are like inner oracles for what is right and true. You know you are doing the right thing when you feel good inside. The valid rules of life are those you make or accept for yourself and that feel right to you.[48]

The inflation of Big Me did not begin in 1990. But in an age epitomized by the selfie and self-promotion, the emphasis on Big Me has become considerably more apparent.

The notion that we should each be guided primarily by what "feels good inside" and by whatever serves Big Me presents obvious challenges to the role of ethics and morality in society. The historian of civilization, William McNeill, observed that "a shared literary canon, and expectations about human behaviour framed by that canon, are probably central to what we mean by civilization."[49] Today, there is little agreement on any "shared literary cannon" or "expectations about human behavior." If, however, there is no consensus on what constitutes moral behavior, then following the "voice of the inner self" becomes more likely. There are potential repercussions that flow from this:

If you believe that the ultimate oracle is the True Self inside, then of course you become emotivist—you make moral judgments on the basis of the feelings that burble up. Of course you become a relativist. One True Self has no basis to judge or argue with another True Self. Of course you become an individualist, since the ultimate arbiter is the authentic self within and not any community standard or external horizon of significance without. Of course you lose contact with the moral vocabulary that is needed to think about these questions.[50]

This is powerful language. Trust in the "true self" is diminishing our shared moral vocabulary, even as previous sources of moral instruction are being devalued.

Small wonder, then, that some are hard pressed to explain why any conduct that is legal might simultaneously be unworthy. Detached from any commitment to some agreed-upon aspiration for human conduct, morality has essentially become individualized. If one is causing no tangible harm, and no law prohibits what one proposes to do, why should there be limits? In this context, it is not surprising that any attempt to take issue with the freely chosen behavior of another—when the behavior does not cause harm or injury—is deemed to be "judgmental." After all, "one True Self has no basis to judge or argue with another True Self." The law, then, becomes the only arbiter of morality:

Now in contemporary societies, as both high literacy and ethics are weakening, the norms by which conduct is regulated have increasingly become purely legal. Legality is displacing morality in the subjective conception of right and wrong. Instead of scruples governed by conscience and inner restraints on what can and cannot be done, actions are now explicitly regulated by coercively enforceable laws... This transition from morality to legality makes for a very different attitude toward right and wrong, good and evil, and all other such judgmental issues. The very fact that "judgmental" has become a term of opprobrium is indicative of the changes in mentality that have taken place, for it means that the exercise of personal judgment in ethical matters is no longer valued or inculcated; in fact, it is condemned.[51]

In the twenty-first century, there is a diminished tolerance for evaluating conduct. Whether one deems this to be good or bad, there is no gainsaying that it is a new way of thinking about behavior within society.

Indeed, Sherry Turkle, MIT professor and psychologist, makes the intriguing observation that in the digital age we have become used to being "in a tribe of one, loyal to our own party."[52] In many countries, modernity delinked the individual from being bound to a particular social station and from conforming in thought or activity. It created the freedom to believe as one wanted, the freedom to live according to the dictates of one's own conscience, and the freedom to aspire to any role or position in society. But the range of choice for the individual in modernity was limited by certain constraints. While individuals had autonomy, their choices were narrowed by geography; their lives were lived within the context of local communities with defined identities. The erasing of these boundaries means that the resultant circumstances of individual life are not just different by degree. The "global persona," unconstrained by physical space, has become possible.

Our detachment from the constraints of physical location has implications for the way that we interact. The emblematic picture of our age is that of a gathering of people in a social setting like a café—each more fixated on a screen than on the other humans in the room. This moment-by-moment intrusion of communications devices in our lives has brought about a palpable sea change in the attention we pay to the human beings in our midst. Turkle is of the view that we have entered a phase of being "alone together":

Over the past 15 years, I've studied technologies of mobile connection and talked to hundreds of people of all ages and circumstances about their plugged-in lives. I've learned that the little devices most of us carry around are so powerful that they change not only what we do, but also who we are.

We've become accustomed to a new way of being "alone together." Technology-enabled, we are able to be with one another, and also elsewhere, connected to wherever we want to be... We want to move in and out of where we are because the thing we value most is control over where we focus our attention.[53]

If, previously, customers in the hypothetical café were truly present in the moment because there were few alternatives, now they can "curate their own attention," deciding when to be present in their immediate surroundings and when to enjoy a movie, review patient charts, close a business deal, or chat with a faraway friend.

In Redner's view, what this means is that we are moving from the "individualization" of modernity to what he describes as the "atomization" of the Internet era:

Atomized individuals neither belong to anything nor do they join anything; they become bereft of both communal identity as well as associational membership... Communities and associations are disrupted as more and more people avail themselves of their formal rights to cut themselves off from society to live their own lives, so to speak, but often in solitude by themselves. Personal freedom is interpreted as not being bound to anyone or anything, escaping all ties, responsibilities, and obligations, and being beholden to no one.[54]

Redner is not suggesting that atomized individuals are looking to cut themselves off so as to live in isolation; most desire ongoing human contact and connection. Rather, Redner is using the term "atomization" to point to the attenuation of a sense of obligation to engage on a regular basis with communities, associations, or even family. Whereas previously, connections to the family, the village, or the guild were an inevitable part of the human experience, this is no longer so.

An illustration of this trend can be found in the number of people choosing to live alone. In the US, the share of those living alone has doubled to 28 percent over the last fifty years.[55] Elsewhere, the levels are even higher:

The four countries with the highest rates of living alone are Sweden, Norway, Finland, and Denmark, where roughly 40 to 45 percent of all households have just one person... They have good company. In Japan, where social life has historically been organized around the family, about 30 percent of all households now have a single dweller, and the rate is far higher in urban areas. Germany, France, and the United Kingdom have famously different cultural traditions, but they share a greater proportion of one-person households than the United States. Same for Australia and Canada. And the nations with the fastest growth in one-person households? China, India, and Brazil.[56],[57]

Genesis may have opined that "it is not good for a person to be alone," but many seem to disagree.

What is driving this phenomenon? Prosperity is one answer. Eric Klinenberg, professor of sociology at New York University, states that one reason why people live by themselves is simply because they "can afford to do so."[58] More importantly, Klinenberg posits that the centrality of the individual has now been raised to the level where the "fulfillment of self" transcends all other responsibilities, including those to family. He quotes the demographer Andrew Cherlin who observed of our society that "today one's primary obligation is to oneself rather than to one's partner and children."[59] Klinenberg underscores what a dramatic societal shift this represents:

The rise of living alone has been a transformative social experience. It changes the way we understand ourselves and our most intimate relationships. It shapes the way we build our cities and develop our economies. It alters the way we become adults, as well as how we age and the way we die. It touches every social group and nearly every family, no matter who we are or whether we live with others today.[60]

Klinenberg explains that for a growing number of people the positives of living alone are sufficiently alluring that it has become their preferred option. A woman named Charlotte is perhaps emblematic when she speaks about the source of this contentment:

"When you live alone, there's no compromising," she explains. "I do everything I feel like doing, when I feel like doing it. And it is totally self-indulgent. It's just all about you."... "I don't think I want to tend to a living thing ever again," she says.[61]

This is what Redner means by atomization. The virtual world of constant connectivity has created the potential for freedom from geographic space, freedom from community and association, freedom from human ties, and even freedom from family itself.[62]

It is worth noting that the personalization that the digital world affords—allowing us to self-curate many experiences—is another driver of atomization. There was a time when everybody saw the same movies or TV shows and could readily discuss what they watched. While that remains true for the occasional sensational viewing experience, usually our entertainment choices are so vast, and our interests sufficiently diverse that there is little overlap. Our phones too are highly individualized. Our apps reflect our personalities and predilections to such an extent that even if the technology is familiar, using another's phone can be disorienting. Curation and personalization reinforce our sense of "being in a tribe of one."

We also have the capacity to curate our identities. In a world in which Starbucks coffee can be ordered as a personalized blend that allows for hundreds of individualized combinations, the old binary distinctions of identity (male/female, gay/straight, black/white, Jew/non-Jew, etc.) are being challenged as identity mixes of greater specificity emerge. This phenomenon is, in some measure, an outgrowth of our cultural and technological experiences. Given that "the idea of hybridity has permeated popular culture"[63]—allowing one to cut and paste a little from here and introduce it there—why not apply the same approach to identity? The answer is that this is exactly what is occurring:

> Globalization impacts upon young people in complex ways and forces them to constantly re-think and revise their sense of identity and place within society. Young people's lives are constantly being influenced by new trends, be they cultural, technological or social... They adapt and recreate in their own image, with their peers and other cultural and geographical influences, and develop identities that reflect this complexity. The internet and use of new technologies have been a major factor in enabling young people to recreate their own identities.[64]

There is, consequently, no longer a strong conviction that people necessarily need to feel bound to inherited identities or rigid identity boundaries. Identity itself has become malleable.

Beyond the individual, human relationships are now different from what they were during modernity Giddens observes: "Among all the changes going on in the world, none is more important than those happening in our personal lives—in sexuality, relationships, marriage and the family. There is a global revolution going on in how we think of ourselves and how we form ties and connections with others."[65] The severing of sexuality from reproduction, which began to have full impact in the 1970s, combined with the greater emphasis on individual fulfilment, has altered our understanding of fundamental human ties: "Marriage and the family have become...shell institutions: they are still called the same, but inside their basic character has changed... Today the couple, married or unmarried, is at the core of what the family is."[66] This observation might sound unremarkable, but it represents a fundamental break with what the normative family of modernity used to be: a married couple, dependent on each other for their economic well-being, within the context of a stable household that was intended to be an appropriate environment in which to raise the next generation. For most of modernity, this was the approximate vision of what constituted a family. Not anymore. Nowadays, coupling is primary and that coupling is less likely to be seen as the first steps toward commitment: "We should recognize what a major transition this is. 'Coupling' and 'uncoupling' provide a more accurate description of the arena of personal life now than do 'marriage and the family.'"[67] The writer and columnist, Louise Perry, encapsulates the transformation this way: "In 1968, 8 per cent of children were born to parents who were not married; in 2019 it was almost half... The institution of marriage, as it once was, is now more or less dead."[68]

Marriage, as a result, has become more of a conditional institution to be retained so long as it continues to provide "emotional satisfaction."[69] Perhaps the best evidence that today's marriages are increasingly dependent on individual fulfillment can be found in the reaction to divorce. In just a few decades, attitudes have changed from seeing divorce as scandalous, to resigned acceptance, to embracing it as a befitting alternative:

> Not long ago, someone who was dissatisfied with his or her spouse and wanted a divorce had to justify that decision. Today it's the opposite: If you're not fulfilled by your marriage, you have to justify staying in it, because of the tremendous cultural pressure to be good to one's self.[70]

Marriage has become simultaneously less obligatory and less enduring. Being married and having children are neither the principal goals nor the essential rites of passage that they were previously. This can be readily seen from the number of Americans who are either choosing or finding themselves in the position of remaining single. In 1970, there were 38 million single people in the US, comprising just 28 percent of the population.[71] In 2018, there were 118 million singles and they comprised 47 percent of the population over the age of eighteen.[72] Moreover, if it was once true that being a single adult was seen as regrettable, in the digital era many celebrate it as a life choice. Elyakim Kislev, in his book *Happy Singlehood*, argues that individual happiness is now central and proposes that "having a clear and more benign image of singlehood will allow individuals to freely choose whatever lifestyle fits them best."[73] No matter what one might think of Kislev's stance, it certainly represents what one reviewer called a "world-shifting trend."[74]

In terms of the societal roles available to women and men, Giddens points out that never before has there been a society in which women have been "even approximately equal to men" in the way that is now the case in much of the West. This has produced a "truly global revolution in everyday life."[75] It has also brought about fundamental shifts for children and their upbringing.[76] Today, the basic nuclear family of a husband and wife with their joint children exists in only a minority of households in developed societies. All other households consist of married couples—gay or straight—with no children, married couples with children from previous marriages, unmarried parents raising children, gay and straight people living together with no formal marriage arrangements, single parents (usually women) with children, or single people on their own. While there is broad acceptance of these realities, they nevertheless represent a striking restructuring of family life.

There is, additionally, growing evidence that our sexual functioning is changing, in no small part owing to the extraordinary spread of pornography that the digital environment has enabled:

> In 1991, the year the World Wide Web went online, there were fewer than ninety different adult magazines published in America, and you'd have been hard-pressed to find a newsstand that carried more than a dozen. Just six years later, in 1997, there were about nine hundred pornography sites on the Web. Today, the filtering software CYBERsitter blocks 2.5 million adult Web sites.[77]

We have "progressed" from a world where fewer than a dozen print publications were available to the average adult to a world where every form of sexual functioning imaginable is available on any unfiltered Internet device, often for free. Such expanded availability only materializes if there are consumers. In a comprehensive analysis of 400 million web searches between 2009 and 2010, researchers found that 13 percent—a little more than one in eight—sought erotic content.[78] In 2020, three pornography websites were listed in the top eleven most visited websites in the world. Combined, they received 8.4 billion visits per month— enough on average for every adult Internet user on the planet to visit at least twice a month.[79] And that only accounts for the most prominent three sites out of the millions on offer. This is a level of pornography usage without historic parallel. During the 2020 coronavirus lockdowns, major pornography sites reported increases in traffic of around 20 percent, largely driven by boredom, loneliness, anxiety, or a dearth of other stimuli.[80]

Online pornography, moreover, is qualitatively different to its print predecessor. It is addictive, graphic, and violent at levels that transcend the paper version: "It's not just that digital technology creates unprecedented desire for pornography: The images themselves are shockingly explicit compared to most pre-digital porn."[81] The websites keep people clicking on this explicit material through the use of algorithms that fuel addictive behavior by offering an endless stream of tantalizing images to each individual. Moreover, as with other digital media, virtual pornography has become interactive, such that customers can curate their own personalized experiences, view live performances, or orchestrate tailor-made clips targeted to their own desires.[82] Plainly, this brings with it a host of ethical challenges that are more complex than the questions raised by analog-era pornography. This much, though, is certain: "Never before have men had such easy access to the pleasure-giving chemicals associated with sex without having to go through rituals of courtship."[83]

When it comes to dispensing with "rituals of courtship," sex robots add yet another dimension. Since around 2010, sex robots powered by AI have been available, and are now able to offer verbal responses to their users. They are being promoted not only as sex aids, but as "companions."[84] Touted as a cure for loneliness, sales of sex robots surged during the coronavirus pandemic. We have entered a "digisexual" world in which sex with robots—previously unthinkable—will continue to expand.[85] This raises a host of issues: Can one legitimately marry a robot? If a person married to a human has sex with a robot, does that constitute cheating on one's spouse? Since sex robots can be ordered with precise specifications, do sex robots represent objectification? In whatever way these questions are answered, robots will soon have a meaningful impact on our sexual environment.

Just as the digital age is reconfiguring our families and our sexuality, the role of community is also in flux. Communal organizations that were once pivotal in bringing people together are now struggling. Institutions that previous generations saw as vital parts of communal infrastructure—rotary clubs, unions, political parties, and the like—have receded. As Robert Putnam described in his landmark book, *Bowling Alone*, this phenomenon began in the last quarter of the twentieth century, with a 58 percent drop in attending club meetings, a 43 percent drop in family dinners, and a 35 percent drop in having friends over.[86] These developments highlighted the significant shrinking of shared community: "Genuine communities arise where people are brought together by a stable common life situation, and in contemporary societies this tends to happen very rarely."[87]

Interactions that once made people feel like they belonged to a wider community are also contracting. Little by little, the communications technologies that have arisen since 1990 have diminished the frequency of direct neighborhood encounters:

> The new means of consumption profoundly altered the nature of social relations. In earlier means of consumption, there tended to be more in depth, face-to-face relationships among and between consumers and those who served them... In the new means of consumption, face-to-face relations have been reduced (e.g., at the drive-in window of a fast-food restaurant) or eliminated completely (e.g., in online shopping, on home-shopping networks, and at self-service storage centers)... In fact, the new means of consumption are better characterized by interaction with things than with people. In that sense, they are part of what has been termed the post-social world.[88]

In the "post-social world," lasting connections with those who, in bygone times, contributed to the feeling of being part of a community are less common. The once familiar experience of decades-long in-person relationships between businesspeople and their clients is fast becoming exceptional.

Alongside the diminishing scope of real-world interactions, the powerful dominance of social media has reshaped human interactions. On the positive side, social media has had a salutary impact on the rates of social connectedness. A 2011 Pew Research study showed that Facebook users have a greater number of close relationships, are more trusting, and receive more social support than others.[89] In 2013, the Spanish sociologist, Manuel Castells, expressed it this way:

> If we needed an answer to what happened to sociability in the Internet world, here it is: There is a dramatic increase in sociability, but a different kind of sociability, facilitated and dynamized by permanent connectivity and social networking on the web. Social Networking Sites are living spaces connecting all dimensions of people's experience.[90]

Castells describes a mode of communication and interaction that have taken over large chunks of "sociability" with breathtaking speed.

But the benefits of social media have come with a price. Social media has deeply influenced society as a whole—even those who never use it. Early in the deployment of social media, critics expressed comparatively mild concerns: people were apt to communicate on social media more tersely and impatiently than they did in person; they were likely to share content that was at times inappropriate for a broad audience; peoples' mood was lowered by social media through the impression that others' lives are better than theirs; and there was "mounting evidence to show a link with narcissism."[91] However, as social media evolved, more weighty issues came to the fore. One of the most comprehensive and public indictments of the genre was delivered by a group that was closely involved in the design of major social media platforms. Describing themselves as a "team of deeply concerned tech industry and social impact leaders,"[92] they offer a succinct "ledger of harms" that have been aggravated by social media:

- Making Sense of the World
  - Misinformation, conspiracy theories, and fake news
- Attention and Cognition
  - Loss of crucial abilities including memory and focus
- Physical and Mental Health
  - Stress, loneliness, feelings of addiction, and increased risky health behavior
- Social Relationships
  - Less empathy, more confusion and misinterpretation
- Politics and Elections
  - Propaganda, distorted dialogue & a disrupted democratic process
- Systemic Oppression
  - Amplification of racism, sexism, homophobia and ableism

- The Next Generations
  - From developmental delays to suicide, children face a host of physical, mental and social challenges[93]

These worried innovators provide accompanying evidence for the powerful effects of social media in each of these critical areas. They paint a picture of a tool, used by billions of people for hours every day, that was deliberately created to be addictive, that depletes our ability to focus, amplifies falsehoods, saps empathy, exacerbates discrimination, and regularly undermines mental health. There is, they contend, much that can be done to ameliorate the downsides of social media, but the long-term effects remain concerning.[94]

One aspect of the rise of social media is particularly worth highlighting: the manifest changes that it has brought about in the field of journalism, with ramifications for politics and governance. As the use of social media has proliferated, achieving success in the news business has come to be measured by clicks and "likes." This has far-reaching implications. In 2016, Emily Bell, professor of professional practice at the Columbia Journalism School, wrote:

> Our news ecosystem has changed more dramatically in the past five years than perhaps at any time in the past five hundred. We are seeing huge leaps in technical capability—virtual reality, live video, artificially intelligent news bots, instant messaging, and chat apps... Social media hasn't just swallowed journalism, it has swallowed everything. It has swallowed political campaigns, banking systems, personal histories, the leisure industry, retail, even government and security.[95]

We have become familiar with one of the more worrying outcomes of this reality—the line between fact and unsubstantiated opinion has become blurred:

> Twenty-five years after the first website went online, it is clear that we are living through a period of dizzying transition. For 500 years after Gutenberg, the dominant form of information was the printed page: knowledge was primarily delivered in a fixed format, one that encouraged readers to believe in stable and settled truths...
> This settled "truth" was usually handed down from above: an established truth, often fixed in place by an establishment. This arrangement was not without flaws: too much of the press often exhibited a bias towards the

status quo and a deference to authority, and it was prohibitively difficult for ordinary people to challenge the power of the press. Now, people distrust much of what is presented as fact—particularly if the facts in question are uncomfortable, or out of sync with their own views—and while some of that distrust is misplaced, some of it is not.[96]

Once upon a time, facts had to be checked before being type-set irrevocably on a printed page. Now, facts compete with views of unknown provenance, and these views are presented as if they were facts and are taken seriously by dint of their widespread distribution.

Not only has the integration of a large proportion of news with social media platforms blurred the line between facts and views, it has also altered the material to which people are exposed. On social media platforms, no editorial team decides what constitutes the public interest. Material is not balanced to present both sides of an argument. The algorithms are in control. These algorithms are "designed to give us more of what they think we want—which means that the version of the world we encounter every day in our own personal stream has been invisibly curated to reinforce our pre-existing beliefs."[97] The consequences are well known: social media reinforces our entrenched views. And given that the most extreme voices typically get the most attention, social media does not reward moderates. The result? One writer framed it starkly: "Facebook is an agent of government propaganda, targeted harassment, terrorist recruitment, emotional manipulation, and genocide—a world-historic weapon that lives not underground, but in a Disneyland-inspired campus in Menlo Park, California."[98] It should come as no surprise, then, that this "once in five hundred years" news revolution has had marked political and societal effects.

Our social media saturated epoch has been accompanied by a substantial erosion of privacy. Seemingly with little objection, society has entered what is being referred to as the "post-privacy age,"[99] in which privacy has been extensively dismantled by the reach of technology into every facet of life. In the physical world, it is now nigh impossible in most urban environments to leave one's home without being monitored constantly.[100] It is estimated that the average American is tracked by a camera more than seventy times per day.[101] At virtually every moment that we find ourselves in public, cameras are watching and recording. Indeed, there are approximately 1 billion surveillance cameras installed worldwide—with governmental access to their data. In 2018, the US had one surveillance camera for every 4.6 persons.[102] In China, the country with the most extensive network of watching devices, millions of cameras are already equipped with facial recognition technology.[103] Clearview AI, a controversial company that first came to public notice in early 2020, has developed the ability to take a picture from any surveillance camera and instantly find matches to billions of photos uploaded to social media. By the time the company gained public attention, more than 600 law enforcement agencies in the US were already using its software.[104] This effectively spells the end of any concept of privacy or anonymity in public spaces. None of this even begins to take into account the pervasive use of cellphones for recording pictures and videos.

Many have also voluntarily opened the door to surveillance of their own homes. Millions of Internet-connected cameras have been installed outside and inside private dwellings worldwide. The implication of this phenomenon was well summarized by the headline "Ring and Nest helped normalize American surveillance and turned us into a nation of voyeurs."[105] In the name of increased security, many have become accustomed to watching neighbors and keeping tabs on family members through cameras installed in multiple rooms and external locations.[106] Even assuming that neither hackers nor the government will ever see what these cameras capture, their presence signals a diminution of domestic privacy.

What is true in the physical world is equally the case in the virtual world. Those with low public profiles or little online presence may still be tough to track in cyberspace. But with just a few clicks, one can find out more online about most people than one might hitherto have discovered in multiple face-to-face meetings. We form impressions about others, their standing, their positions, and their appeal based on a composite picture delivered by the Internet—a picture over which the individual has little control. Few have the power to determine how or where they appear online, to delete information that they would prefer did not appear, or to present themselves as they might wish.[107] Once our online activities are factored in, privacy diminishes even further: On every social media platform, what was once private now tumbles into the public domain. The fact that some struggle to articulate why they should limit the public sharing of their inner selves demonstrates how much technology has already altered mindsets.

However, the online privacy losses that are readily apparent to us pale in significance when compared to the data mining that occurs out of sight. Tech companies, large and small, provide the public with an array of ostensibly free services in return for billions of users agreeing to surrender their data. As the maxim goes, "If you're not paying for the product, you are the product."[108] Web activity, email receipts, credit card transactions, and geolocation are all collected. The result of this data mining is that corporations now know an astonishing amount about each one of us:

> Your web browser and some free software…can track everything you do on the web: which sites you visit, what you search, what you buy, and so forth. Meanwhile, some free email clients, in exchange for using their email service, monitor your inbox for things like receipts to get an idea of user spending. Several alternative data companies buy anonymized credit card data from sources like personal finance apps to get more detailed information about how and where people are spending money. The apps on your phone, from your weather provider to your coupon saver, can sell location data to third parties to see what stores people visit and how long they spend there.[109]

As recently as the early 1990s, nobody contemplated that their every click, purchase, inquiry, interest, schedule, and location could be known to others, monetized, and used for commercial purposes. Now, that is precisely what is happening all the time.

The general lack of protest about the evaporation of privacy, leads to two alternative conclusions: Either there is little consciousness of what has been lost, or people consider the surrender of privacy to be a price worth paying. The view that sacrificing privacy is simply the price of entry to the benefits of the digital age appears to be widespread. As one expert succinctly stated, "in the last six or seven years, we've begun to accept that giving up your personal information is a form of currency."[110]

Julie Cohen, professor of law and technology at Georgetown University, provides a salutary reminder about what is at stake when privacy disappears: "Privacy's goal, simply put, is to ensure that the development of subjectivity and the development of communal values do not proceed in lockstep… [P]rivacy is one of the resources that situated subjects require to flourish."[111] Cohen, one scholar remarked, sees privacy

> as an important buffer that gives us space to develop an identity that is somewhat separate from the surveillance, judgment, and values of our society and culture. Privacy is crucial for helping us manage all of these pressures—pressures that shape the type of person we are—and for "creating spaces for play and the work of self-development."[112]

Stated differently, the loss of privacy has consequences for our self-formation. When our lives play out before the cameras, who we become is extensively shaped by outside dictates, and by an unavoidable consciousness of the spectators, rather than by our own internal compass. Thus, the very individualism that became such a prized feature of modernity is, in Cohen's view, threatened by the perpetual monitoring of our conduct. This much is certain: The type of privacy that people regarded as normal up until 1990 is gone.

There is one more critical domain that is being steadily reshaped in the Internet era: our brains, together with the way we think. It appears that having a screen before our eyes from cradle to grave is significantly altering our willingness to converse, our ability to concentrate, and our internal "wiring."[113] The technology writer, Nicholas Carr, explains that when you look at someone on their smartphone, "what you see is a mind consumed with a medium. When we're online, we're often oblivious to everything else going on around us. The real world recedes as we process the flood of symbols and stimuli coming through our devices."[114]

Our devices command our attention. Small wonder that we cannot resist reflexively reaching for our phones. And before long, without us being aware, our brains become structurally transformed:

> One thing is very clear: if, knowing what we know today about the brain's plasticity, you were to set out to invent a medium that would rewire our mental circuits as quickly and thoroughly as possible, you would probably end up designing something that looks and works a lot like the Internet. It's not just that we tend to use the Net regularly, even obsessively. It's that the Net delivers precisely the kind of sensory and cognitive stimuli—repetitive, intensive, interactive, addictive—that have been shown to result in strong and rapid alterations in brain circuits and functions. With the exception of alphabets and number systems, the Net may well be the single most powerful mind-altering technology that has ever come into general use. At the very least, it's the most powerful that has come along since the book.[115]

"The single most powerful mind-altering technology that has ever come into general use." This is an eye-opening statement. In Carr's estimation, not in half a millennium, and perhaps never before, has a technology so recast human brains, and hence the way we interact with the world around us, as the Internet. A review by Harvard and Oxford academics of three decades of scholarly studies on the impact that the Internet has had

on our physiology concluded that "using the internet is physically changing our brains so that we have shorter attention spans and worse
memories."[116]

What are the ramifications of this reality? There are many, but three
hold particular importance: First, our capacity for concentrated thinking
and analytical reasoning is lessening. The Internet is designed in such a
way that it distracts and fragments our attention. It combats our best
efforts at extended contemplation or deep reflection. Patricia Greenfield,
distinguished professor of developmental psychology at UCLA, surveyed
over fifty studies of "the effects of different types of media on people's
intelligence and learning ability." While she discerned positives associated
with Internet use, these came with undeniable costs:

> Our growing use of the Net and other screen-based technologies has led to
> the "widespread and sophisticated development of visual-spatial skills." …But
> our "new strengths in visual-spatial intelligence" go hand in hand with a
> weakening of our capacities for the kind of "deep processing" that under-
> pins "mindful knowledge acquisition, inductive analysis, critical thinking,
> imagination, and reflection."[117]

This is not just a theoretical matter. Carr offers a glimpse into the modifications that are actually taking place:

> The mental functions that are losing the "survival of the busiest" brain cell
> battle are those that support calm, linear thought—the ones we use in tra-
> versing a lengthy narrative or an involved argument, the ones we draw on
> when we reflect on our experiences or contemplate an outward or inward
> phenomenon. The winners are those functions that help us speedily locate,
> categorize, and assess disparate bits of information in a variety of forms, that
> let us maintain our mental bearings while being bombarded by stimuli.[118]

The Internet is shaping our style of thinking to fit the speed and super-
ficiality that are typical of the medium itself. The nature of intelligence will
be different going forward:

> If we take a broader and more traditional view of intelligence—if we think
> about the depth of our thought rather than just its speed—we have to come
> to a different and considerably darker conclusion... What the Net dimin-
> ishes is...the ability to know, in depth, a subject for ourselves, to construct

within our own minds the rich and idiosyncratic set of connections that give rise to a singular intelligence.[119]

Whether changing the nature of intelligence for the billions of people regularly connected to the web should evoke apprehension or acceptance can be debated. What is, however, likely is that our brains and our thought processes are being reconstituted by our digital environment.

Another result of the Internet's capacity to reshape our brains appears to be a decrease in empathy. Daniel Goleman, the author of *Emotional Intelligence*, holds that "[o]ne cost of the frenetic stream of distractions we face today, some fear, is an erosion of empathy and compassion. The more distracted we are, the less we can exhibit attunement and caring."[120] Goleman is particularly concerned that the reduction in face-to-face communication is weakening the capacity of the "social brain." Given that people are considerably less compassionate when they communicate using digital media, Goleman was asked by an interviewer whether he is worried that "there's a whole generation of people growing up...who have always communicated like that?" His response:

> Goleman: Absolutely, and my worry is this: the way in which humans have transferred skills in emotional intelligence, in managing ourselves and in our relationships is through face-to-face interaction, which means that this skill set is not being learned the way it has been in past generations and to the extent that we're communicating by texting, rather than face-to-face, we are communicating where there's no channel for the social brain. You're being deprived, you're being starved, of vital information.
>
> Interviewer: I mean the consequences of that are potentially huge...
>
> Goleman: It's an unprecedented experiment with an entire generation.[121]

The outcome of this "unprecedented experiment" is unknown. There are, however, indications of what might lie ahead: According to a University of Michigan study, "Today's college students are not as empathetic as college students of the 1980s and '90s." The research found that "[c]ollege kids today are about 40 percent lower in empathy than their counterparts of 20 or 30 years ago" and the biggest drop in empathy came "after the year 2000."[122] While the virtual environment provides opportunities to build social initiatives, stimulate concern for causes, and mobilize action, communication from behind a screen seems to be creating a less empathic response than that elicited by face-to-face interaction.

Taken together, the technology and the culture that now surround us have altered not just our brains but something more. David Brooks summarizes:

> First, communications have become faster and busier. It is harder to attend to the soft, still voices that come from the depths... [M]oments of stillness and quiet are just more rare today. We reach for the smartphone.
>
> Second, social media allow a more self-referential information environment. People have more tools and occasions to construct a culture, a mental environment tailored specifically for themselves...
>
> Third, social media encourages a broadcasting personality... People are given more occasions to be self-promoters, to embrace the characteristics of celebrity, to manage their own image... This technology creates a culture in which people turn into little brand managers.[123]

Stillness is elusive, our technological environment is self-referential, and we have become marketing managers adept at self-promotion. What happens under prolonged exposure to these conditions? This:

> The self is less likely to be seen as the seat of the soul, or as the repository of some transcendent spirit. Instead, the self is a vessel of human capital. It is a series of talents to be cultivated efficiently and prudently. The self is defined by its tasks and accomplishments. The self is about talent, not character.[124]

Over the course of three decades, our technology, culture, society, financial system, media, marriages, families, sexuality, privacy standards, and even our mental functioning have changed. Virtually nothing has been left untouched: the way we live, the way we work, the way we interact, the way we communicate, the way we think, and the way we curate and perceive our reality have all been refashioned. As with any major turning point, there have been both substantial gains and genuine losses. What is certain, though, is that on almost every measure that counts, this digital age is thoroughly discontinuous with what preceded it.

NOTES

1. Thomas L. Friedman, *The World is Flat: A Brief History of the Twenty-first Century* (New York: Farrar, Straus and Giroux, 2005), 9–11.
2. Jonathan Sacks, *The Dignity of Difference*, 126–133.
3. "Google's Original X-Man—A Conversation With Sebastian Thrun," *Foreign Affairs*, November/December 2013, accessed August 1, 2022, https://www.foreignaffairs.com/interviews/2013-10-15/googles-original-x-man
4. Sacks, *The Dignity of Difference*, 127.
5. "Total Number of Websites," InternetLiveStats.com, accessed August 1, 2022, http://www.internetlivestats.com/total-number-of-websites/
6. Robert Colville, *The Great Acceleration—How the World is Getting Faster, Faster* (London: Bloomsbury, 2016). The term "great acceleration" was first coined by Australian scientists in 2005.
7. Ibid., 17.
8. Ibid., 19.
9. Friedman, *Thank You for Being Late*, 26.
10. Andrew McAfee as quoted in Friedman, *Thank You for Being Late*, 26.
11. Ibid., 15, 22.
12. Craig Mundie, as quoted in Friedman, *Thank You for Being Late*, 28.
13. Dov Seidman, as quoted in Friedman, *Thank You for Being Late*, 28.
14. The Stanford Encyclopedia of Philosophy noted in 2002 that "[t]he term globalization has only become commonplace in the last two decades, and academic commentators who employed the term as late as the 1970s accurately recognized the novelty of doing so (Modelski 1972)." "Globalization," *Stanford Encyclopedia of Philosophy*, accessed August 1, 2022, http://plato.stanford.edu/entries/globalization/
15. Anthony Giddens, *Runaway World—How Globalization is Reshaping our World* (London: Profile Books, 2002), 6.
16. Redner, *Beyond Civilization*, 14. Others besides Redner hold this view. For example, the British sociologist Martin Albrow has written about this new period and its terminology: "Indeed, if the belief that a new epoch has emerged is based in reality, the evidence for it will be in people's experience and it will surface in an obvious everyday way rather than in philosophical or sociological treatises. Just as Berger's phenomenology of modernization found the directions of the time inscribed in everyday consciousness, in the same way, in the 1990s, we can listen to the new age in the street. Equally, just as the name for the Modern Age arose from the discourse of the period, so the name for the new epoch is already equally in the public mind. Can it be anything other than the 'Global Age'? The end of the 1980s and beginning of the 1990s has seen an explosion in the

use of 'global' and its associated terms. Its use is ubiquitous in advertising, job descriptions, mission statements, journalism and book titles. This itself suggests a conceptual shift." See Martin Albrow, *The Global Age: State and Society Beyond Modernity* (Cambridge: Polity Press, 1996), Kindle Location 495.

17. Ericsson corporation, as quoted in Friedman, *Thank You for Being Late*, 122.
18. Ibid.
19. Juan Enriquez: "Will our kids be a different species?," TED talk, filmed April 2012, accessed August 1, 2022, https://www.ted.com/talks/juan_enriquez_will_our_kids_be_a_different_species?language=en#t-836065
20. Ed Batista, "The Marshmallow Test for Grownups," *Harvard Business Review*, September 15, 2014, accessed August 1, 2022, https://hbr.org/2014/09/the-marshmallow-test-for-grownups
21. Friedman, *Thank You for Being Late*, 146.
22. "Wikipedia: About," Wikipedia.org, accessed August 1, 2022, https://en.wikipedia.org/wiki/Wikipedia:About
23. National Institutes of Health, "Human Genome Project," March 29, 2013, accessed August 1, 2022, https://archives.nih.gov/asites/report/09-09-2019/report.nih.gov/nihfactsheets/ViewFactSheete078.html?csid=45&key=H#H; The NIH report stresses that "all data generated by the Human Genome Project were made freely and rapidly available on the Internet, serving to accelerate the pace of medical discovery around the globe."
24. "Technology Beats Humans At Growing Strawberries In Pinduoduo Smart Agriculture Competition," *Globe Newswire*, December 15, 2020, accessed August 1, 2022, https://www.globenewswire.com/news-release/2020/12/16/2145844/0/en/Technology-beats-humans-at-growing-strawberries-in-Pinduoduo-smart-agriculture-competition.html
25. Redner, *Beyond Civilization*, 292.
26. The Internet of Things, or IoT, refers to "the billions of physical devices around the world that are now connected to the internet, all collecting and sharing data. Thanks to the arrival of super-cheap computer chips and the ubiquity of wireless networks, it's possible to turn anything, from something as small as a pill to something as big as an aeroplane, into a part of the IoT." See Steve Ranger, "What is the IoT? Everything you need to know about the Internet of Things right now," ZDNet, February 3, 2020, accessed August 1, 2022, https://www.zdnet.com/article/what-is-the-internet-of-things-everything-you-need-to-know-about-the-iot-right-now/

27. The metaverse is "an integrated network of 3D virtual worlds. These worlds are accessed through a virtual reality headset—users navigate the metaverse using their eye movements, feedback controllers or voice commands." See Adrian Ma, "What is the metaverse, and what can we do there?" *The Conversation*, May 23, 2022, accessed August 1, 2022, https://theconversation.com/what-is-the-metaverse-and-what-can-we-do-there-179200

28. Friedman, *Thank You for Being Late*, 83.

29. Giddens, *Runaway World*, 9.

30. Moses Naim has described it this way: "Large organizations had a sheen of authority, modernity, and sophistication; today, headlines are being made by small newcomers that are challenging the big powers. And as the advantages of the large-scale, rational, coordinated, and centralized model of organization diminish, the opportunities increase for micro-powers to make their mark using a different model for success." Moses Naim, *The End of Power* (New York: Basic Books, 2013), 74–75.

31. Ibid., 69.

32. "Not Always With Us," *The Economist*, June 1, 2013, accessed August 1, 2022, http://www.economist.com/news/briefing/21578643-world-has-astonishing-chance-take-billion-people-out-extreme-poverty-2030-not

33. The proportion of undernourished people in developing nations fell from 23.3 percent in 1990 to 12.9 percent in 2014; the primary school enrolment rate in those areas reached 91 percent in 2015, up from 83 percent in 2000; by 2015, 103 girls were enrolled in elementary school for every 100 boys, up from 74 girls per 100 boys in 1990; between 1990 and 2015, the global under-five mortality rate declined from 90 to 43 deaths per 1000 live births; in the same period, the maternal mortality ratio was cut nearly in half; between 1990 and 2015, 2.6 billion people gained access to improved drinking water; and between 2000 and 2014, development assistance from wealthy countries to developing countries increased by 66 percent in real terms. See: Were the Millennium Development Goals a success? Yes! Sort of, World Vision, July 3, 2015, accessed August 1, 2022, https://www.wvi.org/united-nations-and-global-engagement/article/were-mdgs-success

34. Naim, *The End of Power*, 4.

35. "Global flows in a digital age: How trade, finance, people, and data connect the world economy," McKinsey Global Institute, April, 2014, accessed August 1, 2022, http://www.mckinsey.com/business-functions/strategy-and-corporate-finance/our-insights/global-flows-in-a-digital-age

36. Julia Kagan, "How Much Income Puts You in the Top 1%, 5%, 10%?" *Investopedia*, June 2, 2020, accessed October 11, 2020, https://www.investopedia.com/personal-finance/how-much-income-puts-you-top-1-5-10/

37. "Distribution of Household Wealth in the U.S. since 1989," The Board of Governors of the Federal Reserve System, accessed August 1, 2022, https://www.federalreserve.gov/releases/z1/dataviz/dfa/distribute/chart/#quarter:123;series:Net%20worth;demographic:networth;populat ion:1,3,5,7;units:shares;range:1989.3,2020.2

38. Juan Enriquez, *Right/Wrong*, (Cambridge: MA: MIT Press, 2020), 76.

39. Emmanuel Saez and Gabriel Zucman, "Exploding Wealth Inequality in the United States," Washington Center for Equitable Growth, October 20, 2014, accessed August 1, 2022, http://equitablegrowth.org/research/exploding-wealth-inequality-united-states/

40. Redner, *Beyond Civilization*, 225.

41. Manfred Steger, *Globalization* (Oxford: Oxford University Press, 2013), 83.

42. Ibid., 84.

43. Thomas Friedman, *The Lexus and the Olive Tree: Understanding Globalization* (New York: Farrah, Strauss, and Giroux, 2000), 260.

44. Redner, *Beyond Civilization*, 143.

45. Ibid., 202.

46. Ibid., 290.

47. David Brooks, *The Road to Character*, (New York: Random House, 2015), 6.

48. Ibid., 249.

49. William H. McNeill, "The Rise of the West after Twenty-Five Years" in Stephen K. Sanderson, *Civilizations and World Systems* (Walnut Creek: AltaMira Press, 1995), 309.

50. Brooks, *The Road to Character*, 259.

51. Redner, *Beyond Civilization*, 110.

52. Sherry Turkle, "The Flight from Conversation," The New York Times, April 21, 2012, accessed August 1, 2022, http://www.nytimes.com/2012/04/22/opinion/sunday/the-flight-from-conversation.html?pagewanted=all

53. Turkle, "The Flight from Conversation."

54. Redner, *Beyond Civilization*, 350.

55. Esteban Ortiz-Ospina, "The rise of living alone: how one-person households are becoming increasingly common around the world," Our World in Data, December 10, 2019, accessed August 1, 2022, https://ourworldindata.org/living-alone

56. Eric Klinenberg, *Going Solo—The Extraordinary Rise and Surprising Appeal of Living Alone* (New York: The Penguin Press, 2012), 9–10.
57. By 2015 "Japan had 16.84 million single-person households...accounting for 32.5% of the total. Only 28% of all households had two members, and just 18.3% had three. It is now more common in Japan to live alone than with a spouse or a child." See "Japanese say 'I don't' to marriage in record numbers," Nikkei Asian Review, July 2, 2016, accessed August 1, 2022, https://asia.nikkei.com/Economy/Japanese-say-I-don-t-to-marriage-in-record-numbers
58. Klinenberg, Going Solo, 10.
59. Ibid., 13.
60. Ibid., 6.
61. Ibid., 94–95.
62. In this context, it is worth noting that the increased tendency to work remotely brought about by the coronavirus pandemic will likely expand atomization, as many who were accustomed to spending their workdays in the presence of others have continued to work in locations that are physically separated from human contact. While constantly connected virtually, they are remote not just geographically, but in human terms as well. The job might well get done but gathering by the "water cooler," and all that goes with it, are a lesser part of the experience.
63. John Germov and Marilyn Poole (eds.), *Public Sociology* (Sydney: Allen & Unwin, 2011), 191.
64. Douglas Bourn, "Young people, identity and living in a global society," *Development Education and Research*, Issue 7, Autumn 2008, Centre for Global Education, accessed August 1, 2022, https://www.developmenteducationreview.com/sites/default/files/article-pdfs/bourn%20focus%204.pdf
65. Giddens, *Runaway World*, 51.
66. Ibid., 58.
67. Ibid., 59.
68. Louise Perry, *The Case Against the Sexual Revolution – A New Guide to Sex in the 21st Century* (Cambridge: Polity Press, 2022), 163–164.
69. Anthony Giddens, *Modernity and Self-Identity, Self and Society in the Late Modern Age* (Cambridge: Polity, 1991), 89.
70. Klinenberg, *Going Solo*, 13.
71. Jesse Singal, "The New Science of Single People," *New York Magazine*, August 16, 2016, accessed August 1, 2022, http://nymag.com/scienceofus/2016/08/the-new-science-of-single-people.html
72. "Age and Sex Composition in the United States: 2018," United States Census Bureau, July 11, 2019, accessed August 1, 2022, https://www.

census.gov/data/tables/2018/demo/age-and-sex/2018-age-sex-composition.html

73. Elyakim Kislev, *Happy Singlehood: The Rising Acceptance and Celebration of Solo Living* (Oakland: University of California Press, 2019), 5.

74. Susan Waggoner, "Happy Singlehood: The Rising Acceptance and Celebration of Solo Living," *Foreword Reviews*, March/April, 2019, accessed August 1, 2022, https://www.forewordreviews.com/reviews/happy-singlehood/

75. Giddens, *Runaway World*, 12.

76. The sociologist, Manuel Castells, who has no argument with feminism or "sexual liberation," is nevertheless worried about children in the digital age: "The main victims of this cultural transition are children, as they have been increasingly neglected under current conditions of family crisis... The solution is not an impossible return to an obsolete, and oppressive, patriarchal family. The reconstruction of the family under egalitarian relations, and the responsibility of public institutions in securing material and psychological support for children are possible ways to alter the course toward mass destruction of the human psyche that is implicit in the current unsettling life of millions of children." See Manuel Castells, *The Power of Identity*, Second Edition, (Oxford, Wiley-Blackwell, 2010), 235.

77. Ogi Ogas and Sai Gaddam, *A Billion Wicked Thoughts: What the Internet Tells Us About Sexual Relationships*, (New York: Penguin, 2011), Kindle Location 273.

78. Ibid., Kindle Location 365.

79. Graham McGrath, "More people visit XVideos and Pornhub than Netflix and Amazon each month," *Extra.ie*, August 2, 2020, accessed August 1, 2022, https://extra.ie/2020/08/02/must-see/people-visit-pornhub

80. "Pornography is booming during the covid-19 lockdowns," *The Economist*, May 10, 2020, accessed August 1, 2022, https://www.economist.com/international/2020/05/10/pornography-is-booming-during-the-covid-19-lockdowns. See also Joshua Grubbs, "Porn use is up, thanks to the pandemic," *The Conversation*, April 8, 2020, accessed August 1, 2022, https://theconversation.com/porn-use-is-up-thanks-to-the-pandemic-134972

81. Damian Thompson, *The Fix* (London: Harper Collins, 2012), 197.

82. Ibid.

83. Ibid., 230.

84. Fiona Andreallo, "Robots with benefits: How sexbots are marketed as companions," *The Conversation*, November 14, 2019, accessed August 1, 2022, https://theconversation.com/robots-with-benefits-how-sexbots-are-marketed-as-companions-126262

85. Carlyn Beccia, "Are You Digisexual?—Purchases of Sex Dolls Surged in 2020," *Medium*, December 21, 2020, accessed August 1, 2022, https://medium.com/sexography/are-you-digisexual-purchases-of-humanoid-sexbots-surged-in-2020-cddf978d6e29

86. Robert Putnam, "Bowling Alone: The Collapse and Revival of American Community" accessed August 1, 2022 at http://bowlingalone.com/

87. Redner, *Beyond Civilization*, 211.

88. George F. Ritzer, *Enchanting a Disenchanted World: Continuity and Change in the Cathedrals of Consumption*, 3rd Edition (Los Angeles: Pine Forge Press, 2010), 37.

89. Keith Hampton, Lauren Sessions Goulet, Kristen Purcell, "Social networking sites and our lives," Pew Research Center, June 16, 2011, accessed August 1, 2022, https://www.pewresearch.org/internet/2011/06/16/social-networking-sites-and-our-lives/

90. Manuel Castells, "The Impact of the Internet on Society: A Global Perspective," *OpenMind*, accessed August 1, 2022, http://www.jour.auth.gr/wp-content/uploads/2015/06/Castells-The-Impact-of-the-Internet-on-Society-A-Global-Perspective.pdf, 16–18

91. Ray Williams, "Do Facebook and other Social Media Encourage Narcissism?," *Psychology Today*, June 13, 2013, accessed August 30, 2015, https://www.psychologytoday.com/blog/wired-success/201306/do-facebook-and-other-social-media-encourage-narcissism

92. "Who We Are," Center for Humane Technology, accessed November 24, 2020, https://www.humanetech.com/who-we-are#our-story

93. "Ledger of Harms," Center for Humane Technology, October 11, 2020, accessed November 24, 2020, https://ledger.humanetech.com

94. "Together, we can align technology with humanity's best interests," Center for Humane Technology, accessed November 24, 2020, https://www.humanetech.com/rebuild

95. Emily Bell, "Facebook is Eating the World," *Columbia Journalism Review*, March 7, 2016, accessed August 1, 2022, http://www.cjr.org/analysis/facebook_and_media.php

96. Katharine Viner, "How Technology Disrupted the Truth," The Guardian, July 12, 2016, accessed August 1, 2022, https://www.theguardian.com/media/2016/jul/12/how-technology-disrupted-the-truth?CMP=share_btn_fb.

97. Ibid.

98. Adrienne Lafrance, "Facebook is a Doomsday Machine," *The Atlantic*, December 15, 2020, accessed August 1, 2022, https://www.theatlantic.com/technology/archive/2020/12/facebook-doomsday-machine/617384/

99. Andy Newman, "Secret Lives of Real Pets," *The New York Times*, July 22, 2016, accessed August 1, 2022, http://www.nytimes.com/2016/07/24/nyregion/secret-lives-of-real-pets.html

100. As far back as 1999, British researchers estimated that "in an urban environment, on a busy day, a person could have their image captured by over 300 cameras on thirty separate CCTV systems." Clive Norris, Mike McCahill, and David Wood, "The Growth of CCTV: a global perspective on the international diffusion of video surveillance in publicly accessible space," *Surveillance & Society*, CCTV Special (eds. Norris, McCahill and Wood) 2(2/3): 110–135, 2004, accessed August 1, 2022 https://ojs.library.queensu.ca/index.php/surveillance-and-society/article/view/3369/3332, 112.

101. Drew Engelbart, "Caught on Camera: Americans are captured on an estimated 70 security cameras each day," KDVR.com, February 11, 2018, accessed August 1, 2022, https://kdvr.com/news/trending/caught-on-camera-americans-are-captured-an-estimated-70-security-cameras-each-day/

102. Elly Cosgrove, "One billion surveillance cameras will be watching around the world in 2021, a new study says," CNBC, December 6, 2019, accessed August 1, 2022, https://www.cnbc.com/2019/12/06/one-billion-surveillance-cameras-will-be-watching-globally-in-2021.html

103. Arjun Kharpal, "China's surveillance tech is spreading globally, raising concerns about Beijing's influence," CNBC, October 8, 2019, accessed August 1, 2022, https://www.cnbc.com/2019/10/08/china-is-exporting-surveillance-tech-like-facial-recognition-globally.html

104. Kashmir Hill, "The Secretive Company That Might End Privacy as We Know It," *The New York Times*, January 18, 2020, accessed August 1, 2022, https://www.nytimes.com/2020/01/18/technology/clearview-privacy-facial-recognition.html

105. Drew Harwell, "Ring and Nest helped normalize American surveillance and turned us into a nation of voyeurs," *The Washington Post*, February 18, 2020, accessed August 1, 2022, https://www.washingtonpost.com/technology/2020/02/18/ring-nest-surveillance-doorbell-camera/

106. The main argument advanced for installing all these cameras—in both public and private locations—has always been security. It is true that, at least in the US, both violent crime and property crime have declined since the start of the digital era. (See John Gramlich, "What the data says (and doesn't say) about crime in the United States," Pew Research Center, November 20, 2020, accessed August 1, 2022, https://www.pewresearch.org/fact-tank/2020/11/20/facts-about-crime-in-the-u-s/. According to FBI data, "the violent crime rate fell 49% between 1993 and 2019, with large decreases in the rates of robbery (-68%), murder/non-

negligent manslaughter (-47%) and aggravated assault (-43%). …Meanwhile, the property crime rate fell 55%, with big declines in the rates of burglary (-69%), motor vehicle theft (-64%) and larceny/theft (-49%).") It is important to remember, though, that these declines have been accompanied by an increase in cybercrime during the same period. Hence, surveillance devices that contribute to drops in physical crime can simultaneously serve as an avenue for the growth in cybercrime.

107. Europeans do have the right to request the removal of Google links about themselves following a ruling by the European Court of Justice in 2014. In the year following the ruling, Google approved approximately 40 percent of the requests that were made. Succeeding in having a link removed is no simple matter. See Sophie Curtis, "EU 'right to be forgotten': one year on," *The Telegraph*, May 13, 2015, accessed August 1, 2022, http://www.telegraph.co.uk/technology/google/11599909/EU-right-to-be-forgotten-one-year-on.html

108. Rani Molla, "Why Your Free Software is Never Free," *Recode*, January 29, 2020, accessed August 1, 2022, https://www.vox.com/recode/2020/1/29/21111848/free-software-privacy-alternative-data

109. Ibid.

110. John Mello Jr., "Experts Forecast the End of Privacy as We Know It" *TechNewsWorld*, December 18, 2014, accessed August 1, 2022, https://www.technewsworld.com/story/81501.html

111. Julie Cohen, "What Privacy is For," *Harvard Law Review*, May 20, 2013, 126 Harv. L. Rev. 1904, accessed August 1, 2022, https://harvardlawreview.org/wp-content/uploads/pdfs/vol126_cohen.pdf, 1911.

112. Jathan Sadowski, "Why Does Privacy Matter? One Scholar's Answer," *The Atlantic*, February 26, 2013, accessed August 1, 2022, http://www.theatlantic.com/technology/archive/2013/02/why-does-privacy-matter-one-scholars-answer/273521/. Here, Sadowski explains and then quotes Cohen's work.

113. See, for example, Sherry Turkle's *Alone Together*. See also Emily Drago, "The Effect of Technology on Face-to-Face Communication" accessed October 11, 2020, https://www.elon.edu/docs/e-web/academics/communications/research/vol6no1/02DragoEJSpring15.pdf   14–15, for a review of the literature. See also Victoria Dunckley, "Gray Matters: Too Much Screen Time Damages the Brain," *Psychology Today*, February 27, 2014, accessed August 1, 2022, https://www.psychologytoday.com/blog/mental-wealth/201402/gray-matters-too-much-screen-time-damages-the-brain

114. Nicholas Carr, *The Shallows—What the Internet is Doing to our Brains* (New York: W. W. Norton and Company, 2010), 167.

115. Ibid., 165.

116. Mike Wright and Ellie Zolfagharifard, "Internet is giving us shorter attention spans and worse memories, major study suggests," *The Telegraph*, June 6, 2019, accessed August 1, 2022, https://www.telegraph.co.uk/technology/2019/06/06/internet-giving-us-shorter-attention-spans-worse-memories-major/

117. Patricia Greenfield, "Technology and Informal Education: What is Taught, What is Learned," as cited in Carr, *The Shallows*, 195.

118. Carr, *The Shallows*, 196.

119. Ibid., 195, 197.

120. Daniel Goleman, *Focus: The Hidden Driver of Excellence* (New York: Harper, 2013), 107.

121. Daniel Goleman, "Why Aren't We More Compassionate?" NPR, December 19, 2014, accessed August 1, 2022, http://www.npr.org/programs/ted-radio-hour/371276520/just-a-little-nicer

122. Diane Swanbrow, "Empathy: College students don't have as much as they used to," *Michigan News*, University of Michigan, May 27, 2010, accessed August 1, 2022, https://news.umich.edu/empathy-college-students-don-t-have-as-much-as-they-used-to/

123. David Brooks, *The Road to Character*, 250–251.

124. Ibid., 252.

REFERENCES

Age and Sex Composition in the United States: 2018, United States Census Bureau, July 11, 2019, accessed August 1, 2022, https://www.census.gov/data/tables/2018/demo/age-and-sex/2018-age-sex-composition.html.

Albrow, Martin. *The Global Age: State and Society Beyond Modernity*. Cambridge, Polity Press, 1996.

Andreallo, Fiona. "Robots with benefits: How sexbots are marketed as companions," *The Conversation*, November 14, 2019, accessed August 1, 2022, https://theconversation.com/robots-with-benefits-how-sexbots-are-marketed-as-companions-126262.

Batista, Ed. "The Marshmallow Test for Grownups," *Harvard Business Review*, September 15, 2014, accessed August 1, 2022, https://hbr.org/2014/09/the-marshmallow-test-for-grownups.

Beccia, Carlyn. "Are You Digisexual?—Purchases of Sex Dolls Surged in 2020," *Medium*, December 21, 2020, accessed August 1, 2022, https://medium.com/sexography/are-you-digisexual-purchases-of-humanoid-sexbots-surged-in-2020-cddf978d6e29.

Bell, Emily. "Facebook is Eating the World," *Columbia Journalism Review*, March 7, 2016, accessed August 1, 2022, http://www.cjr.org/analysis/facebook_and_media.php.

Bourn, Douglas. "Young people, identity and living in a global society," *Development Education and Research*, Issue 7, Autumn 2008, Centre for Global Education, accessed August 1, 2022, https://www.developmenteducationreview.com/sites/default/files/article-pdfs/bourn%20focus%204.pdf.

Brooks, David. *The Road to Character*. New York, Random House, 2015.

Bucher, Gabriela. "COVID-19 has shown us the true extent of global inequality. In 2021, let's commit to ending it," World Economic Forum, January 25, 2021, accessed August 1, 2022, https://www.weforum.org/agenda/2021/01/covid19-inequality-virus-report-oxfam/.

Carr, Nicholas. *The Shallows–What the Internet is Doing to our Brains*. New York, W. W. Norton and Company, 2010.

Castells, Manuel. "The Impact of the Internet on Society: A Global Perspective," *OpenMind*, accessed August 1, 2022, http://www.jour.auth.gr/wp-content/uploads/2015/06/Castells-The-Impact-of-the-Internet-on-Society-A-Global-Perspective.pdf.

Castells, Manuel. *The Power of Identity*, Second Edition, Oxford, Wiley-Blackwell, 2010.

Cohen, Julie. "What Privacy is For," *Harvard Law Review*, May 20, 2013, 126 Harv. L. Rev. 1904, accessed August 1, 2022, https://harvardlawreview.org/wp-content/uploads/pdfs/vol126_cohen.pdf.

Colville, Robert. *The Great Acceleration–How the World is Getting Faster, Faster*, London, Bloomsbury, 2016.

Cosgrove, Elly. "One billion surveillance cameras will be watching around the world in 2021, a new study says," CNBC, December 6, 2019, accessed August 1, 2022, https://www.cnbc.com/2019/12/06/one-billion-surveillance-cameras-will-be-watching-globally-in-2021.html.

Curtis, Sophie. "EU 'right to be forgotten': one year on," *The Telegraph*, May 13, 2015, accessed August 1, 2022, http://www.telegraph.co.uk/technology/google/11599909/EU-right-to-be-forgotten-one-year-on.html.

Distribution of Household Wealth in the U.S. since 1989, The Board of Governors of the Federal Reserve System, accessed August 1, 2022, https://www.federalreserve.gov/releases/z1/dataviz/dfa/distribute/chart/#quarter:123;series:Net%20worth;demographic:networth;population:1,3,5,7;units:shares;range:1989.3,2020.2.

Drago, Emily. "The Effect of Technology on Face-to-Face Communication" accessed October 11, 2020, https://www.elon.edu/docs/e-web/academics/communications/research/vol6no1/02DragoEJSpring15.pdf.

Dunckley, Victoria. "Gray Matters: Too Much Screen Time Damages the Brain," *Psychology Today*, February 27, 2014, accessed August 1, 2022, https://www.psychologytoday.com/blog/mental-wealth/201402/gray-matters-too-much-screen-time-damages-the-brain.

Engelbart, Drew. "Caught on Camera: Americans are captured on an estimated 70 security cameras each day," KDVR.com, February 11, 2018, accessed August 1, 2022, https://kdvr.com/news/trending/caught-on-camera-americans-are-captured-an-estimated-70-security-cameras-each-day/.

Enriquez Juan: "Will our kids be a different species?," TED talk, filmed April 2012, accessed August 1, 2022, https://www.ted.com/talks/juan_enriquez_will_our_kids_be_a_different_species?language=en#t-836065.

Enriquez, Juan. *Right/Wrong*, Cambridge, MA, MIT Press, 2020.

Friedman, Thomas. *Thank You for Being Late: An Optimist's Guide to Thriving in the Age of Accelerations*. New York, Farrar, Straus and Giroux, 2016.

Friedman, Thomas. *The Lexus and the Olive Tree: Understanding Globalization*. New York, Farrah, Strauss, and Giroux, 2000.

Friedman, Thomas. *The World is Flat: A Brief History of the Twenty-first Century*. New York, Farrar, Straus and Giroux, 2005.

Giddens, Anthony. *Modernity and Self-Identity, Self and Society in the Late Modern Age*. Cambridge, Polity, 1991.

Giddens, Anthony. *Runaway World–How Globalization is Reshaping our World*. London, Profile Books, 2002.

Global flows in a digital age: How trade, finance, people, and data connect the world economy, McKinsey Global Institute, April, 2014, accessed August 1, 2022, http://www.mckinsey.com/business-functions/strategy-and-corporate-finance/our-insights/global-flows-in-a-digital-age.

Globalization, *Stanford Encyclopedia of Philosophy*, accessed August 1, 2022, http://plato.stanford.edu/entries/globalization/.

Goleman, Daniel. "Why Aren't We More Compassionate?" NPR, December 19, 2014, accessed August 1, 2022, http://www.npr.org/programs/ted-radio-hour/371276520/just-a-little-nicer.

Goleman, Daniel. *Focus: The Hidden Driver of Excellence*. New York, Harper, 2013.

Google's Original X-Man—A Conversation With Sebastian Thrun, *Foreign Affairs*, November/December 2013, accessed August 1, 2022, https://www.foreignaffairs.com/interviews/2013-10-15/googles-original-x-man.

Germov, John and Poole, Marilyn (eds.), *Public Sociology*. Sydney, Allen & Unwin, 2011.

Gramlich, John. "What the data says (and doesn't say) about crime in the United States," Pew Research Center, November 20, 2020, accessed August 1, 2022, https://www.pewresearch.org/fact-tank/2020/11/20/facts-about-crime-in-the-u-s/.

Grubbs, Joshua. "Porn use is up, thanks to the pandemic," *The Conversation*, April 8, 2020, accessed August 1, 2022, https://theconversation.com/porn-use-is-up-thanks-to-the-pandemic-134972.

Hampton, Keith, Sessions Goulet, Lauen; Purcell, Kristen. "Social networking sites and our lives," Pew Research Center, June 16, 2011, accessed August 1,

2022,   https://www.pewresearch.org/internet/2011/06/16/social-networking-sites-and-our-lives/.

Harwell, Drew. "Ring and Nest helped normalize American surveillance and turned us into a nation of voyeurs," *The Washington Post*, February 18, 2020, accessed August 1, 2022, https://www.washingtonpost.com/technology/2020/02/18/ring-nest-surveillance-doorbell-camera/.

Hill, Kashmir. "The Secretive Company That Might End Privacy as We Know It," *The New York Times*, January 18, 2020, accessed August 1, 2022, https://www.nytimes.com/2020/01/18/technology/clearview-privacy-facial-recognition.html.

Japanese say 'I don't' to marriage in record numbers, Nikkei Asian Review, July 2, 2016, accessed August 1, 2022, https://asia.nikkei.com/Economy/Japanese-say-I-don-t-to-marriage-in-record-numbers.

Kagan, Julia. "How Much Income Puts You in the Top 1%, 5%, 10%?" *Investopedia*, June 2, 2020, accessed October 11, 2020, https://www.investopedia.com/personal-finance/how-much-income-puts-you-top-1-5-10/.

Kharpal, Arjun. "China's surveillance tech is spreading globally, raising concerns about Beijing's influence," CNBC, October 8, 2019, accessed August 1, 2022, https://www.cnbc.com/2019/10/08/china-is-exporting-surveillance-tech-like-facial-recognition-globally.html.

Kislev, Elyakim. *Happy Singlehood: The Rising Acceptance and Celebration of Solo Living*. Oakland, University of California Press, 2019.

Klinenberg, Eric. *Going Solo–The Extraordinary Rise and Surprising Appeal of Living Alone*. New York, The Penguin Press, 2012.

Lafrance, Adrienne. "Facebook is a Doomsday Machine," *The Atlantic*, December 15, 2020, accessed August 1, 2022, https://www.theatlantic.com/technology/archive/2020/12/facebook-doomsday-machine/617384/.

Louise Perry. *The Case Against the Sexual Revolution – A New Guide to Sex in the 21st Century* Cambridge, Polity Press, 2022.

Ma, Adrian. "What is the metaverse, and what can we do there?" *The Conversation*, May 23, 2022, accessed August 1, 2022, https://theconversation.com/what-is-the-metaverse-and-what-can-we-do-there-179200.

McGrath, Graham. "More people visit XVideos and Pornhub than Netflix and Amazon each month," *Extra.ie*, August 2, 2020, accessed August 1, 2022, https://extra.ie/2020/08/02/must-see/people-visit-pornhub.

McNeill, William. "The Rise of the West after Twenty-Five Years" in Stephen K. Sanderson, *Civilizations and World Systems*. Walnut Creek, AltaMira Press, 1995.

Mello, John. "Experts Forecast the End of Privacy as We Know It" *TechNewsWorld*, December 18, 2014, accessed August 1, 2022, http://www.technewsworld.com/story/81501.html.

Molla, Rani. "Why Your Free Software is Never Free," *Recode*, January 29, 2020, accessed August 1, 2022, https://www.vox.com/recode/2020/1/29/21111848/free-software-privacy-alternative-data.

Naim, Moses. *The End of Power*. New York, Basic Books, 2013.

National Institutes of Health, "Human Genome Project," March 29, 2013, accessed August 1, 2022, https://archives.nih.gov/asites/report/09-09-2019/report.nih.gov/nihfactsheets/ViewFactSheete078.html?csid=45&key=H#H.

Newman, Andy. "Secret Lives of Real Pets," *The New York Times*, July 22, 2016, accessed August 1, 2022, http://www.nytimes.com/2016/07/24/nyregion/secret-lives-of-real-pets.html.

Norris, Clive, McCahill, Mike and Wood, David. "The Growth of CCTV: a global perspective on the international diffusion of video surveillance in publicly accessible space," *Surveillance & Society*, CCTV Special (eds. Norris McCahill and Wood) 2(2/3): 110–135, 2004, accessed August 1, 2022 https://ojs.library.queensu.ca/index.php/surveillance-and-society/article/view/3369/3332.

Not Always With Us, *The Economist*, June 1, 2013, accessed August 1, 2022, http://www.economist.com/news/briefing/21578643-world-has-astonishing-chance-take-billion-people-out-extreme-poverty-2030-not.

Ranger, Steve. "What is the IoT? Everything you need to know about the Internet of Things right now," ZDNet, February 3, 2020, accessed August 1, 2022, https://www.zdnet.com/article/what-is-the-internet-of-things-everything-you-need-to-know-about-the-iot-right-now/.

Ogas, Ogi and Gaddam, Sai. *A Billion Wicked Thoughts: What the Internet Tells Us About Sexual Relationships*. New York, Penguin, 2011.

Ortiz-Ospina, Esteban. "The rise of living alone: how one-person households are becoming increasingly common around the world," Our World in Data, December 10, 2019, accessed August 1, 2022, https://ourworldindata.org/living-alone.

Pornography is booming during the covid-19 lockdowns, *The Economist*, May 10, 2020, accessed August 1, 2022, https://www.economist.com/international/2020/05/10/pornography-is-booming-during-the-covid-19-lockdowns.

Putnam, Robert. "Bowling Alone: The Collapse and Revival of American Community" accessed August 1, 2022 at http://bowlingalone.com/.

Redner, Harry. Beyond Civilization: Society, Culture, and the Individual in the Age of Globalization. London, Routledge, 2013.

Riess, Helen. *The Empathy Effect*. Boulder, Sounds True, 2018.

Ritzer, George. *Enchanting a Disenchanted World: Continuity and Change in the Cathedrals of Consumption*, 3rd Edition. Los Angeles, Pine Forge Press, 2010.

Sacks, Jonathan. *The Dignity of Difference*. London, Continuum, 2002.

Sadowski, Jathan. "Why Does Privacy Matter? One Scholar's Answer," *The Atlantic*, February 26, 2013, accessed August 1, 2022, http://www.theatlantic.com/technology/archive/2013/02/why-does-privacy-matter-one-scholars-answer/273521/. Here, Sadowski explains and then quotes Cohen's work.

Saez, Emmanuel & Zucman, Gabriel. "Exploding Wealth Inequality in the United States," Washington Center for Equitable Growth, October 20, 2014, accessed August 1, 2022, http://equitablegrowth.org/research/exploding-wealth-inequality-united-states/.

Singal, Jesse. "The New Science of Single People," *New York Magazine*, August 16, 2016, accessed August 1, 2022, http://nymag.com/scienceofus/2016/08/the-new-science-of-single-people.html.

Steger, Manfred. *Globalization*. Oxford, Oxford University Press, 2013.

Swanbrow, Diane. "Empathy: College students don't have as much as they used to," *Michigan News*, University of Michigan, May 27, 2010, accessed August 1, 2022, https://news.umich.edu/empathy-college-students-don-t-have-as-much-as-they-used-to/.

Technology Beats Humans At Growing Strawberries In Pinduoduo Smart Agriculture Competition, *Globe Newswire*, December 15, 2020, accessed August 1, 2022, https://www.globenewswire.com/news-release/2020/12/16/2145844/0/en/Technology-beats-humans-at-growing-strawberries-in-Pinduoduo-smart-agriculture-competition.html.

Thompson, Damian. *The Fix*. London, Harper Collins, 2012.

Total Number of Websites, InternetLiveStats.com, accessed August 1, 2022, http://www.internetlivestats.com/total-number-of-websites/.

Turkle, Sherry. "The Flight from Conversation," The New York Times, April 21, 2012, accessed August 1, 2022, http://www.nytimes.com/2012/04/22/opinion/sunday/the-flight-from-conversation.html?pagewanted=all.

Viner, Katherine. "How Technology Disrupted the Truth," The Guardian, July 12, 2016, accessed August 1, 2022, https://www.theguardian.com/media/2016/jul/12/how-technology-disrupted-the-truth?CMP=share_btn_fb.

Waggoner, Susan. "Happy Singlehood: The Rising Acceptance and Celebration of Solo Living," *Foreword Reviews*, March/April, 2019, accessed August 1, 2022, https://www.forewordreviews.com/reviews/happy-singlehood/.

Were the Millennium Development Goals a success? Yes! Sort of, World Vision, July 3, 2015, accessed August 1, 2022, https://www.wvi.org/united-nations-and-global-engagement/article/were-mdgs-success.

Who We Are, Center for Humane Technology, accessed November 24, 2020, https://www.humanetech.com/who-we-are#our-story.

Wikipedia: About, Wikipedia.org, accessed August 1, 2022, https://en.wikipedia.org/wiki/Wikipedia:About.

Williams, Ray. "Do Facebook and other Social Media Encourage Narcissism?," *Psychology Today*, June 13, 2013, accessed August 30, 2015, https://www.psychologytoday.com/blog/wired-success/201306/do-facebook-and-other-social-media-encourage-narcissism.

World Inequality Report 2022, World Inequality Lab, December 7, 2021, accessed August 1, 2022, https://wir2022.wid.world/executive-summary/.

Wright, Mike and Zolfagharifard, Ellie. "Internet is giving us shorter attention spans and worse memories, major study suggests," *The Telegraph*, June 6, 2019, accessed August 1, 2022, https://www.telegraph.co.uk/technology/2019/06/06/internet-giving-us-shorter-attention-spans-worse-memories-major/.

CHAPTER 5

Changing Mentalities

Modernity is over. Its questions, its societal structures, and its struggles are passé. So is its Judaism. Sooner or later, Reform and Conservative Judaism will become entries in the history books, alongside modernity itself. Pockets of strength will likely continue for decades, but the waning years have arrived. This assertion is not intended as a mark of disrespect for the movements of modernity. Quite the opposite. No movement lasts a thousand years—nor should it. Movements belong to a specific time that calls forth a particular response. They belong to a certain thought milieu. For any movement to retain relevance and galvanize hundreds of thousands of adherents well into a second century of existence is no small feat. It is an accomplishment worthy of admiration. From the mid-nineteenth to the late twentieth century, Conservative and Reform Judaism helped millions fuse their Jewishness with modernity in ways that allowed their followers—not all, but many—to live as both engaged Jews and citizens of the modern world.

That reality is no more. No longer does the conversation presume the existence of a Jewish community that lives on the margins of society, seeking to fit in. No longer is there a prominent debate over how the findings of science and history can mesh with Torah. No longer is there a robust discussion about how much autonomy Judaism might afford individuals. Outside Orthodoxy, no longer is there an appeal to knowledgeable authority figures to provide instruction on how to live an authentic Jewish life.

The original version of the chapter has been revised. A correction to this chapter can be found at https://doi.org/10.1007/978-3-031-17992-1_9

Twenty-first-century concerns diverge from those of modernity on vital issues that go far beyond technology. The multiple transformations of the digital era have resulted in what the journalist and foreign policy expert Moses Naim calls a "Mentality revolution." This Mentality revolution "reflects the major changes in mindsets, expectations, and aspirations"[1] that stem from all that has happened since 1990. Naim describes the Mentality revolution this way:

> Globalization, urbanization, changes in family structure, the rise of new industries and opportunities, the spread of English as a global lingua franca—these have had consequences in every sphere, but their effect has been most fundamental at the level of attitudes. Indeed, the signal effect of these changes is the ever-increasing salience of aspiration as a motivator of our actions and behaviors. Desiring a better life is a normal human trait, but aspiration toward specific examples and narratives of how life could be better, not some abstract notion of improvement, is what drives people to take action. …The more contact we have with one another, the greater the extent to which contact breeds aspiration. …The combination of emerging global values and the increase in aspirational behavior poses the strongest challenge of all to the moral basis of power.[2]

The digital age has revamped human expectations. Our values, standards, and norms have been remade. Naim points to the "ever-increasing salience of aspiration" as a motivator for human thinking and behavior. This should not be understood solely in materialistic terms. Rather, aspiration, in this context, is expressed by a desire to maximize individual control and curation of our life experiences with the greatest degree of personalization possible. Given the breathtaking scope of choice that is now available to those with an Internet connection, it is usually possible to find precisely what we want in the midst of many alternatives, and we can often have whatever it is that we seek fashioned to our personal specifications. This possibility to fulfill our individual desires with tailor-made solutions contributes to the altered mentality.

This is not just autonomy on steroids. The notion of individual autonomy was an outgrowth of the widespread access to knowledge that the printing press unleashed. Autonomy allowed people to make a range of choices in their lives that had previously been limited by regal fiat or religious dictate. But, as we have seen, the autonomy of modernity was limited by one's location and the resources, attitudes, cultural norms, and identity patterns of that place.

Now the Internet has opened possibilities that stretch far beyond the autonomy model of modernity. When Henry Ford famously said that a "customer can have a car painted any color he wants so long as it is black," he spoke as an authority figure telling people that things had to be done according to the company's dictates. When, later, one could choose one's car color from a limited range of half a dozen alternatives, that was autonomy—there were choices to be made, but the sellers constrained the choices. When one can order a vehicle with any color, pattern, or image that one's heart desires, that will represent a move that is truly emblematic of our age of aspiration. This third paradigm (whatever color or pattern you dream of) enables individuals to tell the authorities what it is that the authorities should produce. Each person creates their own vision, limited only by imagination, and those in a position to deliver are expected to respond—or be bypassed. The third paradigm differs from the second not merely in the greatly expanded range of choices but in the fact that the locus of power has shifted from what were once authority figures to the individual. It is the individual who now tells the corporation how its product ought to be produced, rather than the business bosses offering whatever suits them. Or, put differently, "the twentieth century was all about getting you to love the things we make. And the twenty-first is all about how to make the things you love."[3] This represents the core of the "mentality of aspiration."

This mentality is also a central feature of what we might call "hyper-individualism." Given that the fulfillment of personal aspirations has become central, it follows that the product, service, experience, or program that any individual receives will frequently be unique to that person. As businesses and organizations look to cater to individual expectations, so the end product becomes ever more distinctive. When combined with the focus on Big Me, the prevailing sense of being in a "tribe of one," and the time spent alone with our personal devices, hyper-individualism has become a reality that cannot be ignored.

A logical question then arises about the place of authority in the digital age: If the printing press led to the contraction of ecclesiastical authority and the rise of the nation state, where does the Internet lead? The probable answer is that the power of authority figures will diminish further as the expectation of individuals that their customized wishes will be satisfied grows. Hyper-individualism will make the exercising of authority more challenging in almost all areas that are not governed by secular law.

The implications for Judaism are sizeable. Both the Reform and Conservative movements regarded it as axiomatic that even in the non-Orthodox context rabbis had some measure of authority. That is why rabbinic decisions, like those surrounding marriage officiation, carried weight. But in the Internet era, even that measure of authority is dissipating. Jewish weddings provide an example of how the ground has already shifted: The typical twentieth-century Jewish wedding usually took place in the home community of the bride or groom. The venue might have been a synagogue or one of several function halls frequented by that community. The officiant was almost always one of the local rabbis. There may have been some variations in the language of the ceremony, but the liturgy was largely predictable. There were some autonomous choices to be made, but, for the most part, the template was familiar. Twenty-first-century Jewish weddings are noticeably different. "Destination weddings" in locations far from the homes of all the participants are on the rise. Why be limited to a community of origin, when the entire guest list can fly to the destination of one's choice? Why be restricted by a small range of venues or a limited list of caterers when one can select whatever view or gourmet delights one craves? Moreover, the growing trend to ask a friend or a family member to act as the officiant demonstrates that many couples see no reason to limit the choice of who leads the ceremony to members of the clergy, especially if the local rabbi hardly knows the participants. While most jurisdictions still require a justice of the peace or ordained minister to officiate, this restriction is easily circumvented by obtaining online ordination. The newly minted clergy-person will, naturally, produce whatever liturgy the couple instructs, since the novice officiant is unlikely to be devoted to any particular rite.

Even overlooking what instant ordination says about perceptions of clergy status, it is worth considering what it implies about the nature of authority generally. As late as the 1990s, having an authority figure officiate at a wedding was key. The rabbi or judge provided the imprimatur of the official acceptance of the marriage in the eyes of God, or society, that imbued the couple's relationship with publicly sanctioned standing. Nowadays, that form of authority is of little interest. Today, the officiant is usually tasked with beautifying and uplifting the moment according to the couple's wishes; nothing more. One of the most popular wedding planning websites even proposes the option of "no officiant," meaning, in practice, self-officiation.[4] A bride who chose this course explained her thinking succinctly when she stated, "We didn't do anything that we had to, only exactly what we wanted to."[5] Hyper-individualism. The questions that agitated a series of twentieth-century debates as to which wedding ceremonies merited rabbinic officiation are yesterday's problems. There is no longer any need to bother with an officiant who is uneasy about the nature of the match or who will not conform to the couple's wishes. Couples can choose the officiant who mirrors their desires precisely.

Whether one regards this as a positive or negative development is not the issue. What is important is that this reframing represents a noticeable step beyond autonomy. The customers are telling the authorities what "product" they want the authorities to produce. The authorities are no longer in charge of determining the parameters of the available choices, as they once were in modernity. One Conservative rabbi encapsulated her role this way: "My success as a rabbi will be measured to the extent that I can help people access their own authentic understanding of themselves as Jews."[6] Insofar as the role of the rabbi has shifted from one who teaches and instills a commitment to *halakhah* or the adoption of fixed Jewish customs and observances to one who "helps people access their own authentic understanding of themselves as Jews," this signals a clear move toward the consumer's view of how the "product" should be shaped. This is the "mentality of aspiration" in action. It is too early to know how this mentality will extend to the broader structures of Jewish law and practice. Its implications, though, will not be restricted to weddings.[7]

All of this demonstrates that we have entered uncharted Jewish terrain where tough questions lie ahead, particularly for those outside of Orthodoxy: Should rabbis attempt to satisfy the aspirations of Jews who want to personalize their Judaism, or should Judaism obligate Jews to perform certain required actions that are not subject to individualization? Is Judaism a system of laws and practices, however loosely understood, or is it a set of desiderata, components to be ordered in the pursuit of a life of self-fulfillment?

Any form of Judaism that is designed to grapple with the challenges that have already arisen in the Internet age will need to contend with a long list of additional questions: If being Jewish has become "part of a larger identity mosaic for today's Jews,"[8] then what should be the Jewish attitude toward hybrid identities? Is the premium placed on being "good to oneself" in the context of marriage and family appropriate? Can the choice to remain single be coherently accommodated within Jewish views of family? Does atomization raise concerns? Is the weakening of communal organizations a phenomenon that needs to be tackled? Is the easy availability of pornography concerning? Is the diminution of privacy an issue that needs to be addressed? Should limits be proposed for human communications via screens, given the impact that these devices have upon the brain and human interactions? Should the rise of a global culture and its eclipsing of local cultures be lauded or critiqued? Should the power of social media be countered? Are the existing rules of *lashon ha-rah* ("the bad use of the tongue"—Jewish conventions on speech) sufficiently robust or do they need to be reappraised? If empathy is diminishing and stillness is elusive, do these problems require solutions? And there are, to be sure, many other fundamental questions that arise from the impact of the digital revolution.

It is perfectly plausible that there will be more than one credible Jewish answer to these questions. The history of *halakhah* yields multiple instances of Jewish communities utilizing the same sources yet arriving at different conclusions. As the Talmud teaches, *eilu v'eilu*[9]—varying responses can be Jewishly authentic so long as each position emerges from a process of applying salient insights from classic sources to contemporary realities. What is critical is that Judaism should provide lucid views on the major issues confronting today's Jews. If Jews are called upon to exhibit conduct that exemplifies the finest forms of justice and righteousness, then it follows that the teachers of Judaism need to shape appropriate Jewish behavioral paths within the altered circumstances of the twenty-first century.

It is possible to envisage how Jewish responses to some of the emerging questions posed above might be framed. Consider, for example, the issue of privacy. Jewish sources are unambiguous about the importance of robust privacy provisions. Through the centuries, privacy regulations were enacted to protect individuals from inappropriate visual scrutiny, to ensure the privacy of correspondence, to guard against sudden intrusion, and to ensure confidentiality.[10] There can be no denying that "the general prohibition against infringing upon privacy as well as the specific prohibition against accessing another's records without that person's explicit consent are...deeply rooted in Jewish law."[11] In truth, though, while privacy concerns may be "deeply rooted in Jewish law," they represented a comparatively small part of the *halakhah*.

It is evident, though, that the rise of the Internet has greatly magnified the issue of privacy: "Accelerated technological development, the weaknesses of cyberspace, and difficulties in security pose new and exciting challenges to Jewish law concerning the application of ancient principles to our times."[12] Nevertheless, in the context of this heightened risk to privacy, there is no observable implementation of Jewish privacy principles to current conduct in cyberspace. Rabbi Asher Meir, a Jewish ethicist, shines a light on this subject while considering the question of whether it is permissible to use online tools to gather information about somebody else.[13] After examining the sources, Meir concludes that "engaging in a web search that discloses private information not available from a casual 'Googling' is a *halachically* questionable activity." "I think," writes Meir, that "it makes sense to distinguish between a routine Google search or visit to a person's Facebook page and a determined, sophisticated use of powerful online tools which cross the line from casual 'seeing' to 'looking' online and would therefore be forbidden." Meir, moreover, expresses concern that "there are many lesser examples where legitimate curiosity can easily cross the line into unwitting cyber-transgression."[14]

This is striking. Meir holds that engaging in cyber inquiry stimulated by curiosity—behavior that a large number of people consider normal—in fact constitutes *halakhic* transgression. It does not matter that the rest of the world might be doing it or that it might be thought of as unremarkable. For Jews, Meir holds, it is beyond the limits of acceptability. If Meir's reading of the sources were to become what Jewish law expects of Jews, it would differentiate Jewish conduct from that of surrounding society in much the same way that consuming kosher food does. But if Meir's understanding is the correct Jewish approach, there is currently no discernible instruction to Jews that this is the required standard. The fact that some version of Meir's perspective has not yet been incorporated into the teachings and practices of Jewish communities is an indication that a distinctive Jewish approach to Internet privacy is yet to crystallize.

Time, however, is of the essence. It is quite possible, therefore, that in short order our genetic, physical, and psychological profiles will be far more accessible to corporations and governments.[15] Could the *halakhic* heritage offer a useful way to approach these weighty challenges? A potential Jewish response would logically prioritize the historic Jewish commitment to robust forms of privacy. It should, furthermore, stress the significance of explicit consent on the part of those being surveilled, as well as emphasizing the *halakhic* distinction between casual "seeing" and systematic investigation.

A similar case can be made about *lashon ha-rah*. There is voluminous writing covering speech in Judaism. It is an issue of sufficient seriousness that the tradition maintains that "death and life are in the power of the tongue" (Proverbs 18:21). The *halakhic* provisions surrounding *lashon ha-rah* are considerably more restrictive than the speech laws of contemporary nations because they aspire to a lofty goal: not just avoiding gross infractions but attempting to minimize the damage that we inflict on our fellow human beings through speech. Maimonides held that any comment, even if true, that might ultimately cause financial loss, physical pain, mental anguish, or appreciable damage is in the category of *lashon ha-rah* and is forbidden.[16] The Chofetz Chaim, considered the leading modern authority on *lashon ha-rah*, clarifies that the ban on *lashon ha-rah* is not limited to what is said orally: "This *issur* (prohibition) of *lashon hara* obtains whether it is actually spoken by mouth or stated in a letter. There is also no difference whether he speaks it explicitly or by sign. In all modes, it is in the category of *lashon ha-rah*."[17] Though the Chofetz Chaim could not have anticipated the digital age, his reference to "all modes" indicates that *lashon ha-rah* is to be resisted no matter where it is expressed. That would undoubtedly include an expectation of circumspect conduct when commenting on websites, participating in social media interchanges, texting, or communicating via any of the multiple platforms that are now available.

The potential for *lashon ha-rah* to lead to damage in the digital era is obviously far more extensive than it was in the analog age. Given that people express themselves in online communication with considerably fewer restraints than in face-to-face interactions, abusive language, hurtful encounters, and cavalier attacks on character, reputation, and well-being have dramatically expanded. Not only has the pool of victims grown, but the severity of the transgressions has worsened, and the number of people who witness misconduct—those affected by "secondhand" *lashon ha-rah*—has mushroomed. Research in 2017 showed that 41 percent of Americans—up from 35 percent in 2014—had experienced offensive name-calling, purposeful embarrassment, physical threats, ongoing provocation, sexual harassment, or stalking online. Fully 66 percent of respondents said they had witnessed this behavior directed toward others.[18] By 2020, the share of those experiencing online *lashon ha-rah* had plateaued, but the gravity of the incidents had escalated. As one researcher put it, the proportion of those who "experienced more severe forms of harassment...or multiple forms of harassing behaviors online [has]...risen substantially in the past three years."[19]

There is, however, little evidence that the mandate to be exemplars in the field of *lashon ha-rah* has been embraced with determination by twenty-first-century Jews. Surveying major Jewish websites that permit public comment reveals that, with few exceptions, *lashon ha-rah* is rife. It is, moreover, difficult to assert that the social media feeds of Jews are characterized by speech restraints. Notwithstanding the magnified potential for damage to others, there does not seem to have been a concentrated Jewish effort to curb online *lashon ha-rah*. It is, however, hard to see how any sensitive application of Jewish thought could fail to emphasize the consequences of speech infractions that inflict so much online misery. But when it comes to digital *lashon ha-rah*, Jews seem to have acquiesced to the standards of surrounding society. Any form of Judaism that is concerned about the core issues of the digital age would do well to address cyber *lashon ha-rah* as a matter of high importance.

A third example of an area where Jewish wisdom could offer an alternative approach is in the area of hyper-individualism that trusts in the virtue of our inner selves and amplifies our self-importance. It is worth recalling the oft-repeated Hasidic teaching attributed to Rabbi Bunam: A balanced individual is one who has two pockets, each containing a note upon which is written a single sentence. On one note are the words "for my sake alone was the world created," while the second note contains the declaration that "I am nothing but dust and ashes." In the digital age, the message of the first note has been enthusiastically embraced, while the contents of the second note have largely been dismissed.

If humility is becoming rarer, while narcissistic tendencies are rising, then this trend is hardly compatible with Jewish values. Jewish tradition prefers that the ego occupies less space. One of the best-known lines about human duties comes from the prophet Micah: "God has told you what is good, and what the Lord requires of you—only to do justice and to love goodness, and to walk humbly [modestly] with your God" (Micah 6:8). The clear expectation is that our task is to promote the Divine agenda—with conscious humility. Judaism emphasizes that the Jewish role in the world is to engage in *Kedushat HaShem*, the sanctification of the Divine name, not our own names.

It is not by chance that the Torah stresses the great humility of Moses as his preeminent character trait. Nor can it be just happenstance that the Talmud gives priority to the positions of Beit Hillel because they taught their opponents' teachings and cited those with whom they disagreed before stating their own case (Eruvin 13b). As Elliot Dorff, professor of Jewish theology at the American Jewish University, expresses it:

Modesty is clearly an important value in Judaism. In the Bible and Rabbinic literature, it is a character trait associated with some of Judaism's most prominent representatives. Nobody was ever as humble as Moses. One should strive to be as humble as Hillel. Rabbi Judah the Prince, redactor of the Mishnah, was so humble that his disciples all failed to be like him in this virtue; as the Talmud puts it, "When Rebbe died, humility disappeared."[20]

The respect accorded to these prominent exemplars stems from the fact that their humility made them experts in the "dissipation of ego," and they modeled how to live in a way that "took up appropriate space."[21]

On today's social media platforms, there is little evidence that humility or "taking up appropriate space" are significant concerns. But while Moses, Hillel, and Judah HaNasi became prominent figures, each articulated a stance that eschewed self-promotion. Why is this important? Because humility is a measure of the balance between the attention paid to oneself and the attention paid to others. The more time we spend on self-promotion, the less time and space there is for other-promotion. It is hardly surprising that a society marked by hyper-individualism is a more shrill and less tolerant society, with large numbers unprepared to consider views that contradict their own. Humility is about questioning our individual importance and about seeking to highlight the worthy qualities of others. Humble people grant that positions with which they disagree nevertheless deserve a full hearing; they concede that there are other agendas beside their own that are worthy of attention. But if this is what humility is, then in the digital age humility is in retreat.

There is no noteworthy difference between Jews and non-Jews in this area; neither is there any meaningful effort to urge Jews to reign in self-referential tendencies. A cyber-age Judaism that seeks to communicate foundational Jewish priorities would likely conclude that emphasizing the value of humility—contra the trends of contemporary culture—could have a salutary effect. But these foundational Jewish ideas have not been translated into a concerted Jewish project.

There are, then, multiple areas where Jewish responses could be formulated to address some of the weighty challenges of our accelerating age. It would be a mistake, though, to conclude that Jewish initiatives should be limited to those behaviors that Jews might be prepared to adopt. Historically, the insights of Judaism were thought to be intended solely for Jews. Pushed to the margins of history, Jews lived apart. While Jewish ideas did permeate the surrounding civilization, this was not a design feature. Rabbinic literature prohibited teaching Torah to non-Jews and rejected the notion that non-Jews might assume their own version of

Shabbat or other quintessentially Jewish practices. The arrival of modernity did little to change this pattern. While Jews no longer lived separately and a greater awareness of Judaism grew, little consideration was given to the role of Judaism in broader society. Even contemplating this type of approach has generally seemed foreign to most Jews. Setting aside concerns about antisemitism, Jews have long been of the view that the wisdom of Jewish law is not supposed to be promoted beyond the Jewish people. Twenty-first-century technology has, however, enabled small groups to reach a global audience as never before. Moreover, for millions of non-Jews, it is no longer a given that the ideas of Judaism must ipso facto be unworthy, as was once the case.

This raises a peculiarly twenty-first-century question: Does Judaism offer solutions for human problems that might prove helpful beyond the Jewish people? Some will hold that the answer to this question is obvious. There are 613 commandments that apply to Jews, whereas non-Jews are expected to do no more than observe the seven Noahide laws.[22] But is it really that straightforward? If it is a Jewish aspiration that others might come to live by higher ethical standards as a result of Jewish modeling, does it not make sense to promote suitable Jewish insights more broadly? Is there not a certain logic to rethinking Jewish reticence in this area and, where it is welcome, disseminating Jewish ideas to a wider audience?

An example: In the US, the law does not require individuals to render assistance at the scene of an accident. Professionals who nevertheless decide to do so are shielded from liability by what are known as "Good Samaritan" laws.[23] By contrast, Israel has a law called the *Lo Ta'amod al Dam Rei'ekha Law* (you shall not stand idly by while your neighbor bleeds) which, based on an injunction in the Torah, explicitly requires that bystanders render assistance.[24] Clearly, from a Jewish standpoint, the Torah's legislation represents the ideal conduct. If Jewish law (as well as the law of Israel) stipulates conduct that is seen to be ethically prefered, does it not make sense for Jews to propose that the optimal approach should be the standard for all?

Hunting represents a further case in point. Hunting for recreational or sporting purposes is prohibited by Jewish authorities because of the gratuitous suffering of animals that is involved. The *halakhic* scholar Rabbi J. David Bleich wrote: "Jewish law clearly forbids any act which causes pain or discomfort to an animal unless such act is designed to satisfy a legitimate human need. All authorities agree that hunting as a sport is forbidden."[25] Plainly, though, it matters not one bit to the afflicted animal whether its anguish is caused by a Jew or a non-Jew. Indeed, one of the seven Noahide laws prohibits a non-Jew from consuming a limb torn from a live animal, presumably to limit cruelty and to promote a higher ethic. If, then, recreational hunting is forbidden to Jews because it represents an ethical transgression, why would the same reasoning not apply to non-Jewish conduct? If Judaism cares about the harm done to animals and aspires to raise ethical standards, it makes sense to oppose hunting for all.

There are additional illustrations. The climate crisis has led some to think about a wider application of the institution of *shmitah*, the sabbatical year commanded in the Torah (Exodus 23:10–11, Leviticus 25:1–7). From the perspective of Jewish tradition, *shmitah*—the "release" of the land or letting the land lie fallow—is an injunction that pertains only to Jews and is to be practiced only in the land of Israel. The permission for non-Jews to continue farming within Israel itself indicates that there is no intent that *shmitah* should be extended to other populations or locations.

Those who have attempted to discern the deeper significance of *shmitah* have, however, concluded that desisting from farming the land every seventh year can have salutary environmental effects. It can also offer a revitalized perspective on stewardship, given that *shmitah* emphasizes God's ownership of the land and is accompanied by the cancellation of loans made to the poor. Seen through this lens, *shmitah* becomes "a core Jewish value—one that, like Shabbat…has the power to transform society."[26] Those who view *shmitah* this way have taken steps to bring *shmitah* "from an obscure law dealt with mainly by Israel's Orthodox to a new Jewish ethos being discussed across the United States, Europe, Israel, and even on the floor of [the] Knesset."[27] Its proponents contend that *shmitah*, a particularistic commandment which was a niche Jewish practice for centuries, could become a response to contemporary global issues: "At a time when the world seems to be on fire—as we are inundated with…climate-change-induced meteorological havoc—*shmita* could become a part of the solution."[28]

There will be disagreements on the question of whether *shmitah* is well suited to dealing with our contemporary challenges. But the fundamental issue here is not about the merits of *shmitah* per se but rather about whether Jews should now begin mining Jewish concepts and practices with the aim of spreading them to a larger audience. Some will remain concerned that such a project might conflict with the rabbinic texts that restrict Jewish practice and learning to Jews. But Rabbi Yechiel Yaakov Weinberg in his *Seridei Eish* (2:55) holds that this prohibition does not apply to a non-Jew who "studies [the Torah] due to his love of wisdom and in order to familiarize himself with the Torah of Israel."[29] Writing in the early twentieth century, Rabbi Weinberg could not have envisaged the potential for propagating Jewish ideas that now exists. Perhaps, in the digital age, allowing the "Torah of Israel" to be imparted more widely not only might prove to have few substantive downsides but also could be a potent way to further Jewish goals. There can be little doubt that such an endeavor would go beyond the normative Jewish approach of modernity. The digital age offers intriguing possibilities for Jewish concepts and ideas to have a greater influence on the global agenda.

In the long run, it will not be the job of Reform or Conservative Judaism to respond to the challenges of the digital revolution or to fashion new Jewish directions. Even if the movements of modernity were to attempt to take on these tasks, they would be less than ideal vehicles. Their understandable historic impulse to help Jews adapt to their environment is not the appropriate toolkit for the digital age. They are like the film manufacturer, Kodak: While the people who once worked at Kodak moved on to live and prosper in a digital world, Kodak itself was not suited to make the leap. Built for a different age, Kodak is remembered as an icon of modernity that recorded innumerable "Kodak moments" in the nineteenth and twentieth centuries. But Kodak, once so dominant, could not be repurposed for the Internet era. So it is for the Conservative and Reform movements. Their DNA comes from a different time.

History has moved on. The movements of modernity have tried valiantly to adapt by embracing new technology platforms, streamlining their organizational structures, becoming more telegenic, and reimagining synagogue models and offerings. They have become inclusive, welcoming, and committed to diversity. They have adjusted to the cultural outlook of contemporary Jews. They have sought to rethink affiliation models, time demands, and financial expectations. These efforts have been commendable. But they represent updated "engagement strategies," while the core content has remained much the same. Modernity may be gone, but Reform and Conservative Judaism are still held in its thrall, still eager to embrace the surrounding culture and to help Jews feel at home in it. The movements of modernity have websites and Facebook pages, Twitter feeds, and Zoom accounts, but they lack a comprehensive response to the manifestly different mindset of our emergent age.

The digital era connects much of the planet via an information platform of unprecedented breadth and openness. For Jews, modernity was chiefly about integration and incorporation. As we have seen, the major hurdles of the age revolved around how Jews could fit into the societies of the nascent nation states and how Judaism itself could accommodate novel intellectual disciplines. The questions of the digital age are almost the inverse: When total integration, at least for individuals, is presumed, should any boundaries remain sacrosanct in the name of community, identity, or culture? When atomization is a palpable and expanding phenomenon, what will bind those human atoms together? When all ideas and every moral viewpoint can be accessed and entertained, does following a set path or accepting a particular narrative make sense? In an age epitomized by mobility and aspiration are limits desirable, and if so, how should they be established and who should determine what they are? In short, viewed from a Jewish perspective, the digital age is no longer about adapting Jews and Judaism to a slowly opening world of belonging and enlightenment; it is about asking how human beings should optimally function within the cacophonous tumult of an accelerating epoch of hyper-emancipation, hyper-connectivity, and hyper-individualism.

This altered vista cannot be incorporated with equanimity into existing forms of Judaism. New vehicles will be required. It is important to emphasize that while the nature of the journey will change, the destination will not. The core elements of Jewish life and thought will remain—engaging with God, Torah, Israel, Jewish law, and Jewish time, as translated into patterns of living structured by *mitzvah, halakhah*, and mores. As was true throughout Jewish history, thoughtful encapsulations of Judaism will still begin with the question: "What does the tradition that emerges from Torah expect of us?" The answer is not to make Jews feel comfortable and safe in the world or to help Jews adapt to their environment. Rather, it is to sanctify God's name and to increase *tzedakah u'mishpat*, righteousness, and justice, through conduct that is worthy of a discerning people. Reaching these goals will require focusing on how Judaism might optimally function within a digital society in order to hone civilization itself.

Through the millennia, Jewish texts have discussed how to promote human flourishing within unanticipated circumstances, thereby allowing Jews to apply the accumulated wisdom of the ages to periods of flux. Given the nature of the questions that now confront humanity, there is an opening for Jewish thought to generate ideas that are capable of improving the human condition in this complex era. Indeed, it is conceivable that the relevance of Judaism and the contributions it could make might well be enhanced in the years ahead. Addressing these matters in a timely fashion is particularly pressing because the "great acceleration" is not slowing down. In fact, the transformed landscape is by no means static; to the contrary, the road ahead is about to head directly into terra incognita.

Notes

1. Naim, *The End of Power*, 11.
2. Ibid., 69.
3. Tom Wujec of Autodesk, as quoted in Friedman, *Thank You for Being Late*, 106.
4. Andrea Fowler, "8 Special People To Consider Having Officiate Your Wedding Ceremony," *The Knot*, accessed August 1, 2022, https://www.theknot.com/content/people-to-consider-for-officiant
5. "A Bohemian DIY Wedding at Leroux Creek Inn and Vineyards in Hotchkiss, Colorado," *The Knot*, accessed August 1, 2022, https://www.theknot.com/real-weddings/a-bohemian-diy-wedding-at-leroux-creek-inn-and-vineyards-in-hotchkiss-colorado-album
6. Emma Green, "We're Headed Toward One of the Greatest Divisions in the History of the Jewish People," *The Atlantic*, July 16, 2017, accessed August 1, 2022, https://www.theatlantic.com/politics/archive/2017/07/intermarriage-conservative-judaism/533637/
7. In this context, it is worth thinking about current popular terminology: "Innovation" is in vogue; "entrepreneurs" are highly prized; "startups" and "thinking outside the box" are applauded. All these terms express a desire to move beyond previous authority structures, and they all laud a mode of thinking that bespeaks an unlimited number of possible outcomes.
8. Anna Greenberg, "Grande Soy Vanilla Latte with Cinnamon, No Foam… Jewish Identity and Community in a Time of Unlimited Choices," *Reboot*, 2006, accessed August 1, 2022, http://www.acbp.net/pdf/pdfs-research-and-publications/Latte%20Report%202006.pdf, 7.
9. "These and those"—Tractate Eruvin 13b records: "For three years there was a dispute between Beit Shammai and Beit Hillel, the former asserting that '*halacha* is in accordance with our views,' and the latter contending that '*halacha* is in accordance with our views.' Eventually, a *bat kol* (heavenly voice) rang out and announced: 'these and those are both the words of the living God—both views represent a valid understanding of Torah law—but in practice, the halacha follows Beit Hillel."
10. David Golinkin, "A Responsum Regarding the Right to Privacy," *Responsa in a Moment*: Volume 1, Issue No. 4, December 2006, accessed August 1, 2022, https://schechter.edu/a-responsum-regarding-the-right-to-privacy-responsa-in-a-moment-volume-1-issue-no-4-december-2006/

11. Aviad Hacohen and Gabi Siboni, "Ubiquitous Presence: Protecting Privacy and Forbidding Intrusion into a Person's Records in Jewish Law," *Cyber, Intelligence, and Security*, Volume 2, Number 3, December 2018, p. 24, accessed August 1, 2022, https://www.inss.org.il/wp-content/uploads/2019/01/Hacohen-Siboni.pdf

12. Ibid.

13. Asher Meir, "Internet Privacy in *Halakhah*," *"Jewish Action,"* Winter 2014, accessed August 1, 2022, https://jewishaction.com/religion/jewish-law/internet-privacy-halachah/

14. Ibid.

15. Jerry Adler, "Smile, Frown, Grimace and Grin–Your Facial Expression Is the Next Frontier in Big Data," *Smithsonian Magazine*, December 2015, accessed August 1, 2022, http://www.smithsonianmag.com/innovation/rana-el-kalioubi-ingenuity-awards-technology-180957204/?no-ist

16. Maimonides, *Mishnah Torah, Hilchot De'ot*, 7:5.

17. Chofetz Chayim, Part One, *The Prohibition Against Lashon Hara*, Principle 1:8.

18. Monica Anderson, "Key takeaways on how Americans view—and experience—online harassment," Pew Research Center, July 11, 2017, accessed August 1, 2022, https://www.pewresearch.org/fact-tank/2017/07/11/key-takeaways-online-harassment/

19. Drew Desilver, "Q&A: What we've learned about online harassment," Pew Research Center, January 13, 2021, accessed August 1, 2022, https://www.pewresearch.org/fact-tank/2021/01/13/qa-what-weve-learned-about-online-harassment/

20. Elliot Dorff, "Modest Communication," Teshuvah of the Committee of Jewish Law and Standards, June 19, 2019, accessed August 1, 2022, https://www.rabbinicalassembly.org/sites/default/files/modest_speech.final.june.pdf

21. David Booth, Ashira Konigsburg, and Baruch Frydman-Kohl, "Modesty Inside and Out: A Contemporary Guide to Tzniut," Teshuvah of the Committee of Jewish Law and Standards, February 2, 2017, accessed August 1, 2022, https://www.rabbinicalassembly.org/sites/default/files/modesty_final.pdf

22. The "Talmudic designation for seven biblical laws given to Adam and to Noah…and consequently binding on all mankind. Beginning with Genesis 2:16, the Babylonian Talmud listed the first six commandments as prohibitions against idolatry, blasphemy, murder, adultery, and robbery and the positive command to establish courts of justice (with all that this implies). After the Flood a seventh commandment, given to Noah, forbade the eating of flesh cut from a living animal (Gen. 9:4)." See "Noahide Laws,"

Britannica, accessed August 1, 2022, https://www.britannica.com/topic/Noahide-Laws

23. Brian West and Matthew Varacallo, "Good Samaritan Laws," National Center for Biotechnology Information, September 20, 2020, accessed August 1, 2022, https://www.ncbi.nlm.nih.gov/books/NBK542176/

24. David Schonberg (translator) "*Lo Ta'amod 'Al Dam Re'ekha*," ASSAI–Vol IV, No 1, February 2001, accessed August 1, 2022, http://www.daat. ac.il/daat/kitveyet/assia_english/porat-1.htm

25. J. David Bleich, "Judaism and Animal Experimentation," *Tradition*, 22(1), Rabbinical Council of America, Spring, 1986, 22.

26. David Krantz, "*Shmita* Revolution: The Reclamation and Reinvention of the Sabbatical Year," *MDPI*, August 8, 2016, accessed August 1, 2022, https://www.mdpi.com/2077-1444/7/8/100, 1.

27. Ibid.

28. Ibid., 25.

29. David Brofsky, "The Conversion Candidate during the Process of Converting," Torat Har Etzion, December 19, 2019, accessed August 1, 2022, https://etzion.org.il/en/halakha/yoreh-deah/topics-yoreh-deah/conversion-candidate-during-process-converting

References

A Bohemian DIY Wedding at Leroux Creek Inn and Vineyards in Hotchkiss, Colorado, *The Knot*, accessed August 1, 2022, https://www.theknot.com/real-weddings/a-bohemian-diy-wedding-at-leroux-creek-inn-and-vineyards-in-hotchkiss-colorado-album.

Adler, Jerry. "Smile, Frown, Grimace and Grin–Your Facial Expression Is the Next Frontier in Big Data," *Smithsonian Magazine*, December 2015, accessed August 1, 2022, http://www.smithsonianmag.com/innovation/rana-el-kaliouby-ingenuity-awards-technology-180957204/?no-ist.

Anderson, Monica. "Key takeaways on how Americans view—and experience—online harassment," Pew Research Center, July 11, 2017, accessed August 1, 2022, https://www.pewresearch.org/fact-tank/2017/07/11/key-takeaways-online-harassment/.

Bleich, J. David. "Judaism and Animal Experimentation," *Tradition*, 22(1), Rabbinical Council of America, Spring, 1986.

Booth, David; Konigsburg, Ashira and Frydman-Kohl, Baruch. "Modesty Inside and Out: A Contemporary Guide to Tzniut," Teshuvah of the Committee of Jewish Law and Standards, February 2, 2017, accessed August 1, 2022, https://www.rabbinicalassembly.org/sites/default/files/modesty_final.pdf.

Brofsky, David. "The Conversion Candidate during the Process of Converting," Torat Har Etzion, December 19, 2019, accessed August 1, 2022, https://

etzion.org.il/en/halakha/yoreh-deah/topics-yoreh-deah/conversion-candidate-during-process-converting.

Chofetz Chayim, n.d. Part One, *The Prohibition Against Lashon Hara*, Principle 1:8.

Desilver, Drew. "Q&A: What we've learned about online harassment," Pew Research Center, January 13, 2021, accessed August 1, 2022, https://www.pewresearch.org/fact-tank/2021/01/13/qa-what-weve-learned-about-online-harassment/e

Dorff, Elliot. "Modest Communication," Teshuvah of the Committee of Jewish Law and Standards, June 19, 2019, accessed August 1, 2022, https://www.rabbinicalassembly.org/sites/default/files/modest_speech.final.june.pdf.

Fowler, Andrea. "8 Special People to Consider Having Officiate Your Wedding Ceremony," *The Knot*, accessed August 1, 2022, https://www.theknot.com/content/people-to-consider-for-officiant.

Friedman, Thomas. *Thank You for Being Late: An Optimist's Guide to Thriving in the Age of Accelerations*. New York, Farrar, Straus and Giroux, 2016.

Golinkin, David. "A Responsum Regarding the Right to Privacy," *Responsa in a Moment*: Volume 1, Issue No. 4, December 2006, accessed August 1, 2022, https://schechter.edu/a-responsum-regarding-the-right-to-privacy-responsa-in-a-moment-volume-1-issue-no-4-december-2006/.

Green, Emma. "We're Headed Toward One of the Greatest Divisions in the History of the Jewish People," *The Atlantic*, July 16, 2017, accessed August 1, 2022, https://www.theatlantic.com/politics/archive/2017/07/intermarriage-conservative-judaism/533637/.

Greenberg, Anna. "Grande Soy Vanilla Latte with Cinnamon, No Foam… Jewish Identity and Community in a Time of Unlimited Choices," *Reboot*, 2006, accessed August 1, 2022, http://www.acbp.net/pdf/pdfs-research-and-publications/Latte%20Report%202006.pdf.

Hacohen, Aviad and Siboni, Gabi. "Ubiquitous Presence: Protecting Privacy and Forbidding Intrusion into a Person's Records in Jewish Law." *Cyber, Intelligence, and Security*, Volume 2, Number 3, December 2018, p. 24, accessed August 1, 2022, https://www.inss.org.il/wp-content/uploads/2019/01/Hacohen-Siboni.pdf.

Krantz, David. "*Shmita* Revolution: The Reclamation and Reinvention of the Sabbatical Year" Religions 7, 2016: no. 8: 100.

Maimonides, n.d. *Mishnah Torah, Hilchot De'ot*, 7:5.

Meir, Asher. "Internet Privacy in *Halakhah*," "*Jewish Action*," Winter 2014, accessed August 1, 2022, https://jewishaction.com/religion/jewish-law/internet-privacy-halachah/.

Naim, Moses. *The End of Power*. New York, Basic Books, 2013.

Noahide Laws, *Britannica*, accessed August 1, 2022, https://www.britannica.com/topic/Noahide-Laws.

Schonberg, David. (translator) "*Lo Ta'amod 'Al Dam Re'ekha*," ASSAI–Vol IV, No 1, February 2001, accessed August 1, 2022, http://www.daat.ac.il/daat/kitveyet/assia_english/porat-1.htm.

West, Brian and Varacallo, Matthew. "Good Samaritan Laws," National Center for Biotechnology Information, September 20, 2020, accessed August 1, 2022, https://www.ncbi.nlm.nih.gov/books/NBK542176/.

CHAPTER 6

The Future

HYPER-ETHICS

There is every reason to believe that the technological and civilizational changes that will unfold over the next several decades will be far more momentous than those which have transpired since 1990. The human brain is structured to anticipate that life will proceed along a linear path, making it hard to grasp that the gradual changes that marked every previous epoch have now been replaced by progress on an exponential scale. Ray Kurzweil has observed that the first fourteen years of the twenty-first century produced as much technological progress as did the entire twentieth century. In Kurzweil's view, it is reasonable to expect that in the course of the twenty-first century we will witness 1000 times as much technological progress as occurred throughout the twentieth century.[1] Quantum leaps forward will become commonplace. This has significant implications. One thousand years ago, predicting what the world would be like fifty years in the future was reasonably easy. Regimes might come and go, but the nature of individual life remained much the same. Today, we can be certain that very little about the world fifty years from now is likely to look anything like the present.

The future, then, will bring with it a systemic challenge. Juan Enriquez, an academic and expert in the life sciences, describes the hurdle succinctly: "We are in an age of exponentially changing technologies. Ergo, we are in an age of exponentially changing ethics."[2] Exponentially changing ethics.

D. Schiff, *Judaism in a Digital Age*, https://doi.org/10.1007/978-3-031-17992-1_6

Let's call it *hyper-ethics*. Jewish ethical responses, it is worth recalling, are not cast in stone. The Torah, by way of illustration, regarded levirate marriage (marriage of a widow to the brother of her deceased husband) as an appropriate practice; today's arbiters of Jewish law see levirate marriage differently. Attitudinal changes of this type and magnitude used to take place over centuries. In the course of one lifetime, there might have been one or two significant ethical reappraisals, and they would have occurred gradually. Hence, ethics felt largely fixed. Like the layout of the streets in the city in which one grew up, a road might be reconfigured occasionally, or a new one built, but this was relatively rare. The street grid was a given—once it was firmly set in one's mind, it could be traversed assuredly for decades.

No longer. The arrival of hyper-ethics rewrites the ethics rule book. Enriquez describes it this way: "What we consider to be right, ethical, and normal is changing at an unprecedented speed. Some of the pillars of certainty, of faith, of what we have held to be self-evident and eternal truths have shifted—and they continue to shift rapidly."[3] Our new reality looks like this: In the span of a few decades, the norms around dating, sexuality, marriage, and childbearing have already changed more than once. And these rapid transitions are not limited to relationship ethics. It is like opening the door one morning to find that the city grid has been rearranged— and having that happen several times during your life in all parts of town. Not only does it make remembering how to navigate difficult, but it makes ethics seem flexible and malleable rather than stable and certain. Who knows what the right way to go might be next year? Additionally, hyper-ethics means that each emerging area of technology requires ethical consideration of its own. No stream of Judaism can be shielded from these disruptions. Jewish thinkers need to grapple with the reality that ethics has become an area that is no longer slow and steady; rather, ethics are now subject to repeated, swift recalculations.

Adding to the complication is the fact that our technological prowess is on a far faster track than our capacity for ethical deliberation. To illustrate: Scientists are currently working on "gene drive" technology that will wipe out whole populations of insects, such as mosquitoes carrying the Zika virus. There are, however, questions about the wisdom of employing the technology. One skeptical researcher observed, "I'm sure we'll be able to do it before people can agree if we should."[4] In a hyper-ethical world, the time frame for engaging in critical ethical deliberations is shortening, even as the agenda of urgent ethical discussions is lengthening. Under such conditions, the urge to simply go ahead and use available technologies often wins the day.

In addition to hyper-ethics, new fundamental questions have arisen about the sources of our ethics. Do our ethical responses emerge from sacred texts, from the power of reason, or are they simply fashioned around the practical realities of what is possible and seems unobjectionable? Enriquez makes a powerful case that technology itself is decisive in molding ethics: "One of the biggest drivers of ethical upheaval and change is technology. Technology provides alternatives that can fundamentally alter our notion of what is Right and Wrong."[5] Enriquez postulates, for example, that the abolition of slavery owed far more to the fact that industrialization obviated the need for human labor than it did to a virtuous commitment to rectifying a fundamental wrong.[6] Technology also reshaped sexual ethics, with the pill yielding the sexual revolution and in vitro fertilization (IVF) decoupling conception from intercourse. Looking forward a few years to the time when renewable energies become cheaper than hydrocarbons, Enriquez suggests that our attitudes to those who burn fossil fuels will likely take a decidedly negative turn.[7] This insight—that technology is a primary driver behind ethics—helps clarify why ethical transformation has gone into overdrive since the digital age began. As we rapidly assimilate new technologies into our lives, those technologies are, in turn, redrawing the boundaries of our ethics.

All of this prompts the question of whether inherited traditions from centuries ago can maintain relevance as ethical perceptions change at breakneck speed. Enriquez points out that to go to an archeology museum, is to walk "through room after room full of dead gods." This, he posits, is because "most religions refuse to recognize that ethics can and do change," and hence they are "lousy" at evolving and learning, such that "99 percent of all religions went extinct or are seriously endangered."[8] In previous ages this "religion extinction" process happened slowly. But the pace may well be faster in the years ahead. Enriquez holds that the only way that a religion can survive is if it is prepared to reevaluate and revisit its ethical stances in a manner that is relevant to today's ethics conversations.

If, though, technology is driving ethics, then ethics can hardly be regarded as a thoughtful vision of what truly constitutes the highest good. Rather, according to this view, ethics is more an expression of what is available, affordable, and seemingly benign to a large number of people. This implies that ethics is more reactive than proactive: Our ethics take form as a response to what is technologically possible, rather than as an attempt to steer technological developments according to a predetermined set of ideals. But the fact that technology often yields positive ethical advances does not mean that this is always the case. If one of the effects of the contraceptive pill was to make consenting sexual relationships with somebody one has just met ethically acceptable, it is not obvious that this constitutes an ethical advance. Is it plausible that those who hold that sex belongs in marriage are behaving in an ethically inferior way to those who take a freer approach? Or is the reverse the case? The pill certainly changed what was ethically permissible, but the technology did not necessarily result in an outcome that represented a definitive ethical improvement. Social media is another case in point: As noted previously, notwithstanding the prodigious gains in our ability to interact, algorithm-driven social media platforms appear to have made less ethically appealing conduct normative.

It follows that it is not enough to hold that our ethics are largely driven by technology and that there is little to be done but sit back and wait to see where the ride takes us. There are numerous instances where a sound philosophy of what is right and wrong needs to precede any decision to permit a particular technology. Take the case of autonomous weapons systems driven by AI: While AI might indeed "make the battlefield a safer place for military personnel," there is a real potential that weapons guided by encoded instructions could result in horrendous loss of life.[9] As a result, there are those who advocate that such autonomous weapons technology should be banned before it can be used. Note the prioritization. Demonstrating that a particular technology does not undermine human well-being is a necessary condition for its activation. This might seem obvious when discussing technologies that could lead to multiple human deaths. But human well-being involves ethical concerns that are far broader than life and death issues. We cannot simply rely on technology automatically leading to a more virtuous world or assume that societal responses to new technologies will inevitably produce positive ethical results.

Indeed, if we do not devote sufficient thought to the ethics of technologies prior to their use, it seems certain that we will, at times, end up with untoward outcomes. David Zvi Kalman, a Fellow at the Shalom Hartman Institute, describes the predicament this way:

> There's a new technology in town. A few years ago it seemed like a pipe dream, but it's now arrived on the commercial market in a big way. Large corporations are lining up to use it even as watchdogs point out serious

potential for abuse. Reporters look into it, agree that there's a problem, and pen dozens of articles fretting about the downsides, demanding regulation and responsible use. The public grows concerned, and then they grow resigned. Meanwhile, the technology is adopted. Sometimes it is well regulated, more often it is not. There are a few horror stories. We learn to live with it. We move on. This is the ethical life cycle of modern technology, and its major problem is that it doesn't know how to distinguish between technologies that complicate morality and those that destroy it—that is, it lacks the ability to say no, absolutely not.[10]

Therein lies one of the critical predicaments of the internet age. We lack "the ability to say no, absolutely not." We "learn to live with it" and we "move on." We develop "work arounds" to cope with the reality that we have permitted. The technological imperative overwhelms us. Soon we forget that the road not taken may have been preferable. It is like never saying "no" to a child. We adjust to deal with the problematic nature of the resultant adult. But the circumstances are less than optimal, and we live with the awareness that saying "no" at an earlier stage could have made the outcome far better.

Kalman cites facial recognition technology (FRT) as a prime example of the problem: FRT "has continued to rapidly develop and proliferate across different sectors of society despite the certainty that it will be used for abusive and dehumanizing purposes."[11] There may be, states Kalman, "some universe in which the benefits of facial recognition could outweigh the dangers, but it isn't this one."[12] After all, Kalman reminds us, "Technologies like facial recognition are integral to the functioning of China's police state and its imprisonment of hundreds of thousands of Uighurs in forced labor and 'reeducation' camps."[13] Given the scope of the facial recognition data that is already in the hands of governments and technology companies, Kalman contends that the abusive possibilities decisively outweigh the advantages. Kalman concludes that FRT "should have no place in our society whatsoever."[14] But it is almost certainly too late. Not only has the technology been adopted, but there are already signs of an "ethics shift" underway: One commentator wrote that if "citizens willingly permit widespread use of FRT…an argument could be made that they no longer have any reasonable expectation of facial privacy."[15] In other words, notwithstanding the ethical concerns, the fact that many have accepted FRT without complaint is taken as evidence that FRT must be acceptable. If this "argument from silence" is correct, then it means that the public has come to regard what Kalman deems to be a fundamentally dehumanizing technology as being ethically unobjectionable.

Having a coherent theory about what is considered right and wrong and what practices might lead to dehumanization is, therefore, critical for scrutinizing proposed technologies before they are deployed. Emerging technologies might well shape some of our ethics, but that does not obviate the need to have a sound *a priori* ethical framework that can evaluate technologies before they begin to change us. Enriquez acknowledges as much. He suggests that "civilians" should oversee the work of technology companies engaged in shaping algorithms and AI because "human decisions and biases underlie the design and output."[16] But arriving at the best decisions and correcting human biases can only be achieved within an accompanying framework of values that tells us what to prioritize and what to reject. There are good reasons, as Enriquez states, "to apply tough scrutiny… [Because] the choices we make today will determine the future of humanity. Literally."[17]

WHERE ARE WE HEADED?

We can already begin to see how tomorrow's "street grid" is about to be rearranged. The predictions concerning what will happen are eye-opening:

Kurzweil points to three primary areas that are poised to alter the nature of human life fundamentally. The first is the genetic revolution. Having mapped the human genome, we are gaining ever greater understanding of the human genetic structure and how the "software" of life functions. Unlike the hit-and-miss approach of the past, medicine is fast becoming an information science, which will soon yield effective, highly personalized treatments. Gene suppression, enhancement, and repair will become standard, as will drugs that are designed to target the disease of one individual, and the "therapeutic cloning of rejuvenated cells, tissues, and organs."[18] Replacement of body parts, custom manufactured from stem cells, will allow for physical repairs that were previously in the realm of fantasy.

Kurzweil's second area is that of nanotechnology, which has the capacity to create machines that are smaller than 100 nanometers across.[19] According to Kurzweil, the shrinking of machines has proceeded along a relatively predictable curve: The amount of computing power that once occupied a large room now fits comfortably inside a cellphone, so computers that were the size of a cellphone will soon shrink to the size of a blood cell. This means that sophisticated computing devices and microscopic drug delivery vehicles—all connected to the cloud—will become normal features inside our bodies. They will also transform the essence of human life:

> The implementation of artificial intelligence in our biological systems will mark an evolutionary leap forward for humanity, but it also implies we will indeed become more "machine" than "human." Billions of nanobots will travel through the bloodstream in our bodies and brains. In our bodies, they will destroy pathogens, correct DNA errors, eliminate toxins, and perform many other tasks to enhance our physical well-being. As a result, we will be able to live indefinitely without aging.[20]

The potential lifespan, Kurzweil postulates, will have no effective limit. The greatest impact of nanotechnology will center on the brain. Currently, our cellphones effectively operate as "brain extenders," hooking us into vast networks that aid our memory and enhance our knowledge. Soon, though, the computing functions of a cellphone will likely become an internal brain "add-on":

> The most important and radical application particularly of circa-2030 nanobots will be to expand our minds through the merger of biological and nonbiological, or "machine," intelligence... [W]e will learn how to augment our 100 trillion very slow interneuronal connections with high-speed virtual connections via nano-robotics. This will allow us to greatly boost our pattern-recognition abilities, memories, and overall thinking capacity, as well as to directly interface with powerful forms of computer intelligence. The technology will also provide wireless communication from one brain to another... [T]his intimate connection between our biological thinking and the machine intelligence we are creating will profoundly expand human intelligence.[21]

Even if Kurzweil is only partially correct in this assessment, his prediction portends that we will incorporate an increasing number of nonorganic parts within us and that our brains will be enhanced in ways that will markedly transcend our current capacities.

Kurzweil's third area is that of robotics and AI. Self-driving vehicles will be the tip of the iceberg. Robots that perform a wide range of physical and non-physical tasks and serve a multiplicity of human needs will be ubiquitous. These robots will become sufficiently responsive that humans will increasingly develop relationships with them. Robots will alter our current understanding of work and leisure and how we occupy our time. At some point in the second half of the twenty-first century, robot intelligence—albeit qualitatively different from human intelligence—will come to vastly exceed our own. Kurzweil describes the turning point this way:

> We are very close to the day when fully biological humans (as we now know them) cease to be the dominant intelligence on the planet. By the end of this century, computational or mechanical intelligence will be trillions of times more powerful than unaided human brain power... Artificial intelligence will necessarily exceed human intelligence...[because] machines can share knowledge and communicate with one another far more efficiently than can humans.[22]

Unimpeded by the evolutionary quirks of the human brain, AI will have immense problem-solving powers, as well as the capacity to act on its "conclusions."

Those who are cautious about the predictions of a futurist like Kurzweil might prefer an alternative perspective: In his book *Sapiens*, Yuval Harari, professor of history at The Hebrew University in Jerusalem, frames his view of the future in the context of the past,[23] leading to predictions similar to Kurzweil's. Harari forecasts that—probably within decades, a couple of centuries at most—*Homo sapiens* will disappear. He is not suggesting that we will destroy ourselves, but rather that we will upgrade to a different kind of being. We will produce what will amount to a new species utilizing three pathways: "biological engineering, cyborg engineering (cyborgs are beings that combine organic with non-organic parts), or the engineering of inorganic life."[24]

What Harari refers to as "biological engineering" is essentially congruent with Kurzweil's "genetic revolution." Harari holds that we are presently using but "a fraction of the potential of genetic engineering,"[25] and the road ahead will make all our previous endeavors in this field look like "child's play." In a few decades, biological engineering will probably "make far-reaching alterations not only to our physiology, immune system and life expectancy, but also to our intellectual and emotional capacities."[26] Harari points out that the human genome is only 14 percent larger than the mouse genome, and we have already succeeded in creating mice with improved memories and upgraded learning skills. It is probably only a matter of time before we will be able to overcome the technological barriers to doing the same, and much more, in humans:

The Cognitive Revolution that turned Homo sapiens from an insignificant ape into the master of the world did not require any noticeable change in physiology or even in the size and external shape of the Sapiens brain. It apparently involved no more than a few small changes to internal brain structure. Perhaps another small change would be enough to ignite a Second Cognitive Revolution, create a completely new type of consciousness, and transform Homo sapiens into something altogether different. True, we still don't have the acumen to achieve this, but there seems to be no insurmountable technical barrier preventing us from producing superhumans.[27]

Cyborg engineering is Harari's second pathway through which we will "change the laws of life." Millions of people use glasses, pacemakers, and hearing aids to supplement their natural organs. Soon, inorganic add-ons will become far more extensive. Harari describes bionic limbs that are now being fitted to those who have lost arms or legs. Through neural signals, translated by micro-computers, humans have already successfully operated these limbs by thought alone. Currently, these inorganic limbs are not as capable as their organic counterparts, but they will soon come to be their equal, and before long the day will arrive when these limbs will be able to lift weights and perform movements that their organic counterparts cannot.

Like Kurzweil, Harari posits that the most profound outcome of cyborg engineering will be its application to the brain. He describes the work being done to develop a "brain to computer interface" that will allow the brain to read signals from a computer directly and computers to access the information in our brains. He speculates about what might happen if this allows us to tap into the memories of others, not just as information, but as memories that could be experienced by the recipient:

> What happens to concepts such as the self and gender identity when minds become collective? How could you know thyself or follow your dream if the dream is not in your mind but in some collective reservoir of aspirations? Such a cyborg would no longer be human, or even organic. It would be something completely different. It would be so fundamentally another kind of being that we cannot even grasp the philosophical, psychological or political implications.[28]

Even if the specific technologies that Harari describes do not come to fruition, it seems reasonable to posit that, in one way or another, humans will venture further into the cyborg realm with all the attendant "philosophical, psychological and political" issues that such a move portends.

The third pathway Harari foresees is the creation of "inorganic life." He writes that we may be getting close to fashioning inorganic beings that could constitute life. For example, computer viruses might be programmed with a random mutation that could enable them to transform themselves, "evolve" in unpredictable ways, and take on a life of their own. Ultimately, this might result in the creation of a brain that "runs" on a computer utilizing sophisticated software. This would be a breakthrough of immense proportions: "If successful, that would mean that after 4 billion years of milling around inside the small world of organic compounds, life will suddenly break out into the vastness of the inorganic realm, ready to take up shapes beyond our wildest dreams."[29] If this actually comes to be, it would challenge our understandings of what it is that constitutes life itself.

In his book, *Homo Deus*, Harari presents three propositions which, in his view, already have broad support:

1. Science is converging on an all-encompassing dogma, which says that organisms are algorithms and life is data processing.

2. Intelligence is decoupling from consciousness.

3. Non-conscious but highly intelligent algorithms may soon know us better than we know ourselves.[30]

The first proposition holds that everything humans experience, including all our thoughts, emotions, and sensations, is the product of extraordinarily complex and sophisticated "biochemical data-processing" algorithms.[31] Broadly defined, an algorithm is "a methodical set of steps that can be used to make calculations, resolve problems and reach decisions."[32] From Harari's standpoint, this means that ascribing any independent reality to such concepts as God, religion, or souls is fanciful. Human functioning and thoughts are the products of the biochemical algorithms that govern us. Nothing more. It follows that religious precepts are essentially stories that do not describe anything that actually exists. Harari goes further: The tenets of humanism that were so emblematic of modernity are also artificial. Concepts like human free will, autonomy, individuality, or sanctity are also just elegant fictions. In truth, we are inexorably driven by pre-programmed algorithms that make us little different from the rest of the animal world. Ultimately, according to this view, the algorithms that control us could potentially be analyzed, broken down into their component parts, and modified.

Harari's second proposition that "intelligence is decoupling from consciousness" is less unsettling. Historically, we have tended to regard conscious beings as possessing superior intelligence to those without consciousness. Harari makes the case that the development of intelligent algorithms means that consciousness is not necessary for superior intelligence: The fact that a taxi driver is conscious and can appreciate his surroundings is of no value when it comes to the task of transporting his passengers from one point to the next. Indeed, it is likely that a self-driving vehicle with "knowledge" of the road features, the surrounding vehicles, and the traffic conditions ahead has greater "intelligence" for the purpose of getting passengers efficiently and safely from one point to the next than does a conscious driver.[33] Today, many intelligent algorithms are already an indispensable part of our environment. Collectively, they represent a form of "intelligence" that is unattainable by individual humans, yet no consciousness is involved.

Harari's third point that highly intelligent algorithms may soon know us better than we know ourselves requires no leap of imagination. According to one study, it is already true that "if you happen to have clicked 300 Likes on your Facebook account, the Facebook algorithm can predict your opinions and desires better than your husband or wife."[34] In the view of the researchers, the day will likely come when we will consult algorithms to make a host of critical life decisions, including selecting a life partner, because the algorithms will know more about us and our fellow humans than we ever could.[35] Harari holds that once the algorithms have access to data from medical sensors within our bodies and can combine this information with an accurate understanding of our psychological and emotional states, they will indeed know more about us than we do. At that point, it will be questionable whether humans are the highest form of intelligence on Earth.

Beyond the perspectives of a futurist and a historian, Juan Enriquez and the life sciences academic and entrepreneur Steve Gullans offer another angle. They emphasize that their account of where technology is headed is not science fiction but "based on science fact." Grounding their work in advances that have already occurred, they seek to chart how these discoveries will "profoundly change tomorrow."[36] Enriquez and Gullans concur with Harari's view that *Homo sapiens* will, within decades, become a different species. They use the term *Homo evolutis* to denote the fact that, for the first time in history, humans have the capacity to oversee our own evolution. Whereas Darwin's view of evolution posited a process of natural selection and random mutation, humans have already instituted unnatural selection and nonrandom mutation. According to Enriquez and Gullans, "half the landmass on Earth is now covered by what humans want, not by what would naturally grow without the intervention of our species."[37] Humans have transformed crops, animals, and the natural environment to suit our purposes and serve our needs and desires in a process of "unnatural" selection that would have shocked Darwin.[38] The move from a natural process that was once random and slow to a designed one that is "rapid, deliberate, and intelligent" represents a pivotal transition.

In the digital realm, remarkable developments came about through software—by encoding instructions using ones and zeros. The "evolution revolution" promises to be no less dramatic: DNA, the double helix that stores genetic information, is structured with a four-letter toolbox—nature has "written the entire language of life using four chemical letters: G, C, A and T."[39] It follows that if life is essentially coded, then it too can be engineered, and the human capacity to accomplish this is developing quickly: "Our ability to read, copy, and rewrite life code now accelerates faster than Moore's law for improvements in computers, making it ever faster and cheaper to redesign flowers, develop exotic foods, build bacteria to manufacture therapeutics, and design animals that serve and entertain."[40] Enriquez and Gullans postulate that we are moving toward a future that will allow us to tackle many diseases and to extend life. It will also open the door to upgrading humans in a way that will make "today's plastic surgery, corrections, deletions, augmentations, and enhancements...seem most tame."[41] These "corrections" may even come to be seen as necessary. Humans, for example, may well pursue a range of physical enhancements to facilitate the ability to live on other planets. According to Enriquez, this might not only be a worthwhile step but one that will be required: given "that extinctions are common and natural" on Earth, it might well become "a moral imperative to diversify our species," in order to keep humanity viable.[42]

Enriquez and Gullans state that contemporary science is in the process of producing "an avalanche of discoveries, modifications, rapid changes, small and large," that together imply that already "we are no longer the same."[43] This reality is playing out in a range of fields:

> As the options available to recombine, alter, modify, enhance, adapt, change, vary, increase, decrease, explode, as we develop things like cell engineering, genomics, proteomics, transplant and organ growing techniques, tissue engineering, brain research, and robotics... As each technology becomes standard operating procedure, and as each application spreads, through off label usage, and as it doubles and doubles in power, then each technology

begins to change hundreds, thousands, and perhaps millions of beings. Not just the lives of those who are sick. We are birthing fundamentally different humans in real time.[44]

In addition to the predictions of Kurzweil, Harari, Enriquez, and Gullans, the views of Max Tegmark, professor of physics and cosmology at MIT, offer a picture based on the findings of AI research. Tegmark envisions the possibility that AI might not only perform all human tasks and become "smarter" than we are but that it might come to represent a superior life form that will surpass us entirely:

> Yet despite the most powerful technologies we have today, all life forms we know of remain fundamentally limited by their biological hardware. None can live for a million years, memorize all of Wikipedia, understand all known science or enjoy spaceflight without a spacecraft. None can transform our largely lifeless cosmos into a diverse biosphere that will flourish for billions or trillions of years, enabling our Universe to finally fulfill its potential and wake up fully. All this requires life to undergo a final upgrade, to Life 3.0, which can design not only its software but also its hardware. In other words, Life 3.0 is the master of its own destiny, finally fully free from its evolutionary shackles.[45]

As Tegmark explains it, Life 1.0 is the relatively rudimentary form of existence that simply survives and replicates. In Life 1.0 both the hardware (physical manifestation) and software (information and learning) of the organism advance solely through biological evolution. Life 2.0—uniquely the realm of humans—not only can survive and replicate but designs its own software without waiting for evolutionary advances. Thus, human culture has greatly expanded our knowledge and learning without meaningful hardware upgrades. Life 3.0 will be altogether different. Not only will it be able to survive and replicate, but it will have the capacity to design and upgrade both its software and its hardware. Hence, it will be able to refashion its physical body to adapt to its circumstances, unrestricted by the inherited human body. According to Tegmark, this third iteration of existence, which will enable life to extend far beyond Earth, will center around beings that are imbued with extraordinary intelligence in physical bodies that will likely have little to no similarity to our current organic, carbon-based forms.[46]

TRANSHUMANISM

It is striking to note the similarities between the views of Kurzweil, Harari, Enriquez, Gullans, and Tegmark. Even if their projections do not all come to fruition, and even if the advances take longer than anticipated, the implications for human life will be staggering. Each one points toward a future that is, to some extent, "transhumanist," where transhumanism is understood as seeking "the continuation and acceleration of the evolution of intelligent life beyond its currently human form and human limitations by means of science and technology, guided by life-promoting principles and values."[47] The writer Mark O'Connell has observed that our current focus on technology in advanced societies means that insofar as

> we have hope for the future—if we think of ourselves as having such a thing as a future—it is predicated in large part on what we might accomplish through our machines. In this sense, transhumanism is an intensification of a tendency already inherent in much of what we think of as mainstream culture.[48]

David Gelernter, professor of computer science at Yale, while unimpressed by transhumanism, acknowledges its reach:

> Catch transhumanism any day now, coming soon to a university (and then a high school and then a kindergarten) near you. Transhumanism is the idea that, by gradually replacing more and more bits and pieces of the human body with computer chips and other exquisite machines, we will make life better—and it doesn't matter anyway, because this is the direction of technology and progress. What kind of pitiful Luddite would ask questions?[49]

It is difficult to disagree with the conclusion that "whether people like it or not, transhumanism has arrived."[50]

Those thinkers who see transhumanism as an inevitable part of the future are largely hopeful that the scenarios they describe will constitute progress and that the transcending of current human limits will be navigated successfully. If, after all, it was a step forward when Neanderthals became *Homo sapiens*, why would it not be a similar step forward when *Homo sapiens* come to share the stage with, or yield the stage to, our successors? And if we can achieve the age-old dream of conquering disease and extending life, then, arguably, opportunities for great contentment await. Who will object to the diminution of pain, the increase of pleasure, and the harnessing of unimagined power? According to this logic, these technological projects will inevitably march forward because their fruits are so enticing.

Transhumanists, it should be noted, arrive at their predictions within the context of their own perspectives on the human condition. Harari provides a clear example. As we have seen, Harari regards references to human dignity, rights, or sanctity as constructs that have no reality—tales that will be easily discarded when they outlive their usefulness. Human behavior is determined by biological givens, "hormones, genes, and synapses," while ethics, law, freewill, and political systems are artificial.[51] This outlook leads Harari to conclude that any thought that our lives have more than passing significance is illusory:

> The modern deal thus offers humans an enormous temptation, coupled with a colossal threat. Omnipotence is in front of us, almost within our reach, but below us yawns the abyss of complete nothingness. On the practical level modern life consists of a constant pursuit of power within a universe devoid of meaning. Modern culture is the most powerful in history, and it is ceaselessly researching, inventing, discovering and growing. At the same time, it is plagued by more existential angst than any previous culture.[52]

The stark, cold truth, Harari tells us, is that we live within a meaningless universe. Hence, our lives are meaningless. We come from nothingness and disappear to nothingness, and our years play out on a minute, forgettable stage that hovers above a gaping, cold void. Humans, therefore, have no "predetermined role"; we can do "anything we want"; we are "constrained by nothing." There is no God, but we can become *Homo deus*, humans with godlike powers. No external force can stop us from acquiring prodigious knowledge and developing technologies that will fulfill our every wish. Without God, we will have the power to live as gods. Meaningless gods.

Harari is certainly not the first to aver that humans are little more than biological machines within a universe that produced sophisticated life by sheer chance. His message is clear: Not only have we not yet discerned any meaning to human life, but there is no meaning waiting to be discovered. We are here because of a series of unintended events, and human extinction, while sad, would have little more consequence than the disappearance of the dinosaurs. To be sure, Harari affirms, the currently dominant "religion of humanism" is vitally concerned with human well-being and deplores hurting human feelings. But once it becomes clear that humans have no free will, that we are wholly driven by physical compulsions, and that algorithms can readily know us and predict our predilections better than we can, we will come to understand that human feelings are just variables to be manipulated:

> What, then, will happen once we realize that customers and voters never make free choices, and once we have the technology to calculate, design or outsmart their feelings? If the whole universe is pegged to the human experience, what will happen once the human experience becomes just another designable product, no different in essence from any other item in the supermarket?[53]

Harari opines that the religions of the future will not emerge from centers of theism in the Middle East, but rather from places like Silicon Valley, and will be data-centered rather than human-centered. Eventually, Harari posits, once we have uploaded the contents of our brains to machines, "we might dissolve within the torrent of data like a clump of earth within a gushing river."[54]

This is not exactly a hopeful prediction. Indeed, if this is to be a new religion, then its major truths will likely produce a certain amount of human despair. Harari's narrative is not, however, an inevitable outcome of transhumanism. Tegmark departs from Harari, holding that the universe does in fact have meaning, and so does human life. For Tegmark, the real significance of conscious existence lies in the understanding that "it's not our Universe giving meaning to conscious beings, but conscious beings giving meaning to our Universe."[55] Without beings like us, the universe would be a vast expanse of material without a flicker of anything worthwhile. A museum empty of visitors in the dark of night is a meaningless repository of multi-shaped objects. Only when the lights come on and the visitors arrive to appreciate, to be moved, and to be motivated by the museum is meaning created:

> This makes our cosmic awakening all the more wonderful and worthy of celebrating: it transformed our Universe from a mindless zombie with no self-awareness into a living ecosystem harboring self-reflection, beauty and hope—and the pursuit of goals, meaning and purpose. Had our Universe never awoken, then, as far as I'm concerned, it would have been completely pointless—merely a gigantic waste of space.[56]

It follows from this that "the very first goal on our wish list for the future should be retaining, indeed expanding, biological and artificial consciousness in our cosmos, rather than driving it extinct."[57] If the universe were to revert to being "permanently unconscious because we drive Earth life extinct or because we let unconscious zombie AI take over," that would be an inversion of our very purpose.

For Tegmark, then, conscious beings, capable of perceiving their surroundings and being impacted by beauty, are the source of meaning in what would otherwise be a lifeless cosmos. Given this understanding of humans as generators of meaning, Tegmark sees no reason why the arrival of more sophisticated, conscious AI should spell the end for *Homo sapiens*:

Traditionally, we humans have often founded our self-worth on the idea of human exceptionalism: the conviction that we're the smartest entities on the planet and therefore unique and superior. The rise of AI will force us to abandon this and become more humble... Indeed, human exceptionalism hasn't only caused grief in the past, but it also appears unnecessary for human flourishing: if we discover a peaceful extraterrestrial civilization far more advanced than us in science, art and everything else we care about, this presumably wouldn't prevent people from continuing to experience meaning and purpose in their lives.[58]

According to Tegmark's approach, the arrival of conscious AI need not herald the disappearance of humans. To the contrary, the more we can expand the existence of sentient life on Earth and beyond, the more the universe will come alive with significance.

Those who are hopeful about the benefits of a transhumanist future do acknowledge that perturbing questions abound. Enriquez and Gullans explicitly call for thoughtful intervention from beyond the realm of science:

We can be certain of one thing... The technologies and changes we are talking about are so powerful that they are changing humanity itself...
Of the four big questions: What? How? Who? Why? It best be science that answers the first two, but it best not be science that tries to answer the last two. Leave the latter to priests, poets, artists, philosophers, ethicists, and existentialists.[59]

All too aware that "well intentioned and very smart scientists generated horrors," Enriquez and Gullans call for discussions about morality and ethics to be led by specialists in the humanities.[60] From their viewpoint, given that we are embarked on a journey that will change humanity, new societal and ethical frameworks will become essential.

Harari, too, sees a role for human judgment in charting the way forward. In *Homo Deus*, at the end of a work filled with predictions, Harari grants that humans could decide to travel down a different road:

> The rise of AI and biotechnology will certainly transform the world, but it does not mandate a single deterministic outcome. All the scenarios outlined in this book should be understood as possibilities rather than prophecies. If you don't like some of these possibilities you are welcome to think and behave in new ways that will prevent these particular possibilities from materializing.[61]

Without acts of "prevention," Harari seems to regard it as likely that technological advances will proceed in the direction that he describes. But he does not claim to be certain about his conclusions. Tentatively, he inquires: Do we "miss anything when we understand life as data processing and decision-making? Is there perhaps something in the universe that cannot be reduced to data?"[62] He concludes this way:

> If the curtain is indeed about to drop on Sapiens history, we members of one of its final generations should devote some time to answering one last question: what do we want to become? This question, sometimes known as the Human Enhancement question, dwarfs the debates that currently preoccupy politicians, philosophers, scholars and ordinary people... The only thing we can try to do is to influence the direction scientists are taking. But since we might soon be able to engineer our desires too, the real question facing us is not 'What do we want to become?,' but 'What do we want to want?' Those who are not spooked by this question probably haven't given it enough thought.[63]

Harari is surely correct that one of the most pressing issues that humanity must consider is "what do we want to want?" It follows, therefore, that influencing the "direction that scientists are taking" has become a task of undeniable significance.

Indeed, if we fail to steer as we hurtle forward our creations could easily spin out of control with disastrous consequences. Robert Colville ends *The Great Acceleration* with the warning that the experts in the field "make an extremely convincing case for why we should be alarmed."[64] Cambridge

University, he writes, established a new "Centre for the Study of Existential Risk" because scholars are concerned that "biotechnology, nanotechnology and artificial intelligence create the potential for things to go so wrong so fast and on such a scale that humanity will be unable to react in time: the equivalent of a Flash Crash in the markets, but in the real world."[65] Colville cites the Oxford philosopher, Nick Bostrom, who depicts the coming human interaction with AI as being like children playing with a bomb. In Bostrom's view, the "intelligence explosion" that may emerge from self-learning AI could engulf us before we have a chance to step away. And these dangers could materialize even if everybody plays by the rules and does not cut corners—an unlikely scenario, given the competitive advantages of gaining an edge. As a result, Bostrom deems the advent of superintelligence as "quite possibly the most important and most daunting challenge humanity has ever faced."[66] After surveying the multiple risks, Colville concludes that the responsible path to averting possible ruin begins with attitudinal change: "If there is one thing that has been consistent across the great acceleration, from finance to our social habits to the state of the environment, it has been our willingness to discount future risks in pursuit of present convenience."[67] As Colville sees it, our inability to delay or deny ourselves certain immediate gratifications may have existential implications.

Even if unexpected calamities do not eventuate, there is an alternative school of thought that regards the transhumanist scenarios as being more a threat to our essence than to our existence. This approach advocates resisting moves that would fundamentally transform humanity. David Gelernter minces no words in calling for opposition to what he terms the "Kurzweil cult." Gelernter accuses scientists of having exceeded their mandate in pursuing initiatives that will throw "man off his throne at the center of the universe and reduce him to just one more creature—an especially annoying one—in the great intergalactic zoo."[68] Humans, as far as Gelernter is concerned, exist within a specific context, and if that delicate framework is disrupted, humanity will not survive:

> ...[M]an as we know him is the top growth on a tall tree in a large forest: His kinship with his parents and ancestors and mankind at large, the experience of seeing his own reflection in human history and his fellow man—those things are the crucial part of who he is. If you make him grossly different, he is lost, with no reflection anywhere he looks. If you make lots of people grossly different, they are all lost together—cut adrift from their

forebears, from human history and human experience. Of course we do know that whatever these creatures are, untransformed men will be unable to keep up with them. Their superhuman intelligence and strength will extinguish mankind as we know it, or reduce men to slaves or dogs. To wish for such a development is to play dice with the universe.[69]

"Playing dice with the universe," opines Gelernter, is an irresponsible gamble. He argues that the "human as computational device" analogy is fundamentally flawed insofar as it cannot account for consciousness or subjectivity, both critical features of our humanity that should not be ignored. Preferring to preserve humanism that is rooted in Western religious thought, Gelernter is emphatic that "the sanctity of life is what we must affirm against Kurzweilism and the nightmare of roboticism."[70]

The writer Tara Isabella Burton, in a study of new religions that have emerged in the Internet age, offers a different critique. She describes the type of "techno-utopianism" articulated by the transhumanists as a civil religion in its own right. Techno-utopians see the goal of the universe as optimizing existence.[71] Evolution in this context is a process of natural optimization that leads logically to the pursuit of human optimization by means of our technological tools. Thus, the perfection of the human being is the central goal—a goal to be achieved through a process of hacking ourselves so as to overcome frailty, sickness, and death. Somewhat ironically, the goal of perfecting humans then leads to the obvious next steps in the optimization process: Humans become cyborgs and then ultimately yield the stage to beings that are even more optimal—post-human AI. As Burton puts it, in the techno-utopian worldview, "transcendence comes from what we can create ourselves: the technology that makes us more than human. We, and we alone, are divine. That techno-utopian obsession with self-divinization finds its natural conclusion in artificial intelligence, which is truly post-human."[72] Burton challenges us to inquire: Is nirvana really to be found in superseding human messiness by achieving a world of pure data or one run by AI in which humans are no more than spectators? Is the path of optimization toward human oblivion really the one that makes the most sense?

The scientist and public intellectual Leon Kass also rails against the "arrogant pronouncements of the bio-prophets." Kass maintains that the picture being presented by the transhumanists offers a "shallow philosophy" of what human life constitutes—a philosophy that is made credible because it is cloaked in the "authority of science":[73]

There is, of course, nothing novel about reductionism, materialism and determinism of the kind displayed here; these are doctrines with which Socrates contended long ago. What is new is that, as philosophies, they seem (to many people) to be vindicated by scientific advance. Here, in consequence, is perhaps the most pernicious result of our technological progress, more dehumanizing than any actual manipulation or technique, present or future: the erosion, perhaps the final erosion, of the idea of man as noble, dignified, precious or godlike, and its replacement with a view of man, no less than of nature, as mere raw material for manipulation and homogenization.[74]

Kass has no objection to benefitting from technology but stresses the danger of moving ahead without a coherent intellectual framework. The "full human meaning" of the path upon which we are embarked requires serious contemplation if we are to avoid becoming "creatures if not slaves" of our own creations:

Hence our peculiar moral crisis. We are in turbulent seas without a landmark precisely because we adhere more and more to a view of human life that both gives us enormous power and, at the same time, denies every possibility of nonarbitrary standards for guiding its use. Though well equipped, we know not who we are or where we are going. We triumph over nature's unpredictability only to subject ourselves, tragically, to the still greater unpredictability of our capricious wills and our fickle opinions. Engineering the engineer as well as the engine, we race our train we know not where. That we do not recognize our predicament is itself a tribute to the depth of our infatuation with scientific progress and our faith in the sufficiency of our humanitarian impulses.[75]

But all is not yet lost. With greater awareness, Kass posits, we might still be able to "defend the vestiges of our human dignity."

Hava Tirosh-Samuelson, professor of modern Judaism and history at Arizona State University, is similarly disturbed by what she sees as the diminution of the human within the transhumanist endeavor:

When we reduce humans to information that can be coded on a silicate substrate, we commit a dual sin: We erase the particular features that make an individual person unique, and we forget that much of our concrete Otherness is rooted in our peculiar biological features, namely, our distinctive embodiment as manifested by this body that is unlike any other.[76]

Tirosh-Samuelson is unprepared to accept the assertion that being human primarily centers around information contained in cells that could just as well be downloaded into some different physical structure. Her concern about the transhumanist approach to technology is that it

> harbors deep disdain toward biological embodiment and its metabolic foundation, replacing it with the presumably superior intelligent machine that transcends the limits of the biological, mistakes-prone human body. It is this disdain toward biological materiality and its inherent imperfection that I find ethically unacceptable. We have come to the point when the adage "to err is human" receives a new meaning.[77]

Tirosh-Samuelson takes issue with the fundamental worldview of the transhumanists: "[t]he transhumanist project seems to me to be misguided because of its mechanistic engineering-driven approach to being human, its obsession with perfection understood in terms of performance and accomplishments rather than moral integrity, and its disrespect for the unknown future."[78] Like Enriquez and Gullans, Tirosh-Samuelson cautions that we should not allow scientists alone to chart the course ahead. Far from seeing transhumanism as being an inevitable destination of our age, Tirosh-Samuelson, Kass, Burton, and Gelernter make the case that humanity should insist upon an alternative vision. Urgently.

Confronting the Challenges

There is, then, substantial agreement about the technological trajectory upon which humanity has embarked. It is a future that will see us move from the goal of treating human ailments and abnormalities to one of upgrading ourselves through an array of human enhancements. It is a future that will shift the focus of our technological innovations from machines that are external to the human body to technology that will remake our physical beings and our internal selves. It is a future that will, if we so decide, lead to us sharing our world with new creations: beings that are, for all intents and purposes, "smarter" and more capable than humans. We are, in short, moving toward transformations that will make the first decades of the digital age look like a mere prelude.

Here are some of the likely consequences of the road ahead: First, jobs: As AI becomes more sophisticated, some hold that, with the exception of a small cadre of positions, there will be far fewer jobs. In a 2017 study, researchers from Oxford's Future of Humanity Institute concluded that while jobs in varying sectors will evaporate at different times, overall "AI should be better than humans at pretty much everything in about 45 years."[79] There are those, however, who disagree with this analysis. Kurzweil and Friedman both point to previous periods in history when technology eliminated whole industries—but new fields arose, providing work that was not previously envisaged, and humans remained gainfully employed. The job market of the future, they argue, will demand more advanced technical skills, but there will still be jobs aplenty.[80]

There are, though, two difficulties for those who argue that most people will have work: First, it is unclear whether the masses of people who are employed in relatively low-skill jobs will be able to retool quickly enough and whether educational systems will be sufficiently nimble to ready workers for more demanding roles. Second, even if the first challenge can be met, continued technological advancement makes it probable that AI will still outperform people in numerous areas. Hence, it is probably true that "the idea that humans will always have a unique ability beyond the reach of non-conscious algorithms is just wishful thinking."[81] At some point in the second half of the twenty-first century, it is conceivable that large numbers may be jobless.

Under such circumstances, how will people spend their time? How will the unemployed be supported economically? Will there be any incentive to provide for the needs of the billions of people who no longer contribute economically in any tangible way? Harari maintains that modern liberalism's reason for holding human life in high esteem was not so much grounded in religious sentiment, but came about because "there was abundant political, economic and military sense in ascribing value to every human being."[82] However, Harari conveys, in the years ahead, if most people no longer have productive work, this argument will collapse; there will no longer be any practical reason to ascribe value to human beings. The great majority of humans will serve no worthy purpose:

The most important question in twenty-first-century economics may well be what to do with all the superfluous people...

In the twenty-first century we might witness the creation of a massive new unworking class: people devoid of any economic, political or even artistic value, who contribute nothing to the prosperity, power and glory of

society. This 'useless class' will not merely be unemployed—it will be
unemployable…

What's so sacred about useless bums who pass their days devouring artificial experiences in La La Land?[83]

This is a jarring assessment, thoroughly at odds with our current perception of the infinite value of all persons. Harari describes a world in
which there will be no compelling case justifying why those he labels
"superfluous people" or the "unworking class" or "useless bums" should
even be sustained, let alone regarded as inviolable. Indeed, Harari urges us
to consider the possibility that, in these circumstances, society's elite—
those few who still have some function and who have amassed resources
sufficient to enhance themselves beyond everybody else—may well simply
decide to "let go of the useless third-class carriages, and dash forward with
the first class only."[84]

Will any semblance of human equality be sustainable if such a vision
becomes reality? The economic inequalities of the early twenty-first century may come to look small compared with what lies ahead. Historically,
wealth disparity did not make the "haves" and "have-nots" into fundamentally different beings—the essence of the human experience remained
much the same for rich and poor. To be sure, the rich could avail themselves of medical treatments that might extend their lives marginally or
procedures that allowed them to look or feel more youthful, but aging and
death still proceeded on relatively similar timetables for all. This will almost
certainly change. Healing the sick is an egalitarian enterprise because it
acknowledges that we have a duty to help all attain a certain basic level of
wellness. Upgrading the healthy will be altogether different. It will likely
become an "arms race" of procuring the best memory, the strongest limbs,
or the greatest endurance that money can buy. Those with the most
resources will be first in line. Mandating that certain advances must be
made available to all will not help. As soon as a new norm is achieved,
those with means will pursue the next level:

The great human projects of the twentieth century—overcoming famine,
plague and war—aimed to safeguard a universal norm of abundance, health
and peace for everyone without exception. The new projects of the twenty-
first century—gaining immortality, bliss and divinity—also hope to serve the
whole of humankind. However, because these projects aim at surpassing
rather than safeguarding the norm, they may well result in the creation of a

new superhuman caste that will abandon its liberal roots and treat normal humans no better than nineteenth-century Europeans treated Africans.[85]

Safeguarding equality in this brave new world will require "imaginative and far-sighted policymakers to come up with ways to share the fruits of disruption equally enough that techno-Utopia for the few does not become dystopia for the many."[86]

Even if, somehow, the inequality hurdle can be managed, body enhancements will still pose the challenging problem of how far is too far. Is it acceptable to equip people with x-ray vision or with the ability to hear beyond the current human range? Should we allow for limbs that can lift astounding weights or reach what was once unreachable? And, most importantly, is it legitimate to seek to upgrade or rewire the functioning of the human brain itself? At what point do humans cease to be humans—and does it matter if we transform ourselves beyond recognition? Gelernter offers this thought:

> Whether he knows it or not, Kurzweil believes in and longs for the death of mankind. Because if things work out as he predicts, there will still be life on Earth, but no human life. To predict that a man who lives forever and is built mainly of semiconductors is still a man is like predicting that a man with stainless steel skin, a small nuclear reactor for a stomach, and an IQ of 10,000 would still be a man. In fact we have no idea what he would be.[87]

In designating those beings that will follow *Homo sapiens* as "Homo evolutis" or "Homo deus," the transhumanists effectively concur with Gelernter that humanity, as we currently understand the term, will indeed have become something else.

Moreover, the notion of the human or post-human being constituting an assembly of upgradable parts represents the ultimate commodification of human life. Humans will come to equal the sum of our parts, with each component manufactured according to individual specifications. This raises the question, what will become of identity? If identity is already a complicated mixture assembled from multiple sources, it, too, will become even more pliable. Will any element of our identities or our individual characteristics be regarded as fixed and immutable? Temperament? Personality? Character? Or will these all be endlessly alterable? In different ways, both our bodies and the contents of our brains may well come to be regarded as no more than tradable, interchangeable, temporary modules.

As human life is reshaped, what will become of the family? In the twentieth century, reliable contraception made family planning and the ability to limit family size available to all. Birth control liberated women. At the same time, in much of the West, contraception and increased longevity were accompanied by higher median life expectancies, elevated divorce rates, and fewer births. What will happen if, in the twenty-first century, scientific advances enable us to extend the lifespan further? What will happen if new technologies allow for babies to be born without the need for pregnancy at all—manufactured rather than birthed? What will happen if our growing sophistication with gene editing allows for genetic traits and enhancements that make our offspring altogether different beings from their parents? What will these developments portend for marriage, families, parents and children, and the view of life as a gift to be accepted, no matter the hand we are dealt?

Perhaps none of the developments envisioned by the transhumanist camp promise to be as revolutionary as the prospect of extending human life indefinitely. Kurzweil expects that humans will ultimately be able to overcome death. Assuming that living forever implies a life characterized by robust health and independence and that it is possible to address practical concerns like overpopulation and economic costs, what objection could there be? Kass has an answer. He regards the goal of conquering death as a project that will change us into beings that are not human:

> Conquering death is not something that we can try for a while and then decide whether the results are better or worse—according to, God only knows, what standard. On the contrary, this is a question in which our very humanity is at stake, not only in the consequences but also in the very meaning of the choice. For to argue that human life would be better without death is, I submit, to argue that human life would be better being something other than human. To be immortal would not be just to continue life as we mortals now know it, only forever. The new immortals, in the decisive sense, would not be like us at all. If this is true, a human choice for bodily immortality would suffer from the deep confusion of choosing to have some great good only on the condition of turning into someone else.[88]

Kass makes four arguments as to why we should not seek indefinite life. First, Kass does not believe that adding time will really cause most of us to add any new dimensions to our lives, and he questions whether happiness will be increased by "more of the same." Second, quoting the Psalmist's call to "teach us to number our days," Kass makes the claim that we only make our days count if they are in fact numbered; without a limit we would never take life seriously or live it passionately. Third, "is not our mortality," asks Kass, "the cause of our enhanced appreciation of all that is beautiful and worthy...? How deeply could one deathless human being love another?" Fourth, when considering the question "for what cause would you be willing to sacrifice your life?," an immortal being could have no answer. Only beings who are mortal, opines Kass, can "rise above our mere creatureliness, spending the precious coinage of the time of our lives for the sake of the noble and the good and the holy."[89]

Kass concedes that his arguments will not convince many. The allure of immortality is almost irresistible. But Kass is resolute that we will not achieve bliss by prolonging our lives forever. Indeed, he holds, the opposite is true: By chasing immortality, we "may seriously undermine our chances for living as well as we can and for satisfying to some extent, however incompletely, our deepest longings for what is best."[90] It is possible that in the very pursuit of what we think we want, we may end up remaking ourselves into beings with longer but much flatter lives, living qualitatively impoverished existences that never end. And once the genie is out of the bottle, there will be no possibility of return.

Does Judaism have anything to say on all these issues? How could it not? Judaism is, after all, a system that deals with every aspect of life. It is vitally concerned with the ethical, the holy, and the human. It has always sought the exemplary path toward a good life on both the micro and the macro levels. If the future portends massive transformations that will determine whether human life will be recognizable or even conceivable, then these concerns must be central to any effective expression of Judaism. Momentous change is certain, and the wheels are already in motion. Thoughtful responses will be needed.

This will be no easy task. Fateful choices about belief and practice need to be made. There are multiple examples, beginning with God: Harari speaks as a historian in pronouncing that the era of God is over: "More than a century after Nietzsche pronounced Him dead, God seems to be making a comeback. But this is a mirage. God is dead—it's just taking a while to get rid of the body."[91] Harari proceeds to trace the steps from the humanist revolution that first dismissed God to what he expects will occur in the data revolution:

> At first humans kept on believing in God, arguing that humans are sacred because they were created by God for some divine purpose. Only much later did some people dare say that humans are sacred in their own right, and that

God doesn't exist at all. Similarly, today most Dataists claim that the Internet-of-All-Things is sacred because humans are creating it to serve human needs. But eventually the Internet-of-All-Things may become sacred in its own right.[92]

How will Judaism respond to Harari? Can Judaism entertain the notion that God is a fiction, cherished by the less enlightened but soon to be discarded entirely? If so, what would sustain the idea of human sacredness? If God is dethroned, can a coherent Judaism survive?

Beyond theological questions, what will be Judaism's response to the practical issues that have been raised? What will be the Jewish recommendation for how people should occupy themselves if jobs are rare? James Livingston, professor of history at Rutgers, presents the challenge in these terms:

[T]he impending end of work raises the most fundamental questions about what it means to be human. To begin with, what purposes could we choose if the job—economic necessity—didn't consume most of our waking hours and creative energies? What evident yet unknown possibilities would then appear? How would human nature itself change as the ancient, aristocratic privilege of leisure becomes the birthright of human beings as such?[93]

Does Judaism have a theory of how such a life should best be spent? Is the answer to be found in studying Torah? If not, what are the alternatives? There will be some who will view the prospect of liberating humanity from work as a wonderful turning point, opening possibilities for spending life in pursuit of satisfaction. Is this a vision that Judaism could embrace?

And what about the challenge of all the "superfluous people?" The very idea runs counter to basic tenets of Jewish thought. Should a large number of humans be allowed to wither away and never be replaced? Should they be prevented from reproducing so that their numbers shrink? There is a decisive choice to be made. Jews can resolve that Harari's picture of the future is disturbing and that they want no part of it. They can prefer the prophets of Israel to the bio-prophets. If, however, Jews are truly committed to the classic Jewish perspective, it is important to be cognizant of the implications: It will mean working to contain technological progress to ensure that dehumanizing outcomes do not emerge. It will mean examining each scientific development in terms of its likely impact on humanity.

Such a project is complex. The struggle is made more difficult by the "innovation infatuation" that prefers to embrace what is new without restraint, deferring harder questions until after novel technologies have already been released. Those who want to take up arms against a transhumanist tomorrow will likely find themselves in a countercultural stance, attempting to scrutinize "advances" that the surrounding culture is moving toward embracing. The alternative, of course, is to endorse the thrust of the technological trend, no matter where it might lead. But this approach means acquiescing to a path that could lead to the dehumanization of billions and to the creation of an elite class of super beings. The dilemma is clear: Either insist that the "humans as sacred" principle must be maintained in one form or another, or allow technology to proceed, knowing that human sacredness could be marginalized.

And what should be the response of Judaism to the prospect of body enhancement? Perhaps the closest analogous debate is the *halakhic* discussion of cosmetic surgery. The *halakhic* consensus generally permits cosmetic surgery to assist an individual to look or feel like others, but it does not bless procedures that are pursued for reasons of vanity. There are four Jewish considerations: "the theological implications of 'improving' God's work; the possible risks to life involved in any operation; the Jewish objection to any mutilation of the body; and the ethical censure of human vanity."[94] But, as pointed out earlier, human enhancement in the twenty-first century will focus far more on upgrades than on correcting deficiencies. Will Judaism regard all enhancements as improper because of the hubris involved in seeking to improve upon God's work? Will these enhancements be prohibited as unnecessary mutilations of the body? Will they be considered vanity? Will it make a difference if such procedures become so widespread that they come to represent the "new normal," such that refusing them relegates one to a sub-par status? The direction that Jewish wisdom will advocate remains unknown.

Related to the area of enhancement is the conversation over how children are conceived and what genetic modifications might be acceptable. Since Judaism is pro-natal it has embraced technologies to help couples conceive in circumstances where conception by traditional means is not possible. What, though, will be Judaism's response to tomorrow's mooted technologies? Take the case of in vitro gametogenesis (IVG), which could allow for the reprogramming of adult cells (skin, hair, etc.) into sperm and egg cells. If perfected, IVG could make asexual reproduction the norm rather than the exception. Individuals or couples might well be able to produce a large number of embryos, selecting their preferred embryo based on traits. In the words of Glenn Cohen of Harvard Law School, "IVG has the potential to upend one of the most traditional elements of human culture—our understanding of what parenthood is and how it occurs."[95] Cohen calls for a rigorous debate about what constitutes parenthood. Does Judaism condone the separation of sexuality and conception for those who can conceive naturally? How would Judaism view the selection of embryos for preferred traits if such selections become normative? Would Judaism approve of the use of mechanical wombs, where gestation no longer occurs within the human body? Should genetic editing be allowed in order to "upgrade" a healthy fetus? The answers are by no means obvious.

At the other end of the life cycle lies the question of the indefinite extension of life. Kass reports the experience of appearing on a panel where a rabbi maintained that Judaism would unequivocally embrace life without end:

> Gently needling his Christian colleagues by asserting that, for Jews, God is Life, rather than Love, he used this principle to justify any and all life-preserving and life-extending technologies, including those that might yield massive increases in the maximum human life expectancy. When I pressed him in discussion to see if he had any objections to the biomedical pursuit of immortality, he responded that Judaism would only welcome such a project.[96]

Given Judaism's unswerving affirmation of life, there is reason to believe that this viewpoint has broad rabbinic support.[97] Indeed, Ilia Stambler, an Israeli academic who specializes in the study of longevity, makes the case that Judaism would have no objection to the open-ended extension of life. Stambler cites Maimonides' "Responsum on Longevity" as evidence that Judaism has "no predetermined limit to human life, and therefore efforts toward the prolongation of life are justified." According to Stambler, Genesis demonstrates that death is not the "inexorable destination" of humanity and that living for centuries is admired. He concludes that "the Jewish religious tradition is perfectly supportive of the pursuit of life extension, even radical life extension, perceiving it as a high manifestation of the valuation of life."[98]

Kass demurs: "I am prepared to accept the view that traditional Jewish sources may be silent on these matters... But, in my opinion, such unqualified endorsement of medical progress and the unlimited pursuit of longevity cannot be the counsel of wisdom, and, therefore, should not be the counsel of Jewish wisdom."[99] Tirosh-Samuelson labels the pursuit of immortality as immoral and pronounces open-ended life extension foreign to Judaism: "From the vantage point of Judaism, at least, the ideal of indefinite postponement of death is the highest form of human hubris, yet another example of human rebellion against God, who created humans as finite beings whose life narrative has a beginning, a middle, and an end."[100] We are, according to Tirosh-Samuelson, brought into the world for a limited time and that reality represents the Jewish vision of how things ought to be.

Who is right? If it becomes possible to extend a healthy and vigorous life by many decades, if not indefinitely, what should be the Jewish approach? Under such circumstances, does it remain mandatory to go on living without any foreseeable terminus? Does death become a matter of autonomous choice, the timing of which would be decided upon by the individual? Would suicide be permitted at any age? Or would people be forced to remain alive even if they felt trapped and viewed the prospect of endless life as unappealing? If the timing of death were left up to the individual, what teaching would Judaism offer as to how such a choice ought to be made? Or, like mandatory retirement ages, should there be a "death age" when life should be ended, even though it could still be comfortably sustained? Gelernter may well be right that a human who can live forever will no longer be truly human, but is our humanity strengthened by demanding the arbitrary termination of life through killing people or insisting on their suicide? And what happens if preserving lives through centuries leads to few new lives being created? If those who have lived for extended periods remain vital and feel fresh, is there any reason to give priority to new life over old? So far, there is scant Jewish direction as to how to proceed.

If the Judaism of the twenty-first century aspires to live up to its mandate to be an engine of inspired ideas for human exaltation, then it will need to chart a way forward through this thicket of issues. There can be little doubt that the choices that humans will make over the next several decades will have fateful consequences for the nature of human life going forward. As is evident, there are many intricate questions that require Jewish answers. It is time to offer responses. In order to reply, though, it will be valuable to describe the foundations of Jewish thought that give rise to the perspectives that lie ahead.

Notes

1. Ray Kurzweil, "Reinventing Humanity: The Future of Machine–Human Intelligence," *The Futurist*, March-April 2006, accessed August 1, 2022, http://www.singularity.com/KurzweilFuturist.pdf, 40.
2. Juan Enriquez, *Right/Wrong*, 8.
3. Ibid., 3.
4. Antonio Regalado, "We Have the Technology to Destroy All Zika Mosquitoes," *MIT Technology Review*, February 8, 2016, accessed August 1, 2022, https://www.technologyreview.com/2016/02/08/71597/we-have-the-technology-to-destroy-all-zika-mosquitoes/
5. Juan Enriquez, *Right/Wrong*, 5.
6. Ibid., 109–110.
7. Ibid., 62.
8. Juan Enriquez, *Right/Wrong*, 126.
9. Samuel Gibbs, "Elon Musk Leads 116 Experts Calling for Outright Ban of Killer Robots," *The Guardian*, August 20, 2017, accessed August 1, 2022, https://www.theguardian.com/technology/2017/aug/20/elon-musk-killer-robots-experts-outright-ban-lethal-autonomous-weapons-war
10. David Zvi Kalman, "Levinas Would Have Banned Facial Recognition Technology. We Should Too," *Tablet Magazine*, January 12, 2021, accessed August 1, 2022, https://www.tabletmag.com/sections/news/articles/levnias-facial-recognition-technology
11. Ibid.
12. Ibid.
13. Ibid.
14. Ibid.
15. Val Van Brocklin, "As commercial use of facial recognition expands, what are the implications for police?," *Police1*, December 7, 2017, accessed August 1, 2022, https://www.police1.com/police-products/police-technology/police-software/facial-recognition/articles/as-commercial-use-of-facial-recognition-expands-what-are-the-implications-for-police-WLDPM0L46oGWdsYv/
16. Juan Enriquez, *Right/Wrong*, 231.
17. Ibid., 7.
18. Ibid., 40–42.
19. Ibid., 42.
20. Ibid., 43.
21. Ibid.
22. Ibid., 43–44.
23. Yuval Harari, *Sapiens: A Brief History of Humankind* (New York: Harper Collins, 2015).

24. Ibid., 399.
25. Ibid., 401.
26. Ibid., 403.
27. Ibid.
28. Ibid., 407.
29. Ibid., 409.
30. Harari, *Homo Deus—A Brief History of Tomorrow* (New York: Harper Collins, 2017), 396.
31. Ibid., 106.
32. Ibid., 83.
33. Ibid., 312.
34. Wu Youyou, Michal Kosinski, and David Stillwell, "Computer-Based Personality Judgements Are More Accurate Than Those Made by Humans," *PNAS* 112: 4 (2015), 1036– 40, accessed August 1, 2022, http://www.pnas.org/content/112/4/1036.full
35. Ibid.
36. Juan Enriquez and Steve Gullans, *Homo Evolutis–Please Meet the Next Human Species* (New York: Ted Conferences LLC, 2011), Kindle Location 34.
37. Juan Enriquez and Steve Gullans, *Evolving Ourselves: How Unnatural Selection and Nonrandom Mutation are Changing Life on Earth* (New York: Penguin Publishing Group, 2015), 3.
38. Ibid., 3–4.
39. Emily Singer, "New Letters Added to the Genetic Alphabet," *Quanta Magazine*, July 10, 2015, accessed August 1, 2022, https://www.quantamagazine.org/new-letters-added-to-the-genetic-alphabet-20150710/
40. Juan Enriquez and Steve Gullans, Evolving Ourselves, 4.
41. Juan Enriquez and Steve Gullans, *Homo Evolutis*, Kindle Location 882.
42. Ibid.
43. Ibid., Kindle Location 1331.
44. Ibid., Kindle Location 1533.
45. Max Tegmark, *Life 3.0* (New York: Knopf Doubleday Publishing Group, 2017), 29.
46. Ibid.
47. Max More, early transhumanist thinker, as quoted in "What is Transhumanism?," accessed August 1, 2022, https://whatistranshumanism.org/#about
48. Mark O'Connell, *To Be a Machine* (New York, Knopf Doubleday Publishing Group, 2017), 6.
49. David Gelernter, *The Tides of Mind: Uncovering the Spectrum of Consciousness* (New York: Liveright, 2016), 79.

50. Zoltan Istvan, "The Growing World of Libertarian Transhumanism," *The American Conservative*, August 8, 2017, accessed August 1, 2022, http://www.theamericanconservative.com/articles/the-growing-world-of-libertarian-transhumanism/

51. Harari, *Sapiens*, 236.

52. Harari, *Homo Deus*, 201.

53. Ibid., 277.

54. Ibid., 395.

55. Max Tegmark, *Life 3.0*, 313.

56. Ibid., 22.

57. Ibid., 313.

58. Ibid.

59. Enriquez and Gullans, *Homo Evolutis*, Kindle Locations 1182, 1195, 1201.

60. Ibid., Kindle Location 1282.

61. Harari, *Homo Deus*, 395.

62. Ibid., 394.

63. Harari, *Sapiens*, 413–414.

64. Colville, *The Great Acceleration*, 313.

65. Ibid.

66. Ibid.

67. Ibid.

68. David Gelernter, "The Closing of the Scientific Mind," *Commentary Magazine*, January 1, 2014, accessed August 1, 2022, https://www.commentarymagazine.com/articles/the-closing-of-the-scientific-mind/

69. Ibid.

70. Ibid.

71. Tara Isabella Burton, *Strange Rites—New Religions for a Godless World* (New York: Public Affairs, 2020), 192.

72. Ibid., 196.

73. Leon Kass, *Life, Liberty and the Defense of Dignity—The Challenge for Bioethics* (San Francisco: Encounter Books, 2002), 137.

74. Ibid.

75. Ibid., 137–138.

76. Hava Tirosh-Samuelson, "The Immorality of Immortality," *Religion Dispatches*, June 10, 2009, accessed August 1, 2022, https://religiondispatches.org/the-immorality-of-immortality/

77. Ibid.

78. Ibid.

79. Paul Ratner, "Here's When Machines Will Take Your Job, as Predicted by AI Gurus," *Big Think*, June 4, 2017, accessed August 1, 2022, http://bigthink.com/paul-ratner/heres-when-machines-will-take-your-job-predict-ai-gurus

80. James Bessen, as cited in Friedman, Thank You for Being Late, 207ff.

81. Harari, Homo Deus, 319.
82. Ibid., 308.
83. Ibid., 318, 325, 326.
84. Ibid., 349.
85. Ibid., 350.
86. Colville, *The Great Acceleration*, 313.
87. David Gelernter, "The Closing of the Scientific Mind."
88. Leon Kass, "L'Chaim and its Limits: Why not Immortality?," *First Things*, May, 2001, accessed August 1, 2022, https://www.firstthings.com/article/2001/05/lchaim-and-its-limits-why-not-immortality
89. Ibid.
90. Ibid.
91. Harari, *Homo Deus*, 267.
92. Ibid., 389.
93. James Livingston, "Your job can't save you now," *Quartz*, September 4, 2017, accessed August 1, 2022, https://qz.com/1062038/jobs-arent-the-solution-to-americas-problems-theyre-the-cause/?mc_cid=f132fc1c42&mc_eid=455f18a000
94. Eisenberg, Daniel "Judaism and Cosmetic Surgery," Aish.com, May 9, 2009, accessed August 1, 2022, https://www.aish.com/ci/sam/48955041.html
95. Ekaterina Pesheva, "The Promise and Peril of Emerging Reproductive Technologies," Harvard Medical School, January 11, 2017, accessed August 1, 2022, https://hms.harvard.edu/news/promise-peril-emerging-reproductive-technologies
96. Kass, "L'Chaim and its Limits: Why not Immortality?"
97. See Norbert Samuelson and Hava Tirosh-Samuelson, "Jewish Perspectives on Transhumanism" in Hava Tirosh-Samuelson and Kenneth Mosman, *Building Better Humans?—Refocusing the Debate on Transhumanism* (Frankfurt am Mein: Peter Lang GmbH, 2012), 109. Samuelson and Tirosh-Samuelson write that "Unlike Kass, who argues for restraint based on the 'virtues of morality,' Reform, Conservative, and Orthodox rabbis and ethicists tend to be strongly in favor of 'more life, longer life, new life,' as Kass derogatorily put it."
98. Ilia Stambler, "Longevity and the Jewish Tradition," LongevityHistory.com, 2014, accessed August 1, 2022, http://www.longevityhistory.com/longevity-and-the-jewish-tradition/
99. Kass, "L'Chaim and its Limits: Why not Immortality?"
100. Hava Tirosh-Samuelson, "The Immorality of Immortality."

REFERENCES

Burton, Tara Isabella *Strange Rites—New Religions for a Godless World* (New York: Public Affairs, 2020).

Colville, Robert *The Great Acceleration–How the World is Getting Faster, Faster* (London: Bloomsbury, 2016).

Eisenberg, Daniel "Judaism and Cosmetic Surgery," Aish.com, May 9, 2009, accessed August 1, 2022, https://www.aish.com/ci/sam/48955041.html.

Enriquez, Juan and Gullans, Steve *Evolving Ourselves: How Unnatural Selection and Nonrandom Mutation are Changing Life on Earth* (New York, Penguin Publishing Group, 2015).

Enriquez, Juan and Gullans, Steve *Homo Evolutis–Please Meet the Next Human Species* (New York: Ted Conferences LLC, 2011).

Juan Enriquez, *Right/Wrong* (Cambridge, MA: MIT Press, 2020).

Friedman, Thomas *Thank You for Being Late: An Optimist's Guide to Thriving in the Age of Accelerations* (New York: Farrar, Straus and Giroux, 2016).

Gelernter, David "The Closing of the Scientific Mind," *Commentary Magazine*, January 1, 2014, accessed August 1, 2022, https://www.commentarymagazine.com/articles/the-closing-of-the-scientific-mind/.

Gelernter, David *The Tides of Mind: Uncovering the Spectrum of Consciousness* (New York: Liveright, 2016).

Gibbs, Samuel "Elon Musk Leads 116 Experts Calling for Outright Ban of Killer Robots," *The Guardian*, August 20, 2017, accessed August 1, 2022, https://www.theguardian.com/technology/2017/aug/20/elon-musk-killer-robots-experts-outright-ban-lethal-autonomous-weapons-war.

Harari, Yuval *Sapiens: A Brief History of Humankind* (New York: Harper Collins, 2015).

Harari, *Homo Deus—A Brief History of Tomorrow* (New York: Harper Collins, 2017).

Istvan, Zoltan "The Growing World of Libertarian Transhumanism," *The American Conservative*, August 8, 2017, accessed August 1, 2022, http://www.theamericanconservative.com/articles/the-growing-world-of-libertarian-transhumanism/.

Kalman, David Zvi "Levinas Would Have Banned Facial Recognition Technology. We Should Too," *Tablet Magazine,* January 12, 2021, accessed August 1, 2022, https://www.tabletmag.com/sections/news/articles/levnias-facial-recognition-technology.

Kass, Leon "L'Chaim and its Limits: Why not Immortality?," *First Things*, May, 2001, accessed August 1, 2022, https://www.firstthings.com/article/2001/05/lchaim-and-its-limits-why-not-immortality.

Kass, Leon *Life, Liberty and the Defense of Dignity–The Challenge for Bioethics* (San Francisco: Encounter Books, 2002).

Kurzweil, Ray "Reinventing Humanity: The Future of Machine–Human Intelligence," *The Futurist*, March-April 2006, accessed August 1, 2022, http://www.singularity.com/KurzweilFuturist.pdf.

Livingston, James "Your job can't save you now," *Quartz*, September 4, 2017, accessed August 1, 2022, https://qz.com/1062038/jobs-arent-the-solution-to-americas-problems-theyre-the-cause/?mc_cid=fl32fc1c42&mc_eid=455f18a000.

O'Connell, Mark *To Be a Machine* (New York: Knopf Doubleday Publishing Group, 2017).

Pesheva, Ekaterina "The Promise and Peril of Emerging Reproductive Technologies," Harvard Medical School, January 11, 2017, accessed August 1, 2022, https://hms.harvard.edu/news/promise-peril-emerging-reproductive-technologies.

Ratner, Paul "Here's When Machines Will Take Your Job, as Predicted by AI Gurus," *Big Think*, June 4, 2017, accessed August 1, 2022, http://bigthink.com/paul-ratner/heres-when-machines-will-take-your-job-predict-ai-gurus.

Regalado, Antonio "We Have the Technology to Destroy All Zika Mosquitoes," *MIT Technology Review*, February 8, 2016, accessed August 1, 2022, https://www.technologyreview.com/2016/02/08/71597/we-have-the-technology-to-destroy-all-zika-mosquitoes/.

Samuelson, Norbert and Tirosh-Samuelson, Hava "Jewish Perspectives on Transhumanism" in Hava Tirosh-Samuelson and Kenneth Mosman, *Building Better Humans?—Refocusing the Debate on Transhumanism* (Frankfurt am Mein: Peter Lang GmbH, 2012).

Singer, Emily "New Letters Added to the Genetic Alphabet," *Quanta Magazine*, July 10, 2015, accessed August 1, 2022, https://www.quantamagazine.org/new-letters-added-to-the-genetic-alphabet-20150710/.

Stambler, Ilia "Longevity and the Jewish Tradition," LongevityHistory.com, 2014, accessed August 1, 2022, http://www.longevityhistory.com/longevity-and-the-jewish-tradition/.

Tegmark, Max *Life 3.0* (New York: Knopf Doubleday Publishing Group, 2017).

Tirosh-Samuelson, Hava "The Immorality of Immortality," *Religion Dispatches*, June 10, 2009, accessed August 1, 2022, https://religiondispatches.org/the-immorality-of-immortality/.

Van Brocklin, Val "As commercial use of facial recognition expands, what are the implications for police?," *Police1*, December 7, 2017, accessed August 1, 2022, https://www.police1.com/police-products/police-technology/police-software/facial-recognition/articles/as-commercial-use-of-facial-recognition-expands-what-are-the-implications-for-police-WLDPM0L46oGWdsYv/.

What is Transhumanism?, accessed August 1, 2022, https://whatistranshuman-ism.org/#about.

Youyou, Wu; Kosinski, Michal and Stillwell, David "Computer-Based Personality Judgements Are More Accurate Than Those Made by Humans," *PNAS* 112: 4 (2015), 1036– 40, accessed August 1, 2022, http://www.pnas.org/content/112/4/1036.full.

CHAPTER 7

A Jewish Response

Judaism is a system with a worldview. Foundational elements of the Jewish vision are not malleable. Thus, for Judaism, the notion that the universe has meaning is primary. It is not by chance that the Torah begins with the imposition of order and structure upon a sea of primordial chaos. It is not an accident that the process of creation culminates in the formation of sentient life. For Judaism, meaning emerges in the nexus between intelligent, conscious life and the ability of that intelligent life to comprehend the laws of the universe, appreciate its beauty and wonder, and respond.

This is not a vain pursuit after some non-existent fiction. To assert that we comprehend the universe well enough to state that it is meaningless is hubris. Commenting on Harari's viewpoint, one writer observed:

> Harari shrugs where he should shudder. It is not a minor thing to assert that the main evolutionary advantage of sapiens—their capacity to produce meaning—is a cruel and pointless joke. There is at least one other alternative: that the best of our stories are not frauds but hints, and that the whole unlikely story has led sapiens to a justified belief in their own dignity and purpose. In this case, the myths produced by Homo sapiens would be not the lies we tell ourselves but the truths we dimly perceive.[1]

The truths we dimly perceive. The Jewish narrative is not arbitrary; rather, it corresponds to a fundamental whisper of meaning that Judaism affirms within the universe. That whisper of meaning, the numinous source of light and law and love, is what Jews call God. While Harari

© The Author(s), under exclusive license to Springer Nature Switzerland AG 2023
D. Schiff, *Judaism in a Digital Age*,
https://doi.org/10.1007/978-3-031-17992-1_7

maintains that God will soon be jettisoned, the British historian Paul Johnson perceives reality differently: "The historian might say: there is no such thing as providence. Possibly not. But human confidence in such a historical dynamic, if it is strong and tenacious enough, is a force in itself, which pushes on the hinge of events and moves them."[2] In other words, while Johnson cannot be sure about the Divine, he is certain that trust in Divine benevolence leads to a view of human dignity and purpose that decisively moves history. Even in the digital age, pushing on that hinge remains pivotal.

This narrative has solid foundations. Miguel Nicolelis, a professor at Duke University known for his pioneering work on brain-machine interface technology, regards the human brain as the "true creator" of knowledge, possessed of an endless yearning to understand the universe:

> According to the most accepted human description of events, barely four hundred thousand years after the singular explosive event that gave rise to the cosmos, light finally escaped, traveling across the universe until it encountered someone or something who could reconstruct its epic journey and attempt to give some meaning to it all. On the surface of a little bluish rock, made by the fusion of intergalactic dust about 5 billion years ago, while orbiting a mediocre yellow star, itself lost in an undistinguished corner of an average galaxy, that primordial light encountered beings who longed to understand it and who, using all their evolution-endowed mental faculties and tools, began in earnest to re-create, inside their minds, the path whence that stream of potential information came and what it possibly meant.[3]

The universe began with light. Eventually, that stream of illumination reached humans, and, ever since, we have been trying to make sense of the illuminated cosmos. From Nicolelis' point of view, Harari didn't go far enough with his list of fictions. It is not just human rights, religions, and money that are stories. Physics, too, is a fiction. So is mathematics. Mass and charge are in the same category. Nicolelis writes that they do not exist at all: "What truly exists is the collection of human mental constructs that provide the best and most accurate account, to date, of the natural world that exists out there."[4] To be sure, certain propositions are subject to experimentation while others are not, but ultimately, observes Nicolelis, all of our knowledge structures are no more than human templates for explaining the way our brains have come to perceive and shape a sense of order in the universe. Even space and time, as we think of them, are the products of human brains. If some intelligent alien were to arrive on Earth, it is not likely that such a being would understand space and time the way we do. Hence, Nicolelis concludes, "the cosmos is a mass of potential information, waiting for an intelligent observer to extract knowledge out of it and, almost in the same breath, stamp meaning on it all."[5]

We are, of course, those "intelligent observers." The "mass of potential information" that surrounds us is not a vast array of non-conforming data without potential for comprehensible patterns. Like puzzle pieces that could be put together in different ways to form alternative pictures—albeit with a limited number of reasonable combinations—we scrutinize the universe, reflect on the contours of our knowledge, and continuously fine-tune our understanding. Thus, we create sophisticated narratives about the physical universe that conform with the information that our senses gather. This type of information yields scientific knowledge. But the universe also holds information about moral truths and about the significance of life itself. This yields a different type of narrative that focuses on our place and our purpose; we arrive at these narratives through straining to understand the "truths we dimly perceive." In the words of David Gelernter, "[t]he scientist explains the origins of the universe with a logical argument. The religious believer tells a story…Only the logical argument has predictive power. Only the story has normative moral content. Only a fool would pronounce one superior."[6]

Thus, meaning does not lie in some hidden answer to the riddle of life that is waiting to be discovered. Meaning inheres within a narrative about our state of being—a narrative that best comports with the universe as we perceive it. Tegmark was right when he maintained that we humans essentially create meaning when we cause the vast, still, cosmos to light up with life and appreciation. But there is more to it than that. We are not just museum visitors who bring the darkened halls to life with awe and understanding. In a very real sense, we are also the museum custodians—or at least the custodians of our wing. According to most ancient civilizations, humans were utterly insignificant; only the interaction of the gods was consequential. Genesis swept that idea away. No sooner did God bring the universe into being than humans were charged with an exalted role: the preservation and the refinement of our domain. We bear responsibility for our world and its destiny. Our purpose is not to be passive observers of the cosmos but to be the keepers of life itself.

In *Man's Search for Meaning*, Victor Frankl wrote that life "ultimately means taking responsibility to find the right answer to its problems and to fulfill the tasks which it constantly sets for each individual." "Each man," wrote Frankl, "is questioned by life; and he can only answer to life by answering for his own life; to life he can only respond by being responsible." [7] Meaning is to be found not just in coming to a fuller appreciation and understanding of the universe but in taking responsibility for the flourishing of life. As Frankl understood it, that implies that our primary responsibility should be other-directed:

> By declaring that man is responsible and must actualize the potential meaning of his life, I wish to stress that the true meaning of life is to be discovered in the world rather than within man or his own psyche, as though it were a closed system. I have termed this constitutive characteristic "the self-transcendence of human existence." It denotes the fact that being human always points, and is directed, to something, or someone, other than oneself—be it a meaning to fulfill or another human being to encounter. The more one forgets himself—by giving himself to a cause to serve or another person to love—the more human he is and the more he actualizes himself.[8]

Taking responsibility means being outward-looking, not self-serving. This is a moral statement. Morality begins with taking responsibility—first, in the Garden of Eden, for life itself, and then in the account of Cain and Abel, where we swiftly apprehend that we are indeed our brother's keeper. Here, then, are the key elements of how Judaism sees meaning: Our lives exist to animate an empty cosmos with appreciation and awe; our minds have been endowed with the capacity to perceive the inherent order in the universe and to discern knowledge and law; and we are imbued with a moral responsibility to preserve and strengthen our corner of creation.

Beyond insisting that the universe has meaning, there are additional features of the Jewish outlook. Judaism does not place much emphasis on doctrinal requirements, but certain tenets are widely accepted. Of considerable importance, contra the transhumanist view, Jewish thought affirms both human uniqueness and the exalted status of human beings. It is, after all, no small matter to claim that humans are "created in the Divine image." The Torah is the first text in history to insist on the grandeur and the preciousness of humanity. Genesis starts with God breathing life into humans who are depicted as having a special form of consciousness that includes creativity, free will, self-awareness, and accountability. These elements constitute the major pillars of what the Torah regards as being imitative of the Divine.

Through the centuries, this exalted view of human potential has often been countered. Multiple scientific discoveries led to the conviction that humans are of little note: Astronomy taught that we are not at the center of the universe and that compared to the 13 billion years that the universe has existed, the arrival of *Homo sapiens* around 200,000 years ago is no more than an eyeblink. This perspective made humans appear to be little more than an afterthought. Perhaps just as disturbing, evolution conveyed that humans are descended from primates with scant distinctiveness beyond our enlarged brains. According to this view, humans are nothing more than glorified animals, driven by selfish genes, limited by the chemistry of our bodies, and always at the mercy of powerful psychological and physiological urges that dictate our responses. As a result, some have come to regard it as axiomatic that humans are flukes produced by nature with little claim to higher worth. Given these messages, it is not altogether surprising that there are those who not only see humanity as inconsequential but life as essentially meaningless. Rabbi Norman Lamm, a twentieth-century Jewish scholar, once marveled at the number of serious thinkers who "have become intoxicated with the sense of their own unimportance. Never before have so many been so enthusiastic about being so trivial."[9]

There are, of course, many Jewish sources that contest this thesis of human insignificance. Psalm 8:4–6 captures the Jewish insistence on a balance between human smallness and greatness:

> When I behold Your heavens, the work of Your fingers, the moon and stars that You set in place, what is man that You have been mindful of us, mortal man that You have taken note of us; yet You have made us little less than the angels and adorned us with glory and majesty.

Plainly, being negligible before God does not comport well with the Jewish position that humans have the standing to struggle with God, are empowered to argue with God, and are enjoined not to accept the world as it is. The Torah portrays humans as the culmination of terrestrial creation with good reason: Humans were, and still are, exceptional. Jewish tradition does not postulate that we must be the most rarefied creatures in the universe—the Bible deliberately describes us as being lower than the angels. And Jewish views do not negate the possibility of intelligent life existing elsewhere with capabilities that might exceed that of humans. But Jewish texts do convey that our unique nature nevertheless represents inestimable value and is the source of enduring dignity.

What is unique about humans? The Torah opens with the universe coming into being by means of comprehensible language, a singular gift shared by God and humanity that gave us the power of high-level, abstract communication. But Genesis goes further. The first thing Adam does upon gaining awareness is to name the animals. God does not instruct Adam how to do this, and Adam does not simply follow an ordered pattern. Rather, Adam engages in a creative process of naming that is quintessentially human. Adam's naming endeavor—an activity which, at face value, appears trivial—signifies the human capacity for independent creativity. It is highly improbable that we will ever build AI with a similar capacity. Nicolelis describes the creative abilities of the human brain as nothing short of awe-inspiring, "whether one looks at NASA's latest visual description of the known universe, Michelangelo's frescoes, or the painted walls of the Lascaux cave, there is no way to avoid feeling temporarily breathless, humbled, and, above all, deeply moved by all the splendorous magnificence."[10]

In his book, *Steering Human Evolution*, Yehezkel Dror, emeritus professor of political science and public administration at the Hebrew University, proposes that, since creativity is such an essential part of humanity, the better designation for humans would be "homo creator" rather than *Homo sapiens*. According to Dror, humanity as a species is "radically unique (at least on Earth) in some crucial respects. The most important one is the acquired and continuously increasing capacity of Homo creator…to reshape drastically its future biological-cultural evolution."[11] Genesis made us "co-creators with God" in continuing the enterprise of forming life. It appears that we are nearing the time when that creativity could potentially be applied, as never before, to the development of entirely new categories of life. That power, Dror holds, separates us from any other creature: "All of human life and cultures are permeated by creativity, putting a high divide between humanity and all other forms of life on Earth."[12]

Beyond creativity, there is memory. There is no other earthly being that exhibits "the unique human capability of acquiring, accumulating, and transmitting…knowledge from one generation to another, for hundreds, thousands, or even millions of years."[13] Memory, it is worth noting, is a particular Jewish specialization: for no other group "is the injunction to remember felt as a religious imperative to an entire people."[14] The verb *zachor*, "remember," appears no less than 169 times in the Hebrew Bible. Without memory, there is no identity, no sense of purpose, and no connection to the past. Indeed, without memory, and without assigning meaning to memory, history is an empty vessel: "It was ancient Israel that first assigned a decisive significance to history and thus forged a new world-view."[15] Our present reality is constructed through the meaning that we assign to the events that formed us. We shape our memories, and we are, in turn, shaped by them.

The Jewish concept of memory goes even further. Jewish history begins with the injunction to "remember that you were slaves in Egypt." It is one of the six remembrances that are commanded in Jewish life. But these commandments to remember do not enjoin Jews to simply recall events from long ago. Rather, they anticipate action. There is a clear expectation that those doing the recalling should appreciate the core significance of past events, take personal responsibility for them, and act accordingly. Memory is also the foundation of transmission. Judaism stipulates the importance of remembering because memory is critical in forging links to the future. Memory, then, can be merely recalling something to mind, but it can also be the stimulus for taking initiative and preserving an inheritance of ideas. It is difficult to imagine that AI will ever be fashioned with memory that might operate in a similar fashion.

Memory is remarkable, not just for its role in shaping our destiny but also because of its variability and fragility; it is intimately associated with forgetting. Humans have some memories that are sharp and can be recalled with great accuracy, some memories that are hazy and uncertain, some that seem to have disappeared but can be recalled when prompted, and some that are effectively gone. Forgetting, of course, plays a vital role. It allows us to generalize about past experiences without being overwhelmed by all the trivial details of everything that ever happened to us. While memory, then, is essential to knowing who we are, it is our less-than-firm grip on memory that allows us to progress.

Human uniqueness extends even further. Gelernter writes compellingly about the extraordinary nature of the human mind. While brains are physical structures, the mind depends on the brain but emerges from it in ways that we do not understand. Intelligence clearly represents one particular type of brain output. AI, named for its intelligence features, will likely do a good job mimicking human intelligence or even exceeding it. "Mimicking" is, however, the operative term. AI may well end up being functionally superior to humans, but the way it solves problems will never resemble human thought. The human mind is not just an intelligence machine. Human minds produce emotions and feelings, they contain our subjective view of the world, they are the locus of our reflections and our internal conversations, and they contain our dreams and our daydreams, our fears, our doubts, our loves, concerns, and ambitions. Perhaps most significantly, they are the seat of our consciousness and self-consciousness.

Gelernter draws a distinction between two different functions that humans perform: doing and being. AI is almost exclusively designed for doing; its code is written as a series of instructions for carrying out tasks.[16] By contrast, while much of human life is preoccupied with doing, a considerable slice of it is about being: Imagine lying on a riverbank on a late summer afternoon and gazing up at the sky as you feel the warm sun energize you. Simultaneously, your mind contemplates the shape of the clouds and then wanders to consider what you seek to achieve in the year ahead. Could we design AI that might desire to lie on a riverbank, be energized by the sun, contemplate the clouds, and then let its "mind" spontaneously wander to consider its ambitions? Even if this were to prove possible, it seems unlikely that we would bother. We have no need to create daydreaming AI that lies on riverbanks and reflects. This is particularly true given that, without consciousness, AI would never engage in real reflection, and the goal of constructing AI with genuine human-like consciousness is likely to be unreachable. The operation of the human mind, from Gelernter's viewpoint, is inseparable from the human body and the neurons, chemicals, and biological material that form its physical substrate. Thus, we might well create sophisticated beings running on digital code that have astonishing knowledge and power, but they will never possess anything resembling a conscious, self-aware human mind.[17]

Nicolelis also holds that the unparalleled structure of the brain, together with the distinctive way that the brain encodes information and utilizes energy, is "one of the key reasons why digital computers will never be able to reproduce the intrinsic works and wonders of the human brain."[18] Any true copying of the full extent of human brain functioning necessarily requires the enormously complex variability and flexibility of organic material. Nicolelis writes that the amazing mental abstractions that our brains can produce are "built through noncomputable operations" that involve a massive number of neurons and neuronal electromagnetic fields and much more: "As important as the sheer volume of neurons might be to achieve our present cognitive abilities, it is likely that the unique cabling of our brains was the main driving force behind the emergence of our species' exquisite mental skills."[19] "That is why," Nicolelis holds, "no digital computer will ever come up with a new god or scientific theory by itself."[20] He concludes that it is the human mind, and only the human mind, that has proven capable of assembling a breathtaking body of knowledge from the seemingly disconnected data that surrounds us. Nicolelis expresses awe for

> the preciousness and uniqueness of what we, as a species, have been able to collectively achieve by carefully building such an island of knowledge over millions of years. I say that because until concrete evidence for the existence of extraterrestrial intelligent beings is found, the human universe constitutes the greatest mental accomplishment ever attained by any intelligent life-form.[21]

The human mind, according to this view, is so intricate and astonishing that it is a powerful testament to human uniqueness.

Loren Eiseley, a mid-twentieth-century professor of anthropology and the history of science at the University of Pennsylvania, expressed it this way:

> Lights come and go in the night sky. Men, troubled at last by the things they build, may toss in their sleep and dream bad dreams, or lie awake while the meteors whisper greenly overhead. But nowhere in all space or on a thousand worlds will there be men to share our loneliness. There may be wisdom; there may be power; somewhere across space great instruments, handled by strange, manipulative organs, may stare vainly at our floating cloud wrack, their owners yearning as we yearn. Nevertheless, in the nature of life and in the principles of evolution we have had our answer. Of men elsewhere, and beyond, there will be none forever.[22]

More recently, Nick Longrich, senior lecturer of Paleontology and Evolutionary Biology at the University of Bath, put it in these terms:

> Imagine that intelligence depends on a chain of seven unlikely innovations—the origin of life, photosynthesis, complex cells, sex, complex animals, skeletons and intelligence itself—each with a 10% chance of evolving. The odds of evolving intelligence become one in 10 million. But complex adaptations might be even less likely...[M]aybe each of these seven key innovations evolve just 1% of the time. If so, intelligence will evolve on just 1 in 100 trillion habitable worlds. If habitable worlds are rare, then we might be the only intelligent life in the galaxy, or even the visible universe.[23]

In all likelihood, we represent an exceedingly unusual flickering of intelligence in the universe as a whole. It appears certain, moreover, that the type of intelligence that humans possess does not exist anywhere else; should the flame be extinguished, it will never again be rekindled.

Is all this worthy of preservation? Is the human mind, memory, creativity, language ability, and the multiplicity of other features and capacities that makes us distinctive of lasting value? It is true that we humans do not consistently cover ourselves in glory. Maybe the next link in the chain of evolution that could conceivably follow us will be more knowledgeable, more efficient, and less destructive than we are. Few miss Neanderthals or long to have them back. So, is there any reason to insist on keeping us around?

Judaism's answer to this question is yes. No matter how animated, intelligent, responsive, or reliable our AI creations might become, AI will never attain the combination of qualities that will merit the status of being "created in the image." While it is doubtful whether it will ever make sense to speak of the death of an AI being, it is unlikely that Judaism will ever see such a loss as a diminution of the Divine. It is not enough to be able to pass the Turing test of being functionally indistinguishable from a person. Nor is it enough to possess superintelligence or unmatched problem-solving abilities. The gulf between achieving convincing human-like qualities and being human is almost certainly unbridgeable. Jews are mandated to expand the Divine image in the world, not to lessen it. That goal demands the preservation of humanity. Judaism provides no license to contemplate an alternative.

Even assuming that it were possible to create AI that not only exceeds human intelligence but also possesses all salient human qualities, it would not lead to the conclusion that human beings are expendable. It would still make sense to preserve humans as unique intelligent beings with a singular view of the universe. The irreplaceable human perspective and the poetry inherent within the grandeur and the struggle of human existence are exquisite. That is why Jewish tradition maintains that "anyone who destroys a life is considered by scripture to have destroyed an entire world; and anyone who saves a life it is as if they saved an entire world" (Mishnah Sanhedrin 4:5). Each human life contains the potential for untold significance, and that will remain true even if AI comes to be viewed as functionally superior. If we allow humans to be regarded as "useless," it will return us to that brutal historical perspective that valued human life only insofar as it was economically productive, possessed the strongest muscles, or displayed the highest intelligence. Judaism rejected that viewpoint back then; it rejects it still today.

It follows that if the preservation of humanity is worthwhile, then attempts to alter humans beyond recognition are inconsistent with this goal. So far, the changes wrought by the various devices that we add to our bodies do no more than restore human abilities to their regular range. Artificial skin, blood, and organs that provide similar outcomes to their biological equivalents fall into the same category. However, once we cross the line into the realm of upgrades, linking our brains to external computers, or installing artificial components with physical capabilities that no human has ever experienced, we will be in uncharted territory. As Gelernter points out, if we enter this brave new world of enhancement, it is not clear that we will still be able to define the resultant substantially augmented beings as "human."[24]

Humans, it is important to emphasize, were created to be vulnerable. Adam was lonely and needed the support of a mate. And after we were forced to move away from Eden's tree of life, mortality and frailty became an enduring part of the human equation. Without exception, every human is forced to confront death and lives with the prospect of sickness, weakening, demise, and loss. On some level, we are all aware that everything we have is but lent to us and that our existence is eternally delicate; reversal of fortune could come at any moment. We live with a perpetual sense that the vitality that flows through us will one day ebb. This reality is perhaps the starkest difference between human beings and the Divine; feebleness and transience are decidedly not Godly. Indeed, God's rejection of the Tower of Babel could be understood as a clear demarcation between the eternal, unflagging Divine realm and the human domain—the domain of the vulnerable, where no name is permanent, and no structure lasts forever. Our vulnerability, moreover, is not limited to our physical selves. Our conduct is also fallible, prone as we are to numerous mistakes, countless wrong decisions, and many unfortunate transgressions. Our memory is unreliable, our communications are inaccurate, and our emotions and desires cloud our judgment and decision-making. This is human life; though we dream of longevity, well-being, and nobility, our dreams evaporate with the dawn.

We are less than Divine, and vulnerability is our hallmark. We spend our lives struggling against physical, mental, and emotional imperfections, knowing full well that, in the end, we will not prevail. Our entire worldview and self-understanding have always been shaped by this reality. Until now. Now, for the first time in history, we stand on the threshold of being afforded a plausible way to "turn the dial" so that we will no longer need to accept fallibility. Our eyesight will not dim because our eyes will be replaced with superior versions. We will not "lose a step" because new legs will allow us to outperform the best of today's athletes. Our skin will not sag because a replacement membrane will be reliably supple. Our knowledge will not lack, because all that is knowable will be instantly accessible through a chip in our brains. Our memory will not be hazy because everything we ever saw or heard will be recallable. And on and on. Technological advancements will, if we choose, start to address one vulnerability after another. More than any of the changes that have transpired in the first decades of the digital age, this series of transformations will truly alter the essence of who we are. If individuals are afforded a life without key vulnerabilities—so that we need to deal far less, or not at all, with apprehension about aging, or illness, or forgetting, or being uninformed, or even dying—it will remake the core of who we are.

Plainly, God could have created us with a range of robust physical or mental features that would have made us less transitory and less liable to failings. Alternatively, the evolutionary process could have delivered a sturdier product. Neither did. From a Jewish perspective, this is not a design flaw. God created humans not as perfect, finished beings but as raw material with untold potential to fashion ourselves and our world into something exalted, something Godly. Jewish tradition regards vulnerability as that feature of human life that propels us to do something of lasting value.

It is revealing that the daily Jewish liturgy contains the words, "What are we? What is our life? What is our virtue?…The mighty are as nothing before You, and the renowned as though they had never been." The prophet Isaiah observes that "man is but grass; grass withers, flowers fade" and that, even in the case of the mighty, "hardly has their stem taken root in earth, when God blows upon them and they dry up, and the storm bears them off like straw" (Isaiah 40:7–8, 24). Acknowledging vulnerability and transitoriness is Judaism's way of instilling a sense of urgency that we should make something of our lives within the time frame allotted to us. The great days of Rosh Hashanah and Yom Kippur stress our weakness and imperfection, providing an annual reminder that humans are no more than dust—"a passing shadow, a dream soon forgotten," while the festival of Sukkot communicates the fragility of life as a core theme. Leon Kass expresses it this way: "[t]o know and to feel that one goes around only once, and that the deadline is not out of sight, is for many people the necessary spur to the pursuit of something worthwhile…Mortality makes life matter."[25]

Symbolically, the entire description of the Jewish odyssey through history is a story of vulnerability. It begins with a tiny, weak clan on an improbable journey to an unknown destination. It continues with God coming to the aid of the most vulnerable, oppressed collective on Earth: the enslaved Hebrews. And after that, Jewish history unfolds as one long litany of insecurity: a traumatized tribe crossing a desert to a promised land filled with opposition; a minute kingdom vanquished time and again by every known empire; a wandering, reviled, isolated group forever treated as the stranger; an unprotected collective targeted for denigration and murder by every tyrant; a scattered network of outsiders, always the "other," never fully secure, forever exiled, driven, converted; and a nation permanently threatened, never able to sleep with both eyes closed even when at home. "The Jews," wrote Paul Johnson, "were the emblem of homeless and vulnerable humanity."[26] Unending vulnerability has typified Jewish existence. Can it be by chance that the first people linked to the pursuit of monotheism would be characterized not by strength or dominance but by palpable existential vulnerability?

Human vulnerability raises a fundamental issue: Does the fact that humanity has never known any other reality imply that we are supposed to be vulnerable and that seeking to banish vulnerabilities is improper? There can be no definitive answer to this question, but it seems reasonable to contend that if vulnerability is a primary characteristic of what makes us human, then the steady removal of vulnerabilities will ultimately cause us to become something other than human. It is not possible to say at what point a mounting sense of invincibility will remove us from the human camp, only that it will. If Judaism offers no mandate to bring humanity to an end, nor any hint that God or Jewish tradition would endorse moving toward a post-human world, then relieving humans of the tapestry of vulnerabilities that makes us human is likely to be improper.

It is important to be clear about what this implies. The Jewish duty to heal illness emerges from the Torah itself. Judaism's uncompromising emphasis on saving life means that the battle to overcome illnesses, mend injuries, and restore impairments is not optional. Most cultures have consistently attempted to mitigate vulnerabilities that cause physical suffering.

Judaism is no exception; through the millennia, Judaism has viewed the removal of economic and health vulnerabilities as being critical Jewish responsibilities. In the not-too-distant future, it is likely that what we define as health vulnerabilities will come to include a range of deteriorations that have long been regarded as characteristic of the aging process; these conditions will come to be seen as fully reversible ailments to be treated like all other sicknesses. In this context, physical decline may come to be regarded as unnatural if its deleterious impacts can be medically addressed. It is unlikely that there will be substantive Jewish objections to the production of cures and devices that seek to eliminate conditions that are perceived as preventable.

Given the experience with the coronavirus pandemic, many will contend that human vulnerability is firmly in place with no amelioration in sight. If, however, the futurists are correct, this view may be short-lived. Prior to antibiotics, it seemed unlikely that people would ever live without fear of infection. In just the same way, advances in the twenty-first century, spurred by the coronavirus experience and the speedy development of new vaccines and therapies, will probably make future pandemics less ominous.

But not all vulnerabilities are created equal. It is one thing to provide every person with the same opportunity that some already have to live longer, healthier lives without unbearable financial need. It is another thing entirely to banish death from the equation or to reconfigure human physical capabilities or to connect human brains directly to vast knowledge sources that allow external access to the contents of the brain. All these transformations seek to "perfect" humans by removing vulnerabilities to death, error, or being supplanted. But such perfecting crosses a boundary: it seeks to reconfigure critical features of what makes us human. To pursue these capabilities is to embark upon the road to perfecting humans out of existence.

In telling remarks, the entrepreneur Elon Musk, when explaining why he is researching brain-computer link technology, stressed that humanity must avoid a future where AI outsmarts and exterminates us. From Musk's perspective, either we "join them" by becoming advanced cyborgs or we will be defeated by them: "It's going to be important from an existential threat perspective to achieve a good AI symbiosis."[27]

What Musk is actually promoting is the elimination of a distinct human vulnerability via the elimination of humans. He is essentially swapping one existential threat for another. True, human elements might continue to exist in some form, but only "symbiotically" on terms dictated by AI. Just as a mule is not a horse, a symbiotic being will not be a human. We will have become something else. Nicolelis regards Musk-type proposals as a dead-end that should be strenuously resisted:

> The braincentric view also categorically refutes the contemporary thesis, professed enthusiastically by the worshipers of the artificial intelligence myth, that we and our brains can be reduced to biological machines or automata whose actions and thoughts can be replicated and simulated by mathematical algorithms and digital hardware or software, no matter how elaborate and complex. Unless humanity as a whole decides to take one more crucial step toward self-annihilation by renouncing its birthright as knowledge gatherers and universe creators, the future scenario proposed by some radical artificial intelligence researchers is yet another example of the type of hollow mental fantasy that will take us nowhere.[28]

Musk is right that we need to be vigilant in warding off existential threats to human existence, but the effort will be for naught if the price of doing so is human existence itself. Judaism, from the Torah on, has always insisted on drawing distinctions—between God and humans, between humans and animals, and between the holy and the ordinary. It is difficult to imagine that a coherent approach to Judaism could countenance human-machine hybrids that compromise what it means to be human.

There is another concern about substantive alterations to the human formula. Those who propose extensive human augmentation to reduce our vulnerabilities believe that the outcomes will assuredly improve the human lot. This is, however, not inevitable. As we have seen, there have been a number of technologies that have delivered untoward results.[29] There is little reason to assume that addressing human vulnerabilities by accepting substantial modifications to the human body will *ipso facto* advance human well-being. Additionally, technology-driven evolution will offer numerous transformations within a lifetime, potentially depriving us of any stable sense of the parameters of our own selves. What ought to be of particular concern is that in the name of "health," technology companies will likely attempt to persuade regulators to permit a range of innovations within the human person with unknowable longer-term implications. Our humanity may depend on our thinking twice.

Take memory as an illustration. As humans age, many complain that their memory "isn't what it once was." Almost all who live long enough find that their memory softens; they search for words or names that were once instantaneously accessible. Assuming that innovators find a way to restore memory to "what it once was," would that be a desirable result? If so, would a memory upgrade be even better, offering the possibility to recall the details of conversations from decades ago, and much more? It does not require a scientific background to anticipate some serious pitfalls. Given that our lives are kept in balance by a complex mixture of remembering and forgetting, improving memory by a little too much may afford impressive powers that might prove more detrimental than beneficial. A strengthened memory might create an overwhelming mental cacophony, or it might deny individuals the ability to forget the past. It seems probable that a memory boost that unlocks currently inaccessible memories would lead to marked personality changes. Even if we were able to tweak the formula so that all could be assured of having the same memory capability that they had at age twenty throughout their lifetimes, it is not clear that this would be advantageous. As the decades go by, remembering one's entire history with clarity could easily orient a person toward the past in undesirable ways. "Memory enhancement" will doubtlessly be sold as a way to "get an edge on the competition," "bring back the sharpness of youth," or "upgrade mental fitness"; in reality, it is likely to change us appreciably and unpredictably. More computer-like, we will be far less vulnerable to forgetting, but that will also set us on the track toward becoming entirely different beings.

The Russian psychologist Alexander Luria wrote about the case of a man with a prodigious memory who could barely read because "each time he tried to read, other words and images surged up from the past and strangled the words in the text he held in his hands."[30] It is an illustration of Nietzsche's point that "[l]ife in any true sense is absolutely impossible without forgetfulness."[31] This is true not just for individuals but for communities and cultures as well: "We must know the right time to forget as well as the right time to remember."[32] We must also know what it is that must be remembered and what it is that should be forgotten, for those who cannot forget cannot move forward. Paradoxically, the fact that we do not have iron-clad memories not only makes us human, it empowers us to adapt effectively. Tinkering significantly with the human memory formula could well lead to unexpected harms.

Plainly, no alteration to our vulnerability would be more transformative than the elimination of death itself. For centuries, humans have dreamed of conquering death. To most, it seems unarguable that if we could live forever, enjoying robust vitality, surrounded by family and friends, unbothered by sickness, pain, or economic want, that would be ideal. The Talmud, however, offers an insight that appears to contradict this thinking. It is set in the town of Luz:

> It is the same Luz where, although Sennaherib came and exiled many nations from place to place, he did not disarrange and exile its inhabitants; Nebuchadnezzar, who conquered many lands, did not destroy it; and even the angel of death has no permission to pass through it. Rather, its elders, when weary of life, go outside the city wall and die. (Sota 46b)

Apparently, Luz was an unusual place: Within the city limits, death never visited. According to the Talmud, however, the inhabitants of Luz did not regard this as an unending delight. One by one, though they could have lived forever, they voluntarily stepped outside the city walls to embrace death. What is the Talmud conveying? Perhaps it is trying to teach that the biblical line "There is a time to be born and a time to die" is not descriptive but prescriptive—that dying is a necessary end to life not just because we cannot prevent it, but because life cannot be life if death is not death. If no one's clock ever runs out, then, like a race without a finish line or a story without an ending, life becomes an infinite span that is robbed of drama and poetry, with no genuine purpose or urgency to act.

We have seen that there is a division between those Jewish thinkers who hold that *halakhah* would applaud the pursuit of life without end and those who believe that eternal life would be counter to the tenets of Judaism. One author, after reviewing the literature on the subject, proposed that since the two positions are wholly irreconcilable, perhaps Judaism intends to leave the decision in the hands of each individual: "A person who is productive and finds life meaningful" might choose to extend life indefinitely, whereas somebody who is "suffering like the inhabitants of Luz" might opt to bring life to a close.[33] Can it really be that in a matter so fundamental—so essential to what it means to be human—Judaism would leave such a fateful decision to each individual? This hardly seems consistent with the historic Jewish approach to matters of life and death.

There can be little doubt that, to date, all the *halakhic* rulings on the preservation of life have presumed the inevitability of death prior to 120 years of age. It seems likely, though, that if there comes a time when that presumption no longer holds, *halakhah* will move forward to coalesce around the position that best reflects the Jewish view of what life is supposed to constitute. Yehezkel Dror advises that "…prolonging healthy life expectancy to, say, 200 years profoundly transforms individuals, society and the species as a whole. It should be prohibited until matured humanity decides otherwise."[34] Dror's caution is noteworthy. It is unthinkable that Judaism would allow "profound transformations" for individuals, society, and the human species without serious reflection. Should the prospect of radically extended lives become a reality, it will have a host of ramifications. While Judaism assuredly has a deep commitment to the preservation of life, there are features of human life that serious approaches to Judaism will hesitate to refashion—even in the name of eternal life.

Beyond the fact that banishing death would radically restructure life, another important reason why Judaism will likely find it problematic to embrace the notion of radical life extension relates to the nature of human progress. Human regeneration is heavily dependent on one generation's ideas yielding to the next. At some point, those who are devoted to viewpoints and approaches that were well suited to an earlier time need to yield the stage to those with new ideas. Just as the generation burdened by Egyptian slavery had to die out before it became possible to establish a free nation, so the ideas of any new generation can only truly take hold once those in thrall to the concepts of a bygone time have departed. If every person born during the nineteenth century were still with us, blessed with energy and the capacity to be active and influential, portions of the social progress achieved during the last century would have been impeded. Keeping people alive forever does not mean that they will change their essential core; formative early memories that shape fundamental attitudes are not readily erased. Hence, welcoming life without end might well be regarded as "progress," but it could be a form of progress that will actually stifle progress. Simply excluding those who have reached a certain age from voting or decision-making will not solve the problem. As humans age, the tendency to become jaded from having "seen it all" increases. Any society with a substantial percentage of healthy citizens who have been around for a century or more, together with a smaller percentage of younger people, will be impacted by the attitudinal realities of longevity. It would be odd for Judaism, a system oriented toward the future, to embrace eternal life if this were to hamper generations yet unborn.

From a Jewish perspective, there is one more point to consider when contemplating whether to bless an unending lifespan: idolatry. It is, after all, valuable to inquire what purpose a radically extended lifespan would really be designed to serve. A helpful contemporary definition of a "false god" teaches that "when anything is made an end in itself, rather than as a means to God and goodness...it is a false god."[35] Given this understanding, it is vital to ensure that the decisions that we make about the future do not enshrine a narcissistic attempt to immortalize ourselves. Judaism would assuredly reject the proposition that we should live forever in order to perpetuate ourselves and our own predilections. There is a danger that life itself could become a false god if we seek its extension for the sake of our own personal desires rather than for a greater purpose. The probable response to this concern will be that the more time one has to live, the more one can devote one's life to sanctifying the Divine. Maybe. But that does not appear to be the central focus of those who are most interested in life extension. If extending human life is essentially a self-serving project that results in fewer babies, an ever-aging society, and little fresh wonder to energize the human soul, then it is reasonable to conclude that the aim is not about elevating the human collective. In a Jewish context, the possibility that life extension might amount to a false god means that it should be approached with skepticism. It also makes it conceivable that, should life without end become practical, Judaism might ultimately contend that the citizens of Luz had it right: If human life is to be human life, then death must be death.

There is, then, no escaping the reality that every human life represents an ongoing struggle with vulnerability. It is both the glory and the tragedy of being human. If there is no possibility of tears, of losing what we prize, then there is no possibility of the fullest joy. Many wish fervently for a life without the travails of vulnerability, but whatever type of existence that might be, it would not be human. It is our very vulnerability that instills within us a sense of humility and an understanding of our dependence on others and on God. It is our vulnerability that forces us to look to others for support; it makes family and community indispensable and builds and reinforces the ties of connection, caring, and cooperation among us. The fact that we are each prone to error, weakness, and loss makes us need the compassion, support, and forgiveness of others. We speak of the importance of "showing humanity," particularly when we refer to those who are the most vulnerable. It is a defining element of what makes us human.

An analogy can help elucidate how our human vulnerability might best be understood: The Earth's atmosphere, within which human life flourishes, is an exceedingly narrow band. The conditions that allow life to function without special support exist for just a few miles above the Earth's surface; beyond this narrow band, conditions make life impossible. Likewise, human vulnerability is also a narrow band. Just as any marked increase poses a threat to our well-being, so a noteworthy decrease will irreversibly transform us. Human well-being depends on our ability to address a range of areas where mounting vulnerability creates real risks. In the twenty-first century, however, there is critical work to be done at both ends of the vulnerability band to ensure that human fragility remains inside that narrow range within which our lives can prosper and yet remain genuinely human.

Any thoughtful Jewish approach to the manifold challenges of the twenty-first century must begin with a Jewish theory of how human life ought to be framed within the context of the "truths we dimly perceive." Perhaps the Jewish insight that transformed human existence more than any other was the insistence that every human life contains an element of the Divine. And that, in turn, led to the premium that Jewish law placed on the preservation of human life: "Choose life so that you and your descendants might live" (Deuteronomy 30:19). We humans are, then, both extraordinarily precious, and disquietingly vulnerable at one and the same time. The owner of an exquisite yet delicate vase will naturally establish special rules for how the vase should be handled. If the vase were of little value, the rules would be unimportant because its loss would be trivial. If the vase were indestructible, the rules would also be unimportant because its loss would be nigh impossible. The combination of preciousness and vulnerability leads to particular rules about caring; it is, in short, the foundation of human ethics. We are called upon to treat one another with meticulous care precisely because we are each uniquely exquisite and delicate at one and the same time.

What counsel does Judaism provide as we tackle the myriad of dilemmas before us? Judaism, it seems reasonable to assert, advocates a world in which the great experiment of imperfect, embodied beings seeking to elevate themselves to more exalted level of functioning should continue. That will require preserving humanity in a recognizably human form—which implies placing prudent limits on enhancement. It will require a commitment to the preciousness of human life and to ensuring that humans have an honorable way to contribute to society. It will require a careful analysis of how family life should be structured and how best to nurture it. It will require prioritizing ethics so that ethics constrain our technology and not the other way around. It will require ensuring that the biological, mechanical, and digital beings that we create—no matter how advanced they may be—are devoted to human life and its well-being. And it will require tending to the narrow band of human vulnerability so as to reduce human vulnerability while yet preserving it. There could hardly be a more significant project.

NOTES

1. Michael Gerson, "Myths, meaning and Homo sapiens," *Washington Post,* June 11, 2015, accessed August 1, 2022, https://www.washingtonpost. com/opinions/myths-meaning-and-homo-sapiens/2015/06/11/28660 902-106f-11e5-a0dc-2b6f404ff5cf_story.html
2. Paul Johnson, *A History of the Jews* (London: Weidenfeld and Nicolson Limited, 1987), 587.
3. Miguel Nicolelis, *The True Creator of Everything—How the Human Brain Shaped the Universe as We Know It* (New Haven: Yale University Press, 2020), 7.
4. Ibid., 5.
5. Ibid., 3–4.
6. David Gelernter, *The Tides of Mind*, 22.
7. Victor Frankl, *Man's Search for Meaning* (Boston: Beacon Press, 1992 edition), 77 and 108.
8. Ibid., 110.
9. Norman Lamm, *Faith and Doubt—Studies in Traditional Jewish Thought* (New York: Ktav Publishing House, Inc., 1986), 115.
10. Nicolelis, *The True Creator of Everything*, 7.
11. Yehezkel Dror, *Steering Human Evolution* (New York: Taylor and Francis, 2020), 3.
12. Ibid., 20.
13. Nicolelis, *The True Creator of Everything*, 19.
14. Yosef Haim Yerushalmi, *Zakhor—Jewish History and Jewish Memory* (New York: Schocken Books, 1982), 9.
15. Ibid., 8.
16. Gelernter, *The Tides of Mind*, 2.
17. Gelernter, "The Closing of the Scientific Mind."
18. Nicolelis, *The True Creator of Everything*, 39.
19. Ibid., 24.
20. Ibid., 175.
21. Ibid., 240.
22. Loren Eiseley, *The Immense Journey* (New York: Knopf Doubleday Publishing Group, 1957), 162.

23. Nick Longrich, "Evolution tells us we might be the only intelligent life in the Universe," *The Conversation*, October 18, 2019, accessed August 1, 2022, https://theconversation.com/evolution-tells-us-we-might-be-the-only-intelligent-life-in-the-universe-124706
24. See Chap. 6.
25. Kass, "L'Chaim and its Limits: Why not Immortality?"
26. Paul Johnson, *A History of the Jews*, 586.
27. Stephen Shankland and Jackson Ryan, "Elon Musk shows Neuralink brain implant working in a pig," *C/net*, August 29, 2020, accessed August 1, 2022, https://www.cnet.com/news/elon-musk-shows-neuralink-brain-implant-working-in-a-pig/#.
28. Nicolelis, *The True Creator of Everything*, 303.
29. See Chaps. 4 and 6.
30. Yerushalmi, *Zachor*, 106.
31. Nietzsche, as quoted in Yerushalmi, *Zachor*, 107.
32. Ibid.
33. Shlomo Friedman, "The Immortality Impulse and Jewish Tradition," *Tradition Magazine 52*:2, Spring 2020, Rabbinical Council of America, 47.
34. Yehezkel Dror, *Steering Human Evolution*, 141.
35. Dennis Prager, *Exodus—God, Slavery, and Freedom* (Washington DC: Regnery Faith, 2018), 228.

REFERENCES

Dror, Yehezkel. *Steering Human Evolution*. New York, Taylor and Francis, 2020.
Eiseley, Loren. *The Immense Journey*. New York, Knopf Doubleday Publishing Group, 1957.
Frankl, Victor. *Man's Search for Meaning*. Boston, Beacon Press, 1992 edition.
Friedman, Shlomo. "The Immortality Impulse and Jewish Tradition," *Tradition Magazine 52*:2, Spring 2020, Rabbinical Council of America.
Gelernter, David. "The Closing of the Scientific Mind," *Commentary Magazine*, January 1, 2014, accessed August 1, 2022, https://www.commentarymagazine.com/articles/the-closing-of-the-scientific-mind/.
Gelernter, David. *The Tides of Mind: Uncovering the Spectrum of Consciousness*. New York, Liveright, 2016.
Gerson, Michael. "Myths, meaning and Homo sapiens," *Washington Post*, June 11, 2015, accessed August 1, 2022, https://www.washingtonpost.com/opinions/myths-meaning-and-homo-sapiens/2015/06/11/28660902-106f-11e5-a0dc-2b6f404ff5cf_story.html.
Johnson, Paul. *A History of the Jews*. London, Weidenfeld and Nicolson Limited, 1987.

Kass, Leon. "L'Chaim and its Limits: Why not Immortality?" *First Things*, May, 2001, accessed August 1, 2022, https://www.firstthings.com/article/2001/05/lchaim-and-its-limits-why-not-immortality

Longrich, Nick. "Evolution tells us we might be the only intelligent life in the Universe," *The Conversation*, October 18, 2019, accessed August 1, 2022, https://theconversation.com/evolution-tells-us-we-might-be-the-only-intelligent-life-in-the-universe-124706.

Nicolelis, Miguel. *The True Creator of Everything—How the Human Brain Shaped the Universe as We Know It*. New Haven: Yale University Press, 2020.

Norman Lamm. *Faith and Doubt–Studies in Traditional Jewish Thought*. New York: Ktav Publishing House, Inc., 1986.

Prager, Dennis. *Exodus–God, Slavery, and Freedom* (Washington DC: Regnery Faith, 2018).

Shankland, Stephen and Ryan, Jackson. "Elon Musk shows Neuralink brain implant working in a pig," *C/net*, August 29, 2020, accessed August 1, 2022, https://www.cnet.com/news/elon-musk-shows-neuralink-brain-implant-working-in-a-pig/#.

Yerushalmi, Yosef Haim. *Zakhor–Jewish History and Jewish Memory* (New York: Schocken Books, 1982).

CHAPTER 8

Vehicles for the Road Ahead

What components will be necessary to build the engines of twenty-first-century Jewish life? At the dawn of an era that has changed faster than any in history, it is useful to scrutinize prospective blueprints. Evaluating which elements will best enable Judaism to maximize its contributions in the decades ahead is a different task from assessing what it will take to reinvigorate a commitment to Judaism among a large number of Jews. The first concern relates to how Judaism achieves its purpose. The second focuses on strategies for engaging Jews. While there is an understandable interest in the second question, the first is more consequential. After all, more than Jewish tradition has been concerned with keeping the majority of Jews Jewish, it has been devoted to making Judaism pertinent.

A few observations about engaging Jews are worth noting: The challenges to stimulating Jewish involvement within a milieu of immense distraction are manifest. Any proposal for living in a way that runs against the trends of the age, be it in ethical decision-making, the use of technology, or other areas, will face headwinds. Many will simply find a countercultural path to be too difficult—even if they acknowledge its virtues. Living according to a particular vision, however loosely structured, involves restraints and boundaries and comes with expectations that will make mass support improbable. So be it. Jewish history has always been written by small cohorts. When the Reform and Conservative movements began, they were not striving to become large networks. Rather, they were attempting to bring coherent Jewish answers to the great

© The Author(s), under exclusive license to Springer Nature Switzerland AG 2023
D. Schiff, *Judaism in a Digital Age*,
https://doi.org/10.1007/978-3-031-17992-1_8

intellectual and societal issues of their day, no matter the number of adherents. A new way of thinking that could speak to the pivotal concerns of the age came first. Interest and support followed. The same order of priorities still applies.

The primary focus, then, should be on what will be required for Judaism to prosper in the decades ahead. In this category, there are some clear essentials: The familiar features of contemporary Judaism—the daily, weekly, holyday, and life cycles, the structure of Jewish observance, and the study of text—will all remain vital, for they are the continuous threads that shape Jewish life and give form to Jewish ideals. These foundational elements of Jewish life must support the central endeavor that the hour demands: serious Jewish consideration of the human condition in the digital era. How might this occur? By making a commitment to address the human dilemmas and difficulties that are already before us as well as those that are visible on the horizon. There are, specifically, three areas of Jewish functioning that need rejuvenation: Jewish practice, community, and ideas.

JEWISH PRACTICE

A symphony orchestra will only make beautiful music when all the musicians play from the same score. To produce the desired result, the musicians must all be on the same page. To be sure, the part that each instrument plays is different, but there has to be an agreed-upon set of instructions that commits each performer to play certain designated notes. For an orchestra, there is no viable substitute for a shared musical score that can be translated into music making. The same is true in Jewish life. To achieve their goals, twenty-first-century iterations of Judaism require a framework of shared Jewish practice. Through the centuries, Jews have consistently expressed their understandings of God's score in lived human activity. Without agreed upon norms, there can be no coherent path that is discernibly Jewish. Historically, *halakhah* has always represented shared Jewish practice that is shaped within distinctive parameters.

The path of *halakhah* is built on the foundations of Jewish texts, and it represents the best available insights that govern Jewish conduct. It is a path broad enough to allow for different views. As the scholar of Judaic studies Leon Wiener Dow expresses it, "*Maḥloket*, disagreement, is central to halakha because it allows for divergent understandings of the divine command."[1] Sometimes the *halakhic* path intersects with the paths of other traditions; at other times it diverges. Individuals decide how closely they wish to cleave to the path, but the path itself provides coherence and direction. It is the Jewish way. The Jewish determination to stay connected to the path played no small role in the survival and the significance of Judaism through the millennia. Any vision of Judaism that eschews the path altogether will ultimately yield a loose amalgam of Jews, each on their own route, with few shared coordinates.

Some will object that any call for twenty-first-century Judaism to have *halakhic* contours—no matter how liberally constructed—will be alien to many Jews. According to this view, invoking *halakhah* conjures up the specter of coercive laws designed to inculcate specific modes of ritual observance or religious piety. But those who think of *halakhah* as being essentially a set of fixed rules from bygone times are operating with a narrow caricature. The historian Yosef Yerushalmi sees this approach as misguided: "...*halakhah* is not 'Law,' *nomos* in the Alexandrian, let alone the Pauline, sense. The Hebrew noun derives from *halakhah*, 'to walk,' hence *halakhah*—the Path on which one walks...the complex of rites and beliefs that give a people its sense of identity and purpose."[2] Eliezer Berkovits, a twentieth-century Orthodox rabbi and philosopher, warned about the clear distortions that can result from a *halakhic* approach that is "exiled" into a preoccupation with the written word:

Because of the lack of opportunity for *halakhic* application to real-life situations of national existence, the art and wisdom of such application dried up. Because of *Halakhah's* exile into literature and codification, new authority barriers were erected that seem unsurmountable. The old principle of the acceptance of personal responsibility for *halakhic* decisions, which demanded that the *Dayan* rule according to what his eyes see, has received a new meaning that reads: according to what he sees in some authoritative text.[3]

According to Berkovits, the correct understanding of *halakhah* balances textual precedent with lived experience in a way that is responsive to real-life circumstances.

Berkovits' approach is particularly relevant to our age, when so many significant questions on the agenda lack obvious *halakhic* antecedents. Consider the example of cultivated meat: Unlike plant-based meat substitutes, cultivated meat is meat that is grown from animal cells and provides the same taste and texture as real meat, but no animals die to produce it. When cultivated meat becomes truly indistinguishable from real meat, will the product be considered kosher if the cells are taken from a kosher animal? From the vantage point of *kashrut*, will it be fit for consumption as meat if no slaughter is involved? A harder challenge will be: If cultivated meat is considered kosher in every way, should Jewish law then prohibit the slaughter of animals for consumption as an unethical contravention of the prohibition against causing gratuitous animal suffering? It seems logical that the reply should be in the affirmative, but whatever the response to this question might be, the answer is not currently embedded in a text. This is, of course, not the first time in history that those who elucidate *halakhah* have been called upon to address questions that earlier sources could not have anticipated. Arguably, though, the wide-ranging conundrums raised by the digital era present a greater plethora of novel issues than ever before.

It will not be enough, then, for a *halakhic* response to the Internet age to remain within the boundaries of what is known as *halakhic* formalism. *Halakhic* formalism regards the development of *halakhah* as a process of answering questions by unearthing the most salient precedent within the context of prior legal texts.[4] The alternative to *halakhic* formalism is what Professor Adiel Schremer of Bar-Ilan University terms *halakhic* realism. In contrast to an idealized "platonic search for pure concepts," realism stresses that "[h]alakha should emphasize concrete historical circumstances and social context as determinative in its shaping."[5] It is this type of approach that most likely has the potential to yield *halakhic* insights that will best illuminate the complex path ahead.

Among contemporary thinkers, Berkovits and Schremer are far from alone in calling for a more expansive perception of *halakhah*. Rabbi David Hartman, founder of Jerusalem's Hartman Institute, contends that reframing our conceptualizations of *halakhah* must be a priority:

> It is extremely important that we create a space within our theology, and within our communities, for the legitimate (though not exclusive) positive understanding of halakha as a selective educational system, and not only as a legal system. For modern Jews who seek access to the lived experience of Jewish community, it is not merely a "tactical" mistake to present halakha in terms of principles of authority, obligations, and the sinful consequences of failure to uphold all of the *mitzvot*. It is a failure of the religious imagination and ultimately a failure of the Jewish community. The legalistic weight of halakha should be lifted completely and without theological compunction. Legalism and authoritarianism are not the best ways to educate a person to begin a way of life, and the overemphasis upon absolute authority claims and legalistic minutiae so prevalent among many Orthodox Jews today belies

halakha's essence and does a grave disservice to the profound potential it holds for today's diverse Jewish population.[6]

Hartman is not calling for the *halakhah* to lose its status as a system of law. Rather, he is making the point that the formal legal framing is not the only way that the life of a Jew can be shaped by *halakhic* categories. At its best, the *halakhah* should be "engaged as an open-ended educational framework rather than a binding normative one."[7] Put differently, it should stimulate Jewish practice in a way that inspires Jews to live according to its most worthy teachings.

Chaim Saiman, professor of law at Villanova University, holds that this insistence that the *halakhah* has both legal and educational functions was, in fact, always inherent within the *halakhic* system. It is best to think of *halakhah*, Saiman holds, as existing on a "spectrum or continuum" that moves between two poles. At one pole, the *halakhah* operates as any legal structure does, providing "rules designed to govern human behavior."[8] But at the other, the work of the *halakhah* is instructive, not legislative: "Here, *halakhah* functions as Torah, as an object of Torah study, and even as literature—with 'Torah' used as a catchall phrase to refer to religious teachings and instruction."[9] As far as Saiman is concerned, *halakhah*, correctly understood, does not operate at either pole, but rather it flows between the two:

> The metaphor of opposing poles also suggests that each side exerts a magnetic pull on the range of *halakhah* as a whole. While there is an undeniable appeal to casting *halakhah* as law-like rules of regulatory conduct, the countervailing pressures of Torah study pull in the opposite direction and transform concrete rules of behavior into wellsprings of philosophical and religious thought. In a sense, we can think of the two poles as establishing the goalposts, while the "game" of *halakhah*, and indeed its lived history, plays out on the field between them.[10]

Thus, the *halakhah* functions regularly beyond the "legislative pole." The rabbis, Saiman maintains, had a unique way of thinking about law, insisting that neither its rule-making nor its educational features should be subordinated:

> ...[T]he rabbis' idea of law means that movement between the poles is not only possible but common. The Mishnah and Talmud do not tell us whether a given body of law describes an imagined legal reality, daily practice,

rabbinic aspiration, or some combination thereof. On the contrary, by constantly mixing, matching, and moving among *halakhah*'s meanings, the Talmud signals that, from its perspective, these distinctions are not very significant. This is one of the central insights of the rabbinic idea of law.[11]

The rabbis, in effect, had an approach to law that regarded *halakhah* as a tapestry of different types of responses designed to form the attitudes, norms, and thinking of Jewish society.

Saiman concludes from this that *halakhah* is the core medium for rabbinic expression on all matters related to human functioning: "In Christianity, questions about the nature of humanity are assessed in the context of the theological disciplines; in the modern academic setting, they are discussed in the humanities, the social sciences, biology, or neuropsychology. For the rabbis, the relevant context is *halakhah*."[12] It follows that to see *halakhah* merely as legislation that pertains to narrow religious matters is un-Jewish. More importantly, in the Jewish context, to think about the "nature of humanity" without employing the framework of *halakhah* is tantamount to trying to participate in a conversation while removing oneself from the forum in which the conversation is being held.

Wiener Dow takes this analysis a step further. He rejects the "dissonance of learning something inspiring or admirable and not giving that idea concrete expression." Judaism, he posits, cannot allow for "a wedge that divides between Torah and *halakha*."[13] *Halakhah*, Wiener Dow maintains, is far from a list of rules; rather, it makes holiness concrete within the realm of action. "In crafting the *halakha* as a whole," Wiener Dow maintains, "the rabbis offer a similarly masterful reading of the Torah's most basic injunction and overarching commandment: to testify to the presence of the Divine through our actions by living a commanded life of holiness. Holiness is the path I travel; it is not a destination."[14] Hence, the *halakha* is a set of finely honed tools for actualizing holiness in all our activities: "*Halakha* is Torah as expressed in action... *Halakha* is the infinite divine word of Torah as expressed in the discrete, hard, finite realm of doing."[15] It follows that Wiener Dow sees *halakhah* as a responsive, dynamic inheritance rather than a set of immutable instructions. More critical to its functioning than the decisions made by judges is the way that the *halakhah* is brought to life by individuals and communities: "To live a life of *halakha* is to listen, to be on the way, to experiment, to place oneself on a precarious perch between the received tradition and the reality into which we are thrust by some combination of circumstance and choice."[16]

Wiener Dow's approach to the *halakhah* is rooted in the thought of the twentieth-century philosopher, Franz Rosenzweig. In particular, Wiener Dow builds upon Rosenzweig's distinction between that part of Jewish law that an individual perceives as having personal commanding force in the present and that part which, though legislated, does not yet evoke a personal sense of obligation. Wiener Dow extends this notion to the *halakhah* as a whole. He emphasizes that the individual can never simply be a passive recipient of the law but must play a vital part in making it live: "The aspiration of *halakhah* is to transform the laws into the performance of *mitzvot* in the moment, where we hear the voice of the commander… The ongoing development of *halakha*—which includes it reaching into new, previously-uninhabited places—is fundamentally an invitation to address ourselves to the Divine."[17] When thought of this way, it is plainly imperative that in the digital age the *halakhah* must advance into "previously-uninhabited places" so that new areas of human endeavor might become imbued with Divinity.

Wiener Dow holds that those who are not Orthodox need to be engaged with the *halakhic* system both for their own sake and for the vitality of the *halakhah* itself. Here too, he invokes Rosenzweig to the effect that a non-Orthodox Jew who "sets up tent" outside the building of *halakhah* thereby establishes a clear connection to the "normative" domain of Jewish communal life:

> The protection over her head will not be identical to the roof that the halakha provides, and yet, the placement of the tent across from the entry to the world of halakha indicates that this non-*halakhic* Jew continues to live her life in relationship to normative communal life. Over time, avers Rosenzweig, as more and more tents are erected on its front lawn, the building of halakha may well move. That is the self-reform that characterizes the halakha: it never fully excludes those Jews who live according to their own ability and who insist upon maintaining relationship with the communal norm.[18]

Thus, those who are prepared to dwell in tents that are adjacent to the *halakhic* building can over time become part of the *halakhic* encampment and will have an influence on the direction in which the law flows. Living "in relationship to normative communal life," they impact the contours of the community's shared practice.

Halakhah, according to this metaphor, is not static. This is what Rabbi Moshe Zemer, a twentieth-century proponent of *halakhic* norms in the Reform movement, termed "evolving *halakhah*."[19] For Zemer, the importance of being part of the *halakhic* process is not just that the *halakhah* is designed to encapsulate Torah's teachings in action or to concretize the holy, but that it demands ethical practice:

> *Halakhah* is by nature and practice evolutionary, flexible, ethical, and progressive. It has roots in the distant past, but its methods allow it to deal with contemporary conditions. It can be applied to almost every human situation. Its determinations are a matter not only of ancient law but also of social justice and human rights. In other words, it deals not only with the dry letter of the law but also—and perhaps chiefly—with human beings as human beings and with Jews as Jews.[20]

Zemer claims that "If a ruling is *halakhic*, it must be ethical. If it is unethical, it cannot be *halakhic*."[21] The implication is plain: the *halakhah* cannot become a series of rules that are impervious to the dilemmas of real life. To the contrary, utilizing principles that are inherent within the *halakhah* itself, the *halakhah* must respond to new ethical challenges:

> Change in *Halakhah* is the result of deeper inquiry into and reinterpretation of older texts, employing the rules and principles—themselves enshrined in *Halakhah*—by which the Torah is expounded. Thus, there is no reason why decisors of the present generation may not rule leniently and permit what is at first sight questionable or forbidden, in accordance with the demands of ethics, their conscience, and evolving *Halakhah*.[22]

Revitalization of the *halakhah*, Zemer argues, will require the construction of a *halakhah* that is truly responsive to the conditions in which Jews find themselves.

Perhaps no one has been more direct or blunt about the need to adopt a renewed vison of *halakhah*—true to its original impulse—than Rabbi Nathan Lopes Cardozo. Trained in Orthodox yeshivot, Cardozo, dean of the David Cardozo Academy in Jerusalem, has a perspective that is decidedly divergent from the dominant Orthodox approach. Cardozo rails against the ongoing process of codifying Jewish law that reduces the *halakhah* to a set of fixed legal instructions. The reason for his opposition is that "these great codes of Jewish Law are very un-Jewish in spirit. They present *Halacha* in ways which oppose the heart and soul of the Talmud, and therefore of Judaism itself. They deprived Judaism of its multifaceted halachic tradition and its inherent music."[23] In Cardozo's view, this "un-Jewish" ethos of codification has created an "artificial Judaism suspended in time, which has been rewritten in ways which detrimentally oppose its very living nature." The "obsessive" practice of codification has meant that "Jewish beliefs are constantly being dogmatized and *halachicized* by rabbinic authorities, and anyone who does not accept these rigid beliefs is no longer considered to be a real religious Jew." This leads Cardozo to declare that "over the years we have embalmed Judaism while claiming it is alive because it continues to maintain its external shape."[24] Cardozo calls for the urgent reversal of this process to allow the *halakhah* to "be what it has always been: an anarchic, colorful, and unequaled musical symphony that requires room to breathe."[25]

These are powerful statements. Cardozo maintains that not only should the understanding of *halakhah* as "fixed law" be rejected, but the very attempt to make it into fixed law is antithetical to Judaism. Codification embalms. It "strangles" Judaism so effectively that Orthodox Judaism is "on its way to becoming irrelevant" to anybody who seeks the vitality of a living tradition.[26] Cardozo calls for a *halakhah* that is innovative, rebellious, and divergent enough to make room for dissent. He calls for *halakhah* to be shaped by those who are committed to the system but eschew rigidity:

> Their common ground is their view of this tradition as a river that flows through an often rocky terrain, with many unexpected turns, but which never dries up. These arbiters would never forsake the river. Some will subtly alter its course, pushing against the river's shore in an attempt to widen it, while others would never dare. But not one of them would suggest creating an altogether new river. If that were to happen, all would be lost.[27]

Halakhah is a river that flows. Jews should never abandon the river, but nor should they anchor themselves permanently in one place, unprepared to move with the river's flow. As Cardozo pictures it, the *halakhah*, though based in a core set of texts, must be fluid, with "room to breathe."

Halakhah, then, can be described with varying metaphors: It is the practice that emerges from the conversation of an encampment. It is a colorful, musical symphony. It is the encapsulation of the ethical and the holy in a lived community. It is a river that flows with unexpected turns. It is a way of responding that is built upon unalterable principles but which nevertheless evolves and relates with relevance to contemporary conditions. It is the infinite, divine word of Torah expressed in the realm of doing. It is a unique medium of expression on all matters related to human functioning. In short, *halakhah* bespeaks a distinctive way of looking at the world while being adaptable to new conditions. And here is what *halakhah* is not: It is not codified legislation and it is not a collection of ossified texts contained in dusty volumes without applicability to today's circumstances.

The *halakhic* approach that is likely to be most conducive to our new epoch will be one that displays greater responsiveness than that currently associated with Orthodoxy. Orthodoxy has historically exhibited wariness about modern attitudes and behaviors. When the Chatam Sofer declared "that which is new is forbidden by the Torah,"[28] he did not intend that Orthodoxy should refrain from responding to new societal or technological developments; rather that it should draw the line at changes that might allow modern attitudes to influence Jewish observance. This caution undoubtedly shielded Orthodoxy from much of the vicissitudes of modernity, enabling it to maintain a system of practice that was less exposed to assimilation. But the mindset that regarded anything novel as being suspect also led to a restraint that typically resulted in delayed responses.

Eliezer Berkovits has pointed out the significant disadvantage of holding the zeitgeist at arm's length—particularly when Jews no longer live at a distance from surrounding society:

> Alas, those who have the authority to impose laws of the Torah do not care to understand the nature of the confrontation with the Zeitgeist. They take the easy way out. They do not search for the Word that was intended for this hour, for this generation. If they have the authority, they impose the Word meant for yesterday and thus miss hearing the Word that the eternal validity of the Torah was planning for today, for this generation, for this new hour in the history of the Jewish people.[29]

Being insufficiently cognizant of the zeitgeist impairs the opportunity for Jewish wisdom to have influence and relevance. Responding forthrightly to technological and societal trends should be one key ingredient of future *halakhic* strategy. Another should be developing a proactive *halakhic* impulse. In the digital age, it will not be sufficient for *halakhic* insights to arrive only after the societal or technological changes they are addressing have become normative. To be sure, each technological step forward raises discrete questions that could theoretically be answered in the traditional way—by replying to inquiries that arise after a given innovation has been deployed. But focusing on individual trees does not necessarily produce a desirable forest. In the generation of hyper-ethics, responding incrementally to new societal conditions only after they have already become concrete realities will likely marginalize the *halakhah*.

A *halakhic* approach that is truly adapted to the exponential speed of the digital era will need to exhibit a responsiveness that, while remaining thoughtful and deliberative, can keep pace with across-the-board acceleration. More than that, it will need to anticipate future innovation trends so as to provide guidance on their desirability before society is presented with unavoidable *faits accomplis*. If the *halakhic* process does not position itself ahead of the curve, it risks being ignored. A *halakhic* system of practice that is well adapted to a new iteration of Judaism will be one that can contend seriously with the massive changes before us, can be timely, can be relevant to the lives of twenty-first century Jews, and can grapple convincingly with novel fields of human endeavor.

Jewish Community

In the Jewish tradition, community is not perceived as a utilitarian tool for creating group experiences; it is a value. The Hebrew word for community, *kehillah*, is often accompanied by the word for holiness, *kedoshah*, implying that to live in a community offers a level of exaltation that is unavailable without it. Judaism, furthermore, insists that we are each our "brother's keeper" and that the notion of brother extends beyond relatives. Every day, Jews recite lines that recall the duty to rejoice with bride and groom, to accompany the dead to burial, to visit the sick, and to raise the fallen; these injunctions are not limited to family and friends.

The Jewish emphasis on community is readily apparent in one of the oft-repeated Jewish texts attributed to Hillel in the *Mishnah*: "Do not separate yourself from the community" (*Pirkei Avot*, 2:4). Another rabbinic text emphasizes the point by depicting one who separates from the community in a decidedly negative light:

If one makes oneself like *terumah* ("a portion of produce"), set aside in the corner of the house, and says, 'Why should I trouble myself for the community? What's in it for me to take part in their disputes? Why should I listen to their voices? I'm fine [without them],' this person destroys the world. (*Midrash Tanchumah, Parshat Mishpatim* 2)

The forceful wording underscores the importance that Judaism attaches to being part of communal life. This can be illustrated in numerous ways. There are many religions that teach that praying alone affords the same opportunities as praying in a community; Judaism, however, requires a *minyan* for critical elements of the liturgy, stressing the importance of community and the strength it provides. The Jewish approach emphasizes that a community is more than a group of individuals: "While public prayer could theoretically be regarded as simply many individual selves gathering together, the *minyan* posits the creation of a new existential entity that changes the efficacy and very nature of prayer."[30] In other words, a community is greater than just the sum of its parts; it has a distinctive capacity that emerges from the harmony of a collective that is committed to its members and to a shared endeavor. Indeed, the reason why a true community is regarded as functionally "elevated" is precisely because a community qualitatively transcends a simple collection of people brought together for a specific task. What is possible in community cannot be attained without it.

Another regularly quoted statement about community in classic Judaism is the Talmudic declaration that "all of Israel is responsible one for the other" (*Shevuot* 39a). This declaration teaches that a vital aspect of community is taking personal responsibility for other members of the group. Specifically, the question for Judaism is not "what will community do for me?" but rather "what does community demand of me?" Community implies responsibility. The community in which we live influences and shapes us in ways that those who are more distant cannot emulate. That is why Jews are called upon to take responsibility for the struggles of their neighbors and to try to improve the level of conduct in their neighborhood. One joins a *minyan*, even when one is not keen, so that a person whom one might not know can say *Kaddish* for a lost loved one. A community, then, involves an unswerving commitment to the well-being of its members, including the weak and the unpopular. In community, people deem it essential to notice the unnoticed in the ranks and to be available to take care of their needs. Consequently, community demands physical presence. Being able to discern somebody's absence, to deliver a meal personally, or to share viscerally in the common lived experience of a particular location and social milieu are some of the fundamental markers of community. These features are not available online.

In the Internet era, some contend that it is feasible to experience community online. Often, though, those who make this claim are using the term *community* as a substitute for what is actually an affinity group. To be sure, the bonds between members of an affinity group can be powerful and deep. Real attachments can be formed with people halfway around the world with whom one shares a passion, a stage of life, a perspective, a condition, a hobby, or other commonalities. One can develop close connections with members of such a group, communicate regularly, care about them, support them, help them, and be there for them—at least virtually. But this is not the way that Judaism understands community.

Separation from the community is regarded as a negative in Jewish life because togetherness is community's indispensable glue. The coronavirus pandemic underscored that a community that is restricted to a virtual version of itself is diminished. Lockdowns provided a reminder that not only do most people yearn for physical community, but vital elements are missing when community is inaccessible. Holiness, then, is to be found in physical community precisely because community is the locus of caring, the place where we truly take responsibility for all other community members and for the conduct and standards of the group. Digital age iterations of Judaism should not be indifferent to rising levels of atomization, nor should they regard places of meeting as dispensable. Countering atomization and loneliness by resisting the technologizing of critical human encounters represents a statement about how Jews see others and assume responsibility for their well-being. Any approach to Judaism that is not committed to the centrality of in-person community downgrades a bedrock value. Despite the difficulty of bringing together physical communities in an era in which so much is mediated by screens, it remains a vital value.

The author Jonathan Safran Foer wrote perceptively that "the problem with accepting—with preferring—diminished substitutes is that over time, we, too, become diminished substitutes."[31] Put differently, the less we are in each other's presence, the less each other's presence seems to mean. However, like a person who becomes dehydrated without noticing, we are unwittingly sapped of an ingredient that is vital to our well-being. Leon Wiener Dow insists that any true community must have "spatial dimension": "We know well from our attempts to bridge physical distance through the myriad of mechanisms that technology has put at our disposal, a person on the screen or on the phone can be there for us—but never here with us. The full depth of human existence requires presence in all of its rich connotation."[32] Indeed it does.

It follows that the synagogue—the core communal institution at the heart of Jewish life—continues to be essential. For thousands of years, Jews have derived inspiration, education, and connection from being together in synagogues where they have drawn strength from one another. That is why Jewish law instructs communities to build a synagogue that has prominence (*Shulchan Arukh, Orach Chayim* 150:1). Through the centuries, the synagogue has consistently demonstrated remarkable resilience. In the words of Rabbi David Wolpe of Sinai Temple in Los Angeles, the synagogue "remains home base": "The shul [synagogue] has been the home to Jewish people for thousands of years. …New organizations have their role to play, but the shul is the backbone of Judaism."[33] The synagogue is the lifelong locus around which community revolves. There is little reason to believe that an alternate communal institution will become more central to community life: "Which model will be continuously available throughout the life of a Jew? What happens when you outgrow the organization or the time for the retreat ends? A synagogue is for all ages, at all times. No other institution in Jewish life has that comprehensive commitment."[34] A Jewish community without a synagogue is a Jewish community without a secure tomorrow.

Perhaps one of the reasons why synagogues have always grounded Jewish communal life is because they were adaptable; they served as houses of assembly and study as much as houses of prayer. In the decades ahead, it is quite possible that synagogues will adapt again. They may no longer be establishments with permanent structures. It is conceivable that the focus of their activities might shift. But as accessible institutions where Jews come together to encounter that which is Godly, to be within a holy communal framework, and to contemplate the expectations of Judaism, synagogues will remain fundamental.

Jewish Ideas

Through the millennia of Jewish history, ideas that emerged from the wellsprings of Judaism have influenced human civilization. More than a few Jewish ideas changed the course of history. From the structure of the week to monotheism to universal education, and to caring for those in need, Jewish conceptual thinking has truly "pushed the hinge of history." *Halakhah* was correctly perceived as being "about bold ideas and discovering solutions which nobody ever thought of."[35] Indeed, the observation that in "biblical days the Halacha was astir while the world was sleeping" may not be much of an overstatement.[36]

In the digital age, Jewish ideas have the potential to play the same role once again: "Only when the *halakhah* wakes up and starts to challenge our society with novel ideas and rulings will it once more be the vital mover of Jewish life."[37] There is every reason to see the past as prologue. As essential concerns about what it means to be human become the paramount focus of the century upon which we are embarked, Judaism's long tradition of delving deeply into these matters could again become a valuable resource.

The challenge of retaining our humanity in the decades ahead will demand thoughtful and creative proposals. The Jewish future, consequently, would be well served by establishing a network of twenty-first-century academies, think tanks, and communal forums in order to deliberate on the nature of human life and death, work and leisure, the interface between humans and machines, the impact of algorithms and AI, privacy, sexuality, gene editing, and the host of other areas that call for discerning responses. A structured process to begin thinking Jewishly about the major conundrums that face our digital world should be convened by experts in *halakhah*, tradition, and practice, together with specialists in a broad range of technologies, as well as philosophers, ethicists, and thinkers from other disciplines. The doors of these idea incubators should be open to all who are interested in engaging in the process of considering how to frame Jewish perspectives on the human future. These academies should incorporate the ethos of the "new yeshiva" that Cardozo envisages: "We are in need of a radically different kind of yeshiva: one in which students are confronted with serious challenges to Halacha and its weltanschauung and learn how to respond...where it is not rabbinic authority that reigns supreme, but religious authenticity."[38] Inspiration from foundational sources, combined with a determination to forge the best path forward through the web of complex challenges before us, has the potential to produce beneficial ideas that might prove determinative.

The Talmudic academies that were the source of extraordinary wisdom 2000 years ago also emerged in the wake of a momentous transition. Following the loss of the Temple, the rabbis instituted a network of schools of inquiry that discussed all aspects of existence. Their work constituted a vast conversation on how Judaism, rooted in tradition, could respond to an altered reality. The rabbis of old were not seeking to galvanize the next generation. They were focused on one task: honing Jewish ideas so as to distill the right, Torah based way to offer the best models for uplifting human existence. It was a strategy that proved to be effective and long-lasting.

Some will wonder whether such a project should begin as a specifically Jewish pursuit. Why not bring together diverse groups of thinkers from many backgrounds to pursue solutions jointly? The answer is that human culture and ideas have generally been rooted in particularism. Distinctive approaches to government, religion, economics, morality, the arts, and other domains have emerged from particularistic ways of looking at the world. More importantly, the particularist approach yields multiple different sets of ideas from divergent perspectives so that, when the time comes for a wider conversation, the discussion is informed by a greater range of alternatives than would otherwise be the case.

In contemplating the potential of AI, Max Tegmark provides an illustration of exactly the type of discussion that might be brought to the twenty-first-century study hall:

> To program a friendly AI, we need to capture the meaning of life. What's "meaning"? What's "life"? What's the ultimate ethical imperative? In other words, how should we strive to shape the future of our Universe? If we cede control to a superintelligence before answering these questions rigorously, the answer it comes up with is unlikely to involve us. This makes it timely to rekindle the classic debates of philosophy and ethics, and adds a new urgency to the conversation.[39]

What's meaning? What's life? What is permissible and what is not? Responsible societal advancement in the years ahead will be dependent on answering such questions with intelligence and coherence. It is hard to imagine a more Jewish task. In a breakneck world of hurtling change, Judaism has a renewed opportunity to address the critical issues that are now part of the broader human agenda. Judaism can once again become a significant generator of ideas by grappling seriously with the major issues that face humanity and by crafting significant solutions that are informed by the texts and contours of Jewish tradition. Judaism, after all, does not exist simply to perpetuate itself; rather, applying the wisdom of a millennial heritage is its fundamental *raison d'etre*.

Somewhere out there, just beyond the mist, are new iterations of Judaism that will soon come into view. It is too early to discern their precise form. But this much we know: The arrival of an unheralded epoch in history provides an opportunity for Jewish approaches to make a difference once again. What is at stake in the digital age is no less than what it means to be human in the twenty-first century and beyond. There should, then, be no illusions about the parameters of the task ahead: The period for contemplation will be limited, the questions will be complex, the need will be pressing, and the implications will be vast. Perhaps it is time to move forward.

NOTES

1. Leon Wiener Dow, *The Going—A Meditation on Jewish Law* (Cham: Palgrave Macmillan, 2017), 47.
2. Yerushalmi, *Zakhor*, 113.
3. Eliezer Berkovits, *Not in Heaven—The Nature and Function of Halakha* (New York: Ktav Publishing House, Incorporated, 1983), 91.
4. See Adiel Schremer, "Toward Critical *Halakhic* Studies," Tikvah Center Working Paper, 04/2010, accessed August 1, 2022, http://www.law.nyu.edu/sites/default/files/TikvahWorkingPapersArchive/WP4Schremer.pdf
5. Ibid.
6. David Hartman, Charlie Buckholtz, *The God Who Hates Lies: Confronting and Rethinking Jewish Tradition* (Woodstock: Jewish Lights Publishing, 2011) 50–51.
7. Ibid., 49.
8. Chaim Saiman, *Halakhah: The Rabbinic Idea of Law* (Princeton: Princeton University Press, 2018), 9.
9. Ibid.
10. Ibid.
11. Ibid., 55.
12. Ibid., 62.
13. Wiener Dow, *The Going*, 7.
14. Ibid., 98.
15. Ibid., 42.
16. Ibid., 98–99.
17. Alan Brill, "Interview with Leon Wiener Dow—The Going: A Meditation on Jewish Law," August 28, 2018, accessed August 1, 2022, https://kavvanah.blog/2018/08/28/interview-with-leon-wiener-dow-the-going-a-meditation-on-jewish-law/
18. Ibid.

19. Moshe Zemer, *Evolving Halakhah—A Progressive Approach to Traditional Jewish Law* (Woodstock, Jewish Lights, 1999), chapter 1.
20. Ibid., 38.
21. Ibid., 49.
22. Ibid., 39–40.
23. Nathan Lopes Cardozo, *Jewish Law as Rebellion* (Jerusalem: Urim Publications, 2018), 65–66.
24. Ibid., 66–67.
25. Ibid., 58.
26. Ibid., 59.
27. Ibid., 55.
28. See Chap. 3.
29. Berkovits, *Not in Heaven*, 118.
30. Leon Morris, "Pragmatism versus the Talmudic Process in Reform Judaism: The Minyan as Case Study?" *CCAR Journal*, Summer 2014, 48.
31. Jonathan Safran Foer, "How Not To Be Alone," *The New York Times*, June 8, 2013, accessed August 1, 2022, https://www.nytimes.com/2013/06/09/opinion/sunday/how-not-to-be-alone.html
32. Wiener Dow, *The Going*, 53.
33. David Wolpe, "Shivim Panim," *Sapir*, Volume 6, Summer 2022, accessed August 10, 2022, https://sapirjournal.org/education/2022/08/shivim-panim/
34. Ibid.
35. Cardozo, *Jewish Law as Rebellion*, 40.
36. Ibid., 48.
37. Ibid.
38. Ibid., 41.
39. Tegmark, *Life 3.0*, 279.

References

Berkovits, Eliezer. *Not in Heaven–The Nature and Function of Halakha*. New York, Ktav Publishing House, Incorporated, 1983.

Brill, Alan. "Interview with Leon Wiener Dow—The Going: A Meditation on Jewish Law," August 28, 2018, accessed August 1, 2022, https://kavvanah.blog/2018/08/28/interview-with-leon-wiener-dow-the-going-a-meditation-on-jewish-law/.

Cardozo Nathan Lopes. *Jewish Law as Rebellion*. Jerusalem, Urim Publications, 2018.

Foer, Jonathan Safran. "How Not To Be Alone," *The New York Times*, June 8, 2013, accessed August 1, 2022, https://www.nytimes.com/2013/06/09/opinion/sunday/how-not-to-be-alone.html.

Hartman, David, Buckholtz, Charlie. *The God Who Hates Lies: Confronting and Rethinking Jewish Tradition*. Woodstock, Jewish Lights Publishing, 2011.

Morris, Leon. "Pragmatism versus the Talmudic Process in Reform Judaism: The Minyan as Case Study?" *CCAR Journal*, Summer 2014.

Saiman, Chaim. *Halakhah: The Rabbinic Idea of Law*. Princeton, Princeton University Press, 2018.

Schremer, Adiel. "Toward Critical *Halakhic* Studies," Tikvah Center Working Paper, 04/2010, accessed August 1, 2022, http://www.law.nyu.edu/sites/default/files/TikvahWorkingPapersArchive/WP4Schremer.pdf.

Tegmark, Max. *Life 3.0*. New York, Knopf Doubleday Publishing Group, 2017.

Wiener Dow, Leon. *The Going—A Meditation on Jewish Law*. Cham, Palgrave Macmillan, 2017.

Wolpe, David. "Shivim Panim," *Sapir*, Volume 6, Summer 2022, accessed August 10, 2022, https://sapirjournal.org/education/2022/08/shivim-panim/.

Yerushalmi Yosef Haim. *Zakhor—Jewish History and Jewish Memory*. New York, Schocken Books, 1982.

Zemer, Moshe. *Evolving Halakhah—A Progressive Approach to Traditional Jewish Law*. Woodstock, Jewish Lights, 1999.

Correction to: Changing Mentalities

CORRECTION TO:

Chapter 5 in D. Schiff, *Judaism in a Digital Age*,
https://doi.org/10.1007/978-3-031-17992-1_5

The book was inadvertently published with an incorrect reference which is corrected now in the proofs and given below.

Krantz, David. "*Shmita* Revolution: The Reclamation and Reinvention of the Sabbatical Year" Religions 7, 2016: no. 8: 100.

The updated original version of this chapter can be found at
https://doi.org/10.1007/978-3-031-17992-1_5

Index[1]

[1] Note: Page numbers followed by 'n' refer to notes.

© The Author(s), under exclusive license to Springer Nature
Switzerland AG 2023
D. Schiff, *Judaism in a Digital Age*,
https://doi.org/10.1007/978-3-031-17992-1